# THE
# NOBLE
# VOICE

*Books by Mark Van Doren*

COLLECTED POEMS

JOHN DRYDEN

LIBERAL EDUCATION

THE MAYFIELD DEER

THE NIGHT OF THE SUMMER SOLSTICE
*(Editor)*

THE PRIVATE READER

THE SEVEN SLEEPERS

SHAKESPEARE

TILDA

THE TRANSPARENT TREE

A WINTER DIARY

THE NOBLE VOICE

# THE
# NOBLE
# VOICE

## A STUDY OF TEN GREAT POEMS

### BY MARK VAN DOREN

### HENRY HOLT AND COMPANY

*Copyright, 1946, by*

HENRY HOLT AND COMPANY, INC.

First printing

PRINTED IN THE UNITED STATES OF AMERICA

*To*

CHARLES VAN DOREN

# CONTENTS

I · THE ILIAD        1

II · THE ODYSSEY        45

III · THE AENEID        86

IV · PARADISE LOST        122

V · CONCERNING THE NATURE OF THINGS        148

VI · THE DIVINE COMEDY        172

VII · THE FAERIE QUEENE        231

VIII · TROILUS AND CRISEYDE        257

IX · DON JUAN        283

X · THE PRELUDE        303

INDEX        321

# PREFACE

THE NOBLE VOICE of Calliope, whom Hesiod called
chiefest of the Muses, has sounded steadily since
Homer. It has not sounded all of the time, but whenever it has sounded it has given strength to those
through whom it spoke. It is the source of great poetry
— of great story — and as such it is the subject of this
book. Among the nine sons of Calliope whom I consider there are only three who do not name her. These
are Byron, Wordsworth, and Homer himself. But the
omission does not matter. It is she who makes them
ambitious, and it is her voice which with varying success all nine are trying to match.

Their ten long poems, for Homer of course has two,
are discussed in ten chapters which the reader is at lib-
erty to take in any order he pleases; but I should prefer
that he follow mine, for my subject is single, and this
is the order in which I found it developing itself.
Chronology is observed, but under categories that interest me more than the history of poetry, if there is
such a thing, has ever done. The first four poems are
epic, the next three are philosophical, the two after
that are comic, and the last one is modern. This is a

makeshift classification, particularly in the case of Wordsworth's poem with which I close, but I leave its defense to the chapters themselves, which will show how little or much the labels mean. They overlap from poet to poet, and they are interchangeable at times. But I must not anticipate my text.

The book has three heroes: Homer, Dante, and Chaucer. With them, that is, I find no fault; nor would I with Shakespeare if he were here. He is not here because he is a dramatic poet, and because I have discussed him in another book. In the six who remain I have thought it important to explain as best I could a relative failure. It is only relative, but that does not make it unreal. A lack of candor toward the realities of poetry seems to me the capital crime in criticism, and so nothing can prevent me from saying, for instance, that Milton in my judgment does not wholly succeed. The legend that he does is the worst enemy of his reputation. We should love him for what he is, and for that alone; and so with Virgil, Lucretius, Spenser, Byron, Wordsworth. They are great, or they would not deserve our candor. They would not have survived, even, to invite it.

The nine poets seemed susceptible to treatment in a single volume not because they had a single subject or were conscious of a common enterprise. Chronology permitting, they refer to one another a good deal, and they share such themes as sin, courtesy, and peace; but that is not it either. Their merit as subject matter, quite apart from their intrinsic glory, is that they offer a perspective through poetry which nothing else can give. To know them is the only conceivable way of knowing what poetry can be, and is the only practical way of accumulating the nerve necessary for judgment. I do not suppose that all of my judgments are right, but I can claim that I have formed them in the most generous perspective available. To be satisfied with less than this much perspective is not to be sure that one is talking as much sense as one can.

What is a given poem about? What happens in it? What exists in it? If too little of the world is in it, why is that? If all of the world is there, by what miracle has this been done? Is tragedy or comedy at work, and what is the difference between those two, and what the resemblance? Are the facts of life accounted for in the unique way that poetry accounts for them, and is this poem something therefore that any man should read? Does its author know more, not less, than most men know? Such seem to me the great questions, though they are not regularly asked by criticism. A commoner question has to do with how the poem was written, in what style, and whether well or ill. It is better, I believe, to ask how the poem was conceived — with what wisdom the poet made those silent decisions which precede the composition of a single line. It is hard to find answers, and mine may be wrong in every case. But I confess that I have been ambitious in the endeavor, for I take poetry at its best to be a useful and a beautiful thing.

I am not an expert in any of these poems. I should

like to be an expert in them all, considering them as one; but I do not make the claim. My approach is professional — or, as some experts would put it, amateur. I have not studied any poem, that is, to the exclusion of the rest. Those who do so study Homer or Dante or Milton are very valuable persons, but there are practical questions which they never attempt to answer. The difference between their poet and some other — they see it from one side, and so may not see it at all. I have tried to make these poems comment on one another as in fact I think they do. For they inhabit the same world, and stand or fall by the report of it they give. To be an expert in them all would be to have a perfect knowledge of the world. I do not make the claim.

I am content with the certainty that by most readers half of these poems will be read in translation. That is how I have read them myself, and that is how I have quoted them. It is an interesting fact that Homer wrote in Greek, but what anybody may find in him is vastly more interesting. Nobody fails to find in him, below the level of sound and style, the things that prove him a great poet. Nothing so clearly proves him one as that he survives translation. His structure, his story, is still evident and powerful; and this is true even when his English translator has used prose. I prefer prose translations in general, and only in the case of Lucretius have used verse: the verse of William Ellery Leonard, through which I first made the Roman's acquaintance. The translation I use is in each case the one I know best, nor would I defend it further. But I so much believe in translation that I have not scrupled to quote Chaucer in the modern English of Professor Krapp; and I have gone back to George Gilfillan's edition of Spenser because it is as free as possible of the antique orthography which keeps so many readers away from *The Faerie Queene.* I have removed every such handicap that I could, in the faith that no superfluous barrier should exist between the reader and the work. If I could do so without seeming wayward I would suggest that the reader imagine he was going through all of the English poems in translation. Milton would thus be deprived of his famous style, but the result might be as edifying as it is in the case of Virgil, who without his style confesses his lack of the power to say what Homer in any language says. As for Dante, it never seems to matter how we read him. The immense poet is always there, as Shakespeare is said to be in Russian or Hungarian.

I have not cited book or line for my quotations, because I chose to hope that the reader, if he had not read all of the work in question, might soon do so for himself. If he already has, then he will recognize the quoted fragments. If he has not, he will be free to find a better set. Mine, clearly, are no substitute for the wholes from which they come. The wholes are what this volume has in mind, and they cannot be encountered by too many persons, or too many times.

M. V. D.

*New York, 1945*

# ACKNOWLEDGMENTS

I AM INDEBTED to the publishers of the following translations for permission to quote from them in the chapters which their titles indicate:

Homer: *The Iliad*. With an English translation by A. T. Murray. The Loeb Classical Library. Harvard University Press. Two volumes.

Homer: *The Odyssey*. With an English translation by A. T. Murray. The Loeb Classical Library. Harvard University Press. Two volumes.

Virgil. Translated by John Jackson. Oxford University Press.

Lucretius: *Of the Nature of Things*. A Metrical Translation by William Ellery Leonard. E. P. Dutton and Company.

The *Inferno*, *Purgatorio*, and *Paradiso* of Dante Alighieri. Translated by John Aitken Carlyle, Thomas Okey, and Philip H. Wicksteed. The Temple Classics. London: J. M. Dent and Sons. Three volumes.

*Troilus and Cressida*. By Geoffrey Chaucer. Englished Anew by George Philip Krapp. Random House.

In the chapter on the *Aeneid* I am further indebted to the Harvard University Press for permission to quote from Harold N. Fowler's translation of *The Statesman* in the Loeb Classical Library edition of Plato, Volume III.

# ACKNOWLEDGMENTS

It is a pleasure to state my obligation to those students of Columbia University and St. John's College who have listened to me lecture on these poems and in ensuing discussions have corrected or improved my understanding of them.

I am especially grateful to Mr. Jacob Klein of St. John's College for suggesting the connection between Virgil and Plato which I consider in the chapter on the *Aeneid,* and for permitting me to benefit as I may from his remarkable insight.

# THE
# NOBLE
# VOICE

# I · THE ILIAD

HOMER, with Shakespeare at his side, is still the sovereign poet. The phrase is Dante's, who is third in this strict company which excludes all others. Only these three — yet Chaucer is a fourth — are masters of the main art a poet must learn: the art of standing at the right distance from his matter, of keeping the right relation to it, and of using, along with the knowledge he brings, the knowledge he gains while he goes. With the poet, as with the historian, the position he takes is everything, and we shall not believe him unless he maintains it. But whereas the historian's distance must be great enough to permit a survey of the event from a point where its limits in time are always visible, the poet must seem to annihilate both time and distance — we enter the action, we are there as these things happen, we believe because we see and hear and touch. The distinction is not pure. The poet without perspective has no meaning, and the historian who cannot move up to the particulars of his choice, to battles and meetings and the sending and getting of messages, will not be read to the end. But as a distinction it will do. And Homer understood it perfectly.

Homer's scenes, and the incidents that fill them, are beheld as if in a long dream, or as if in memory. They are fiercely present, yet they have the brightness of things removed, of things threatened by darkness and only by miracle recalled. The ideas Homer had, and he may have had all possible ideas, were had in the right way: they did not prevent him from being a complete poet. Nothing prevented him from believing and loving the deeds and men that he saw, exactly as he saw them. This is the secret of his constant, surprising, and intimate power, a power that no successor has matched, so that he is still unique, the one, the only epic poet. The higher criticism of him is misguided, or is misunderstood, if it seems to deny the identity of a single artist who twice was capable of measuring the intensity with which a hero felt himself — Achilles burning at the center of his poem, Odysseus swimming or scheming or leaning on a long staff at the center of his. The heroes, like the poems, are as different as night and day, but neither success has been achieved again. No other epic poet is so valuable line by line, so rapid over all and yet so rich in each movement that he follows. No other stories are so clear, so important, or so full of unforgettable persons. We still do not know how these persons were made, because they seem to have been made before the poems were written. Yet they were not. It is poetry, not history, that has rendered them so plain in their differences, so round and solid and simple, so permanently themselves, so endlessly discussable. How did Homer do this? Nobody knows.

The conventions about characterization do not apply. The characters of Homer are inseparable from his scenes, as his scenes are from his fables. All is multiple and near, all is one and far away.

Nothing about the *Iliad* is more incredible than its power to make us take as natural the wonders with which it is filled — Achilles and his mother, the beauty of the gods, the eloquence of the men. These things are so natural that we are tempted to think them easy, and Homer naïve, a lucky poet who came early to the art. The temptation is soon conquered if we note what happens to us as we read, and to the poem; if we count the things that collect in it as forces collect to make a world, if we study — though it is hard to do this — the massive way in which so many simple units are joined to produce an effect of huge and complex order. The effort required is never mentioned, it is only made, and made with a success that deceives us. Homer may doubt his ability to remember every name that should go into a list of warriors, and he likes to make much of such minor difficulties. The great difficulties he silently solves. And the greatest difficulty of all he solves at the start. The poem, like the world it contains, is first as well as last a single and great thing.

The world of the *Iliad* is incessantly and everywhere alive. Energy runs through it like a blood stream, heating it to the high color that shows in wine-dark seas, black ships with vermilion prows, gold and silver and bronze objects, fair women, and one golden-haired hero among a host of swarthy comrades. Nor is this color there for decoration. It is put on, or rather it is put in, to stay; it is what gives each surface its depth, its interior animation, as well as a thousand outward appearances of change; the hue of this life is at once indestructible and disturbed. A storm is going on in Nature, a storm that may engulf all phenomena; but the phenomena are fast, and they survive.

The world of the *Iliad* abounds with moving creatures, animal and human, whose images are mixed. The oxen, the sheep, the dogs, the bees, the lions, the boars, the cranes, and above all the horses — the horses, most proud of their capacity to move, most conscious of their necks, their manes, their rippling tails — these share with swarms of men the secret of Homer's life, uttered for them in many a gigantic simile. The men themselves are great and swift, fiery and proud, of exalted stature and magnificent dress; eloquence flows from them like honey, and the epithets by which they are known stream away from them like long hair. It is as if the wind did this, for in such a world the wind is always blowing, as the sea is always heaving, the rivers are always rushing, and the tall trees are trembling to their tops. The gods are in motion too, sliding here from Olympus to show the flash of their eyes before they return along divine tangents; or rising from the grey sea, dripping tears; or slipping again under the waves, which one of them, Poseidon, shows his broad shoulders above, ruling them with his voice and wand.

The landscape of the *Iliad* is rich and energetic, as

befits its contents. It is deep-soiled and thickly wooded; its mountains have many ridges, and its shining seas are peopled with more islands than men know the names of. Honey bees abound, and cool springs gush in hidden glades which patient kine will seek out even though the danger of lions be what it is. The mountains of the gods are crowned with clouds, and perhaps only there the sound of the world comes faintly. Where we stand it is a strong, unceasing sound, a hum or roar which Homer accompanies with his hexameters. It is a sound we understand as well as hear. It explains for us the power of even inanimate objects to participate in the life of this poem. The goblets, the gold-studded staffs, the shields and swords have biographies, have pedigrees; they came here under their own momentum, and they will go hence likewise.

And Meriones gave to Odysseus a bow and a quiver and a sword, and about his head he set a helm wrought of hide, and with many a tight-stretched thong was it made stiff within, while without the white teeth of a boar of gleaming tusks were set thick on this side and that, well and cunningly, and within was fixed a lining of felt. This cap Autolycus on a time stole out of Eleon when he had broken into the stout-built house of Amyntor, son of Ormenus; and he gave it to Amphidamas of Cythera to take to Scandeia, and Amphidamas gave it to Molus as a guest-gift, but he gave it to his own son Meriones to wear; and now, being set thereon, it covered the head of Odysseus.

Such an object is not after all inanimate. It glories in its existence as any creature might. It approaches the distinction of being an Homeric animal — as, from the other side of creation, does one of Homer's greatest men:

And even as when a stalled horse that has fed his fill at the manger, breaketh his halter, and runneth stamping over the plain — being wont to bathe him in the fair-flowing river — and exulteth; on high doth he hold his head and about his shoulders his mane floateth streaming, and as he glorieth in his splendor his knees nimbly bear him to the haunts and pastures of mares; even so swiftly plied Hector his feet and knees, urging on his charioteers, when he had heard the voice of the god.

All the life in the *Iliad* is one life.

It is not, however, monotonous or meaningless. If the *Iliad* is packed with sound, it is not noisy. If it is restless without end, it is not sick of a fever. Its abundant life is brilliant with form. This is because Homer never forgets the great world he seemed to cut away when he concentrated our gaze upon the small strip of Trojan shore where the crowded action takes place. We are given but a fragment of the world to see, just as we are given but a few days of the war, and just as those few days are subdued to the theme of Achilles' wrath. Achilles, outraged by Agamemnon, withdraws from the fighting, and asks Thetis his mother to intercede with Zeus against the Greeks until they shall have suffered enough to suit his pleasure; but when their sufferings include the death of his comrade Patroclus he returns in a new rage and kills Hector. That is the action of the *Iliad*, in one spot and stretch of time. Yet nothing of what Homer knows is missing in the end.

The great world is kept. That is the meaning of the catalogue in the second book, the roll call of countries whence these heroes came. They are homesick for Greece, and puzzled as to why they left it. The good past which their present madness has repudiated returns to plague them with many a remembered beauty. The lineage of cups and spears is a life line to normal experience. The gods are shown in their serene dwelling places — but shown, too, leaving them, drawn here by the terrible importance of tragedy. For neither the great world nor the little one is Homer's subject, but the two together, alternating and competing. The little one escapes into the great one when it can, yet often enough the great one bears back upon it, pressing it into place and silence, and all but crushing the strong men who are its inhabitants. So in a steady rhythm the *Iliad* oscillates between bustle and quiet, between masses of men in motion and one man making music in his hut, between the din of furious battle and the domestic peace of bedchambers, of weaving rooms, and of walls where old men sit like grasshoppers, weak and lily-voiced. Even the fighting has its variety, its great chords and its pauses. The meaning of the *Iliad*, if meaning there must be, is neither in the narrow world it fills nor in the wide one it remembers. It is in the relation between these two — between this much and all.

Nor are the realms confused. Nothing is confused in Homer, because nothing is vague. He gives us one detail at a time, in sharp focus. He is a farsighted poet whose vision penetrates foreground and background with equal ease. He does not run things together as the impressionist, uncertain of his aim, inveterately will. In Homer only one thing at a time is visible, but the others are waiting, silent and apart, to be seen when his attention sweeps to take them in. The *Iliad* would be a less tremendous tragedy were this not true.

For it is a tragedy. The emphasis is upon those pressures at the center, those all but intolerable burdens imposed from without, which are the sign that man is trying more than he can do. The little world of war is the world upon which the *Iliad* lavishes its art. The other world is there, but this is the one that suffers.

The movement of the poem is compounded of great velocity and great weight. Much is carried, but it is swung with surprising speed. The sense of a burden huge to the point of hopelessness is never lost, yet motion never stops; there is still the lightness that art must have if it is not to encumber the earth. It cannot always be seen how Homer accomplishes this miracle, but it is certain that his repetitions help — his refrains, his never-failing epithets, and his far-famed similes. These stitch his fabric solid, reënforcing every thread to the last corner. Our consciousness is kept always at the full; we are not permitted to forget that Achilles is swift-footed, that Agamemnon is king of men, that Nestor is the Gerenian horseman, that silver-footed Thetis is daughter to the old man of the sea, that Odysseus of the many wiles is also a sacker of cities, that Diomedes is good at the war cry, that Aphrodite loves laughter, that Hera sits on a golden throne, and that Zeus, the son of Cronos, is cloud-gatherer and lord over all. Every mortal, every god, takes the full weight of his identity with him wherever he goes, reappearing in the panoply of his several names as he prepares to speak that which we already know; for Homer's creatures take pleasure in declaring themselves even when there is no novelty to disclose, just as the objects with which he surrounds them grow to be eternal objects, seen in the setting of time. So things that are done are done as in ritual, the same words always coming back: "The wind filled the belly of the sail," "And this plan seemed to his mind the best," "All ungentle was the voice he heard," "But why doth my heart thus hold converse with me?"

The great loom of the similes never pauses in its work of weaving Homer's worlds together.

The Trojans came on with clamor and with a cry like birds, even as the clamor of cranes ariseth before the face of heaven, when they flee from wintry storms and measureless rain, and with clamor fly toward the streams of Ocean, bearing slaughter and death to Pigmy men.

Even as when from some place of outlook a goatherd seeth a cloud coming over the face of the deep before the blast of the West Wind, and to him being afar off it seemeth blacker than pitch as it passeth over the face of the deep, and it bringeth a mighty whirlwind; and he shuddereth at sight of it, and driveth his flock beneath a cave; even in such wise by the side of the Aiantes did the thick battalions of youth, nurtured of Zeus, move into furious war.

And he fell to the ground in the dust like a poplar tree that hath grown up in the bottom land of a great marsh, smooth of stem, but from the top thereof branches grow: this hath some wainwright felled with the gleaming iron that he might bend him a felloe for a beauteous chariot, and it lieth drying by a river's banks.

And he bowed his head to one side like a poppy that in a garden is laden with its fruit and the rains of spring; so bowed he to one side his head, laden with his helmet.

Full easily did he cast down the wall of the Achaeans, even as when a boy scattereth the sand by the sea, one that makes of it a plaything in his childishness, and then again confounds it with hands and feet as he maketh sport.

And they ever thronged about the corpse as when in a farmstead flies buzz about the full milk-pails, in the season of spring, when the milk drenches the vessels; even so thronged they about the corpse.

Him the old man Priam was first to behold with his eyes as he sped gleaming over the plain, like to the star that cometh forth at harvest time, and brightly do his rays shine amid the host of stars in the darkness of night, the star that men call by name the Dog of Orion. Brightest of all is he, yet withal he is a sign of evil, and bringeth much fever upon wretched mortals. Even in such wise did the bronze gleam upon the breast of Achilles as he ran.

And as in a dream a man availeth not to pursue one that fleeth before him — the one availeth not to flee, nor the other to pursue — even so Achilles availed not to overtake Hector in his fleetness, neither Hector to escape.

Such masterpieces keep on coming, in dozens, in hundreds; the engine does not tire, for the work it does is done at the heart of the poem. The similes of the *Iliad* are not its ornaments, they are rather the stuff which the fable adorns, they are the basic life over which action creeps like embroidery — gilding it, to be sure, but leaving it no less substantial than it was. No reader in his senses skips them, or misses the significance of their coming at times in flocks and showers, as when the tide of battle rises and wrath grows to a storm; a series of them, one ignited by another, is ever a sign that events of fatal importance are imminent. Nor are they invariably long. When Athene saved Menelaus from death by the arrow of Pandarus she did it quickly, and the words themselves are quick: "She swept it just aside from the flesh, even as a mother sweepeth a fly from her child when he lieth in sweet slumber." The hands of Automedon when he had despoiled Aretus of his armor were "all bloody, even as a lion that hath devoured a bull." And the armor which Hephaestus made for Achilles, though it would have been too much for any other man to wear, fitted his glorious limbs so well that it "became as it were wings to him."

The eloquence of Homer's men, and of his women too, is more than an accident in the *Iliad*. It is also a function of the fury with which a vast world drives in upon its center. The old horseman Phoenix, once the nurse of Achilles, reminds the stubborn hero that Peleus had ordered him to teach the boy "to be both a speaker of words and a doer of deeds." Eloquence was a respected art, in peace as well as war. But now in the ninth year of carnage before Troy it has grown into a desperate art, and the flames that play in it are as fierce as the necessities that move these men to speak. Even Nestor, who is too ancient for anything but talk, must talk of terrible things. He is "sweet of speech," this "clear-voiced orator of the men of Pylos," and words flow from his tongue "sweeter than honey," yet he summons thunder in his effort to quell the wrath of Achilles and Agamemnon:

Nay, hearken unto me; ye are both younger than I. Ere now have I consorted with warriors that were better than ye, and never did they set me at naught. Such warriors have I never since seen, nor shall see, as Peirithous was and Dryas, shepherd of the host, and Caeneus and Exadius and godlike Polyphemus, and Theseus, son of Aegeus, peer of the immortals. Mightiest were these of all men reared upon the earth; mightiest were they, and with the mightiest did they fight, even with the centaurs that had their lairs among the mountains, and in terrible wise did they destroy them.

In the seventh book, chiding the Greek chieftains because they hesitate to volunteer against Hector in single combat, he breaks into wrath of his own sort, moodily remembering the days when men were not children:

I would, O father Zeus and Athene and Apollo, that I were young as when beside swift-flowing Celadon the Pylians and Arcadians that rage with spears gathered together and fought beneath the walls of Pheia about the streams of Iardanus.

And on he goes, while in his words the deep past starts running like a sea, revealing the waves and ocean-creatures, the fabulous man-monsters, of time's oldest meadow, faded from every memory but his. The pages of reminiscence with which, not unlike Polonius, he keeps the impatient Patroclus waiting in the eleventh book to learn for Achilles who it is that has been brought wounded into Nestor's hut, are irrelevant to everything save our suspense, yet they are wonderful as the words of all these afflicted men are wonderful: as those of Odysseus are when he smites Thersites the blasphemer, or argues against going home to Greece, or is spokesman for the embassy to Achilles in the ninth book, beseeching the indispensable hero to return; as those of Hecuba are at the close of the poem, when she rebukes the temerity of Priam, setting off to buy his son's body back from Achilles; as those of Priam are, answering her through his grief:

Seek not to stay me that am fain to go, neither be thyself a bird of ill-boding in my halls; thou shalt not persuade me. For if any other of the men that are upon the face of the earth had bidden me this, whether of seers that divine from sacrifice or of priests, a false thing might we deem it, and turn away therefrom the more; but now — for myself I heard the voice of the goddess and looked upon her face — I will go forth, neither shall her word be vain. And if it be my fate to lie dead by the ships of the brazen-coated Achaeans, so would I have it; forthwith let Achilles slay me, when once I have clasped in my arms my son, and have put from me the desire for wailing.

There, in that last outburst, is the true tone of the *Iliad's* oratory. It is a unique tone, both choked and free. The men and women who speak are full of things they cannot say, and yet they say them. The result is a music at once heavy and clear, like that toward which the tongue of Othello, originally inarticulate, magnificently toils. The heroes of Homer had been taught to deliver themselves of words, but they had not expected that these things would have to be said. They are said under pressures which no man here had imagined far away and long ago in his dear native land.

The density of the *Iliad* tends to be absolute. Its passionate beginning is not easily read by one who comes to it relaxed, as one may come to the *Odyssey*. This opening is compact of anger, terror, and death. Events are already complex — the wrath now not of Achilles but of Apollo, and the pestilence among the host, so that "ever did the pyres of the dead burn thick." Then in no time at all they become complex beyond cure. Homer has started at the moment most ripe for tragedy. His people are packed into a limited space of earth which nine years have made them loathe. They loathe one another and themselves, in disgust and in despair. Nor is it merely the invading Greeks of whom this is true. They are savage with frustration — the freeing of Helen was not to have taken nine years — but so are the Trojans savage, with fatigue and fear and with a special loathing which they feel for Paris, Helen's abductor and effeminate husband. And both sides hate Helen, even while it is the case that no man who gazes at her can resist her beauty.

Thus the *Iliad* begins under the "knotted cord of mighty strife and evil war, a knot none might break

nor undo." "Scant is the breathing-space in war," remarks the poet in his seventeenth book, days later than
this day when wide-ruling Agamemnon was so sorely
vexed, "and with rage was his black heart wholly filled,
and his eyes were like blazing fire." This was the day
when we met our first god in the poem, and he was
nothing like the goddess whose bright charm over-
spreads the opening of the *Odyssey*. "Down from the
peaks of Olympus he strode, wroth at heart, bearing
on his shoulders his bow and covered quiver. The arrows rattled on the shoulders of the angry god, as he
moved; and his coming was like the night." Even of
Pallas Athene it was said, when Achilles turned on that
day to see who had pulled his golden hair: "Terribly
did her eyes flash."

That was the beginning, and all is of a piece thereafter. Achilles has had leisure to reflect that the Trojans never were his enemies; they have harried no kine
of his, abducted no wife. He is here for nothing save
that Agamemnon's brother shall be avenged. And
avenged, ironically, upon a contemptible "ogler of
girls," a curled and pampered Paris, despised and hated
"of all men like black death" — a "strange man,"
Hector says, a man of unstable understanding, says
Helen. Achilles is here for nothing. But so are all the
people of the *Iliad*. A vortex has whirled and sucked
them into its darkness, and in that darkness where there
is so little room their spirits have hardened. "Ever is thy
heart unyielding," says Alexander to Hector. "Thy
heart is unbending," Patroclus tells Achilles. "Of

iron verily is thy heart," cries Hecuba to Priam. The same thing will be said by Telemachus to Penelope, but it will not be true, and it will not be said in a tragedy.

This is a tragedy of strife whose origin can scarcely be remembered, and whose development is altogether out of proportion to that origin. As the sense of disproportion grows, the savagery of what men do increases. The war becomes steadily more abominable. The Greeks will take no Trojan alive — "Let not one escape destruction," Agamemnon runs and shouts to Menelaus, "nay, not the man-child whom his mother bears in her womb; let not even him escape, but let all perish together out of Ilios, unmourned and unmarked." The insults to the body of Patroclus are more than matched by those returned upon the body of Hector. Each chariot paints itself with woeful war. "And with blood was all the axle sprinkled beneath, and the rims round about the car, with the drops that smote upon them from the horses' hooves and from the tires." The details of death grow ever more cruel, ever more grotesque. Mydon's body, pitching on its head in deep sand, remains erect there until his horses kick him horizontal. Peisander's torso, shorn of its arms and head, goes rolling like a round stone amid the throng. As Alcathous falls with a thud, his heart still beats a little so that the spear that has penetrated it quivers at the butt. Harpalion, slain by Meriones, lies "stretched out like a worm on the earth." Heads hang by the skin of the neck, teeth are shaken out, and dying eyes are filled with blood.

But the climax of so much savagery is reached in the great river battle of the twenty-first book, when Achilles drives half of a Trojan army into the Xanthus and slaughters more young men than can be counted while they swim and cry in the deep eddies, confused among their chariots. The river itself, outraged by the loss of so many sons, and unable any longer to pour its waters forth into the bright sea, rushes tumultuously upon Achilles, "raging on high and seething with foam and blood and dead men." The dead men, both on shore and in the stream, already lie rotting. "Many a fish as he leapeth among the waves shall dart up beneath the black ripple to eat the white fat of Lycaon." And even now the eels and fishes deal with the corpse of Asteropaeus, "plucking and tearing the fat about his kidneys." On the adjacent plain are strewn bodies wet only with their recent blood. These the wrathful river, pursuing Achilles as he flies at last in fear, mercilessly overflows, so that "many goodly arms and corpses of youths slain in battle" float there in a new horror. The end comes only when Hephaestus, invoked in Achilles' aid, meets water with fire and burns even the river away.

First on the plain was the fire kindled, and burned the dead, the many dead that lay thick therein, slain by Achilles; and all the plain was parched, and the bright water was stayed. And as when at harvest-time the North Wind quickly parcheth again a freshly watered orchard, and glad is he that tilleth it; so was the whole plain parched, and the dead he utterly consumed; and then against the River he turned his gleaming flame. Burned were the elms and the willows and the tamarisks, burned the lotus and the rushes and the galingale, that round the fair streams of the river grew abundantly; tormented were the eels and the fishes in the eddies.

If Homer is a master of horror, he is also a master of relief from horror. None knows better than he the clean blessing of fire, or the comfort of "sweet Sleep." He does not forget to pause when pause is necessary lest we grow too heavily laden with the terror of his tale. Just when all threatens to be confusion, to be an intolerable heaping up of woe, there comes such a moment of silence as that at the end of the eighth book, when the Trojans rest for the night in their new camp on the plain before the city:

Even as in heaven about the gleaming moon the stars shine clear, when the air is windless, and forth to view appear all mountain peaks and high headlands and glades, and from heaven breaketh open the infinite air, and all stars are seen, and the shepherd joyeth in his heart; even in such multitudes between the ships and the streams of Xanthus shone the fires that the Trojans kindled before the face of Ilios. A thousand fires were burning in the plain and by each sat fifty men in the glow of the blazing fire. And their horses, eating of white barley and spelt, stood beside the cars and waited for fair-throned Dawn.

Sweet seep land distant fire. It is a different relief from that brought by Hephaestus as he consumes the stench along the Xanthus. But then Homer is always different. The brawls and magnanimities of the funeral games for Patroclus are another ingredient of change, inserting laughter between the two grimmest moments of this story.

Yet the story remains tragic, its interludes of peace only intensifying the tread of its doom. Its concentration is complete. Difficult to enter, it is impossible to leave. Homer has been praised for his technical triumph in compressing so much of the Trojan war into so small a compass, for his ingenuity in organizing so much history about the wrath of Achilles. But his theme is vaster than any war, and outreaches history. His theme is the world, which here if anywhere is seen, heard, felt, feared, and pitied at its heart. Here, as would be the case with any heart we had entered, all is closeness, darkness, and the terrible beat of the organ. All is urgency. The hatreds of these heroes cannot rest or cease. There seems to be no time for wisdom. Decisions must be made impromptu, against judgment and even against the will. The poem is packed, its atmosphere is thick. Distances dissolve, so that no artist would succeed who set out to make pictures of what he saw. The *Iliad* cannot be illustrated. It hums with an energy both divine and diseased, both magnificent and calamitous, both beautiful and terrible. Here is the world of man becoming itself, as it were, in crisis. The morals of existence are being made before us — a nebular creation — and we cannot say that they should not have been so made. This war should never have been, but it is senseless to say so. It has become necessary to our knowledge; man has become most noble, most transparent, through his errors.

Zeus, addressing from his height the deathless horses of Achilles as they weep for Patroclus, soliloquizes thus:

Ah unhappy pair, wherefore gave we you to king Peleus, to a mortal, while ye are ageless and immortal? Was it that among wretched men ye too should have sorrows? For in sooth there is naught, I ween, more miserable than man among all things that breathe and move upon earth.

But there speaks the lord of creation, not created — newly created — man. The king of the Brobdingnagians declares, after listening to the best account Gulliver can give of the society he has left at home: "I cannot but conclude the bulk of your natives to be the most pernicious race of little odious vermin that nature ever suffered to crawl upon the surface of the earth." But there speaks, and in a comedy, one who will never see men in the magnificence of their mistakes. It is thus that Homer sees them — both the error and the glory.

The mistakes and the magnificence are telescoped, the landscape of fate is curiously foreshortened. Irony lurks in every line, though we may not know it is there until we have remembered it. Achilles will die young, yet he looks and moves like one who will live forever. This war, bitter to the taste though it is, has so much beauty in it that we cannot glance away. The heroes are subject equally to the gods and to themselves; they are impelled to do what they do, but this does not mean that they lose importance. We watch their war as if we knew it would never end; yet we know it will, and indeed we know that it did. Helen does not love Paris any longer, but she must make love to him when Aphrodite brings him home from battle. Aphrodite, the laughter-loving, cries at her mother's knee because Diomedes has wounded her. Hector is roused to his final wrath, and filled with his final confidence, only because Zeus wishes to hasten the moment when his decree against the Greeks can be recalled; and the Trojans go eagerly in his wake, not knowing that it is to their certain death. When Patroclus returns to the battle which will obliterate him, the only fear of Achilles is that he will do deeds surpassing his, and so lessen his honor. Deiphobus appears outside the walls of Troy as Hector flees Achilles in his last duel and speaks words which seem to be wise: they counsel him to stand his ground and do battle with Achilles man to man. And Hector answers him: "Deiphobus, verily in time past thou wast far the dearest of my brethren, that were born of Hecabe and Priam, but now I deem that I shall honor thee in my heart even more, seeing thou hast dared for my sake, when thine eyes beheld me, to come forth from out the wall, while the others abide within." The irony here is at least twofold. The words are not wise, since Hector has no chance against the man-slayer he has been fleeing; and they are not friendly, because they are spoken in reality by one who knows this. They are spoken by Athene in the guise of Deiphobus, and the real Deiphobus will never learn that great Hector spoke to him thus, using his name in wondrous compliment.

The crowning irony, however, is Thetis' when she

rises a second time from the sea, having heard again her dear child Achilles groaning. She had come the first time at the beginning of the story, when the cause of Achilles' grief was the dishonor done him by Agamemnon, and the loss of his fair-cheeked Briseis. Then we were told how she arrived in answer to his prayer:

So he spake, weeping, and his queenly mother heard him as she sat in the depths of the sea beside the old man her father. And speedily she came forth from the grey sea like a mist, and sate her down before his face, as he wept; and she stroked him with her hand, and spake to him, and called him by name: "My child, why weepest thou? What sorrow hath come upon thy heart? Speak out; hide it not in thy mind, that we both may know."

And we were told how he besought her to intercede with Zeus against the Greeks, and how she did so — indeed, all of the action since that day has been determined by Zeus' promises to her. All of the action, including now the death of the mortal whom Achilles loves best, Patroclus of the embattled body, Patroclus who had worn his famous armor and driven his ageless horses. But Thetis does not know this when in the eighteenth book she hears him again:

Then terribly did Achilles groan aloud, and his queenly mother heard him as she sat in the depths of the sea beside the old man her father. Thereat she uttered a shrill cry, and the goddesses thronged about her, even all the daughters of Nereus that were in the deep of the sea. . . . So saying she left the cave and the nymphs went with her weeping, and around them the waves of the sea were cloven asunder. And when they were come to the deep-soiled land of Troy they stepped forth upon the beach, one after the other, where the ships of the Myrmidons were drawn up in close lines round about swift Achilles. Then to his side, as he groaned heavily, came his queenly mother, and with a shrill cry she clasped the head of her son, and with wailing spake unto him winged words:

"My child, why weepest thou, What sorrow hath come upon thy heart? Speak out; hide it not. Thy wish has verily been brought to pass for thee by Zeus, as aforetime thou didst pray, stretching forth thy hands, even that one and all the sons of the Achaeans should suffer cruel things."

What you wanted has been given you — was it not enough? Too much, Achilles answers. On which irony the entire poem pivots. Thetis and her child who is the best of men have been caught in the net of their success. The success was real, but now success itself has changed its name.

In the shadow of so desperate an irony it is no wonder that Thetis regrets she had ever reared this boy, cursed as she was in bearing him. Zeus had afflicted her once with a mortal husband, Peleus, whose bed she must endure; and here is the result, a hero who is hers but whom she cannot help, however many times she rises and goes to him. Birth into such a world as the *Iliad* inhabits is bemoaned by many another of its persons. Hector wishes that Paris had not been born; and Helen, taking the cue from him, wishes the same thing for herself:

O Brother of me that am a dog, a contriver of mischief and abhorred of all, I would that on the day when first my mother gave me birth an evil wind-storm had borne me away to some mountain or to the wave of the loud-resounding sea, where the wave might have swept me away or ever these things came to pass.

But Hector does not hear the sister of this speech, cried out to him by Andromache after his death:

Ah Hector, woe is me! to one fate, it seemeth, were we born, both of us twain, thou in Troy in the house of Priam, and I in Thebe beneath wooded Placus in the house of Eëtion, who reared me when I was a babe, hapless father of a cruel-fated child; would God he had never begotten me.

There is a special pathos in the numerous pedigrees Homer gives us of youths who are slain, youths whom a gazette would report by name only; but Homer knows who their fathers are, and does not spare us the details of how they will be missed. "Ares, Ares, thou bane of mortals, thou blood-stained stormer of walls," Zeus might have called to the war-god whom he so much abhorred, "thou slaughterest merest innocents, in no good cause." There is "Anthemion's son, the lusty youth Simoeisius, whom on a time his mother had borne beside the banks of Simois, as she journeyed down from Ida, whither she had followed with her parents to see their flocks." There are the two sons of Dares, a priest of Hephaestus, one of whom the god interferes to save from Diomedes, "enfolding him in darkness that his aged priest might not be utterly fordone with grief." Pedaeus, slain by Meges, "was in truth a bastard, howbeit goodly Theano had reared him carefully as her own children, to do pleasure to her husband." Abas and Polyidus were "sons of the old man Eurydamas, the reader of dreams; howbeit they came not back for the old man to interpret dreams for them, but mighty Diomedes slew them." Pandarus, son of Lycaon, is notable not only because it is he who breaks the oath both armies had sworn to desist from general combat until Menelaus and Alexander should settle their quarrel between them, but even more because of what Homer tells us concerning the home he left — and, of course, will never see again. In his case it is horses he will miss, for he came without any of the fine beasts his father had urged him to harness and drive to war. "Howbeit I hearkened not — verily it had been better far! — but spared the horses lest in the multitude of men they should lack fodder, they that were wont to eat their fill. So I left them, and am come on foot to Ilios."

There is Axylus, "Teuthras' son, that dwelt in well-built Arisbe, a man rich in substance, that was beloved of all men; for he dwelt in a home by the high-road and was wont to give entertainment to all." There are the twin sons of Bucolion, whom he had by the fountain nymph Abarbarea when once, while shepherding his flocks, he lay with her in love. There is Iphidamas, son of Antenor —

and Cisseus reared him in his house while he was yet but a little child, even his mother's father. But when he came to the measure of glorious youth he sought to keep him there, and offered him his own daughter; howbeit, a bridegroom newly wed, forth from his bridal chamber he went after the rumor of the coming of the Achaeans. . . . So there he fell, and slept a sleep of bronze, unhappy youth, far from his wedded wife, far from the bride of whom he had known no joy.

The two sons of Merops came here against their father's wish, for he was above all men skilled in prophesying, and he knew they would die; which they do, by Diomedes' hand. "A certain Euchenor" came with the same knowledge from Corinth, but with better reason:

He embarked upon his ship knowing full well the deadly fate to be, for often had his old sire, good Polyidus, told it him, to wit, that he must either perish of dire disease in his own halls, or amid the ships of the Achaeans be slain by the Trojans. . . . Him Paris smote beneath the jaw, under the ear, and forthwith his spirit departed.

But it is Achilles whose man-slaying hands work the worst havoc among the hopes of those who have sent their loved ones to this war. It is Achilles who disembowels Polydorus, son of Priam, who had forbidden the boy to fight "for that among his children he was the youngest born and was dearest in his eyes; and in swiftness of foot he surpassed all. And lo, now in his folly, making show of his fleetness of foot, he was rushing through the foremost fighters, until he lost his life." Lycaon, whom the fishes were to eat, was another son of Priam; Achilles had once before encountered him, as he cut the shoots of a young fig tree in his father's

orchard, and then Achilles merely sold him into cap-
tivity. But he had been ransomed; and now on the
twelfth day he is here again, caught once more and
begging Achilles for his life; in vain, for the two-edged
sword makes him food for eels. The greatest son of
Priam is Hector, whom of all the slain warriors we
know most about. We know his wife Andromache:
how she weaves for him, and how at the very moment
of his death she is having a hot bath prepared for him,
since she thinks he will come home tired from the day's
battle. We know his son Astyanax, who fears the
plumes on his father's helmet, and shrinks away until
Hector, laughing, removes the bronze object with its
horsehair crest and kisses the child, and fondles him
in his arms. No background for death is so rich as
this, unless it be the background for Achilles' death.
But that is not to happen here.

No wonder that in such a poem, where events press
so relentlessly, and every move is so dangerous, the
heroes are often at a loss to know what they should do.

And grief came upon the son of Peleus, and within his
shaggy breast his heart was divided in counsel, whether he
should draw his sharp sword from beside his thigh, and break
up the gathering, and himself slay the son of Atreus, or should
stay his wrath and curb his spirit.

Thus Achilles in his first quarrel, facing Agamemnon.
Athene decides for him then, standing behind him and
tugging at his golden hair. But there is not always a
divinity to shape decisions; though Hector, "divided
in mind" at the Scaean gate because he cannot conclude

whether it is best to drive again into the turmoil or to collect his host within the wall, is visited by Apollo and told to go headlong against Patroclus. Even the gods hesitate and ponder — Zeus as to how he can best make good his promise to Thetis, and Hera as to how she can most effectively beguile her immortal husband. "And this plan seemed to her mind the best — to go to Ida, when she had beauteously adorned her person, if so be he might desire to lie by her side and embrace her body in love, and she might shed a warm and gentle sleep upon his eyelids and his cunning mind." But it is the mortals who find it hardest to think. Odysseus in his poem, thinker that he is by nature, genius, and long habit, will frequently be of double mind. And Aeneas, with such differences as shall appear between him and his Greek forebears, will regularly be rooted by Virgil in one spot, divided even to the point of paralysis. Here in the *Iliad*, however, indecision has its original and proper quality, and a tragic quality because we know so well that every answer must be wrong. "But why doth my heart thus hold converse with me?" It is one of the *Iliad's* refrains, as has been remarked. Menelaus says it over the body of Patroclus. Agenor says it, gathering himself together to await oncoming Achilles. Hector says it, wondering whether he should flee Achilles at the last or stand and fight. Achilles himself says it over Hector's body, unimportant now:

But why doth my heart thus hold converse with me? There lieth by the ships a dead man unwept, unburied, even Patroclus;

him will I not forget so long as I abide among the living, and my knees are quick.

No wonder that in such a poet there is no interest in the familiar devices of suspense. Homer foretells everything, again and again. He knows, or Zeus knows, that the war will last a long time, and that this final year of it will be the most terrible. We are told that Patroclus will die; that Achilles will arm himself again and slay Hector; that the Achaeans will take steep Ilios and sack it; and that the Argives will go back in their ships to their dear native land. We are told all this, and more, because of a greater suspense which we shall then constantly feel. The outcome of a story is one thing to know, but in a great story the outcome is only one thing, if indeed the last thing, in a series. Before it arrives there are a thousand moments on which we hang, suspended in the uncertainty which attends the heartbeat of time. The *Iliad* is a great story, and so it is filled with the kind of suspense that matters. It is the kind that can be felt again in the hundredth reading. We know what will happen, yet as we find ourselves once more imbedded in the ironies of the tale it seems that we do not know. The fears, the illusions, the hopes, the despairs come alive again. And the ironies lose none of their crushing weight; mortality still stings. We wait again while Thetis learns that what she has done for Achilles has failed to make him happy. We remember that Achilles will give the body of Hector back to Priam when he comes, but as we watch the old man coming we share his trepidation. Suspense never leaves us in the *Iliad,* foreshortened as it is into one complex of dark and sore uncertainty.

Even the gods suffer at times where it hurts gods most to suffer, in their serenity. A world is being made, and it is too much for them. They are very brilliant and beautiful, like shooting stars, or in Zeus' case like all the cloud-capped heaven; but before the poem is finished they have had a war among themselves, and rivalries have developed that will reverberate through eternity. They visit the battlefield in every guise — Aphrodite once as an ancient dame, a wool-comber, though to be sure with beauteous neck and lovely bosom and flashing eyes; Athene once as a heron hard by the way, crying unseen by night to guide Odysseus and Diomedes toward the camp of Rhesus where horses, wondrous like the rays of the sun, are waiting to be stolen. They come and go, restlessly, in animal or human form, and sometimes in their own form, terrible to see. It is not their splendor that suffers. As Poseidon rides the waves the sea-beasts gambol beneath him as they always did, for they know their lord, and the sea parts gladly before his car. As Zeus sits among the peaks of Ida the many-fountained, mother of wild beasts and seat of his fragrant altar, he exults in his glory as he always has, "looking upon the city of the Trojans, and the ships of the Achaeans, on the flashing of the bronze, and on the slayers and the slain." His dalliance on this mountain with Hera, when she beguiles him with dreams, sweet sleep, and herself, could not have been more splendid in any golden age:

And beneath them the divine earth made fresh-sprung grass to grow, and dewy lotus, and crocus, and hyacinth, thick and soft, that upbare them from the ground. Therein lay the twain, and were clothed about with a cloud, fair and golden, wherefrom fell drops of glistering dew.

It is not the glory of the gods that is disturbed. It is their sense that human life is simple. They too must go their way into the battle: Hera, Pallas Athene, Poseidon, Hermes, and Hephaestus on the side of Agamemnon's men; Ares, Phoebus Apollo, Artemis, Leto, Xanthus, and Aphrodite on the side of Troy. And the issue is long delayed. Not until the twenty-second book does Zeus hang out his golden scales — "and down sank the day of doom of Hector, and departed unto Hades; and Phoebus Apollo left him." The implication is that Apollo goes reluctantly; puzzled, even, if that is one of the things a god can be.

Yet it must be said again that the *Iliad* is not confused. Its people are, and its one grand event; but Homer is always free to separate a scene from its fellows, and in this scene to create a sudden beauty. "The sun was now just striking on the fields" as in the seventh book the two armies set about burying their fallen comrades — it is a short phrase, and a conventional one, but in its place it accomplishes a wonder. The thousand campfires at the end of the eighth book are famous as far as poetry is known; after millenniums they have lost no sparkle of their brightness. The superb episode of the tenth book, the night expedition of Diomedes and Odysseus, is in itself an epic, tough and fearful in its charm; the best friend of Odysseus, Athene of the flashing eyes, is heard this time, not seen; she gives her sign on the right, and the doughty killers go their way "like two lions through the black night, amid the slaughter, amid the corpses, through the arms and the black blood," disappearing from every Greek eye or ear until Nestor catches the sound of horses coming back.

Then there are the single objects which Homer needs only to mention in order that they should be forever fixed in our memories. There is the oak tree, landmark by the Scaean gate. And there is the "wind-waved wild fig tree" past which Achilles pursues Hector in the ultimate race. These are like the solitary sentences which so often shine forth from the text, bearing a brilliance not to be explained:

So said she; but they ere now were fast holden of the life-giving earth there in Lacedaemon, in their dear native land.

Ah, poor wretch, thy father and queenly mother shall not close thine eyes in death, but the birds that eat raw flesh shall rend thee, beating their wings thick and fast about thee.

Pitiless one, thy father, meseems, was not the knight Peleus, nor was Thetis thy mother, but the grey sea bare thee, and the beetling cliffs, for thy heart is unbending.

Unseen of these great Priam entered in, and coming close to Achilles, clasped in his hands his knees, and kissed his hands, the terrible, man-slaying hands that had slain his many sons.

And now somewhere amid the rocks, on the lonely mountains, on Sipylus, where, men say, are the couching-places of goddesses, even of the nymphs that range swiftly in the dance about Achelous, there, albeit a stone, she broodeth over her woes.

For at thy death thou didst neither stretch out thy hands to me from thy bed, nor speak to me any word of wisdom whereon I might have pondered night and day with shedding of tears.

Or, to consider now the masterpiece of Homer's separate triumphs, they are like the duel between Hector and Achilles — isolated, clear, silent; surrounded, as a climax should be, by distance and a hush. For the Trojans on the walls behold it as a thing far away; only a few objects — the fig tree, the two fair-flowing fountains, the broad washing-tanks where Trojan women cleansed their raiment in the forgotten days of peace — compete for their attention with these two greatest of living men, one of whom is running to his death. The running is what is so silent, so unreal, as if two figures ran in a painting, and one would never overtake the other. It was like a dream, says Homer. But the dream comes to an end; Hector stands, gives battle, and is slain. The silence then is shattered by Hecuba's loud cry from the walls, and by Priam's piteous groan; though indoors Andromache goes on with her weaving, unaware of any dream.

Hector is the greatest man in the poem with the exception of one still greater man, Achilles. More often than others he contemplates the fame which he will some day have. All of them live not only in the conviction that they are doomed but in the clear consciousness that men who come after them will say thus and so. Hector, however, is the most eloquent in his imaginings:

And some one shall some day say even of men that are yet to be, as he saileth in his many-benched ship over the wine-dark sea: "This is a barrow of a man that died in olden days, whom on a time in the midst of his prowess glorious Hector slew." So shall some man say, and my glory shall never die.

Homer's people know they will be famous, and live in the dusky glow which this certainty kindles about their knees. The lives they expect to lose are valuable to them; they are works of art, each one of them unique. "Even in days to come," says Helen to Hector, "we may be a song for men that are yet to be." Agamemnon knows this too, and Diomedes, and Sarpedon, and of course Achilles. It is as if Homer had no work to do in making them what they are; they mold their own images, carefully building out each part and standing off to scrutinize the whole. Each one of them is round and clear, a sharp detail holding its outline amid a host of others.

Odysseus, shorter than the other men but broader of shoulder, the bellwether of the herd, the ram of thick fleece, will shine more perfectly in his own poem; though here too he is complete, both in the tenth book when he leads home the horses of Rhesus and later on when he argues with Achilles that food and drink are necessary before Patroclus shall be avenged. Telemonian Aias, the man mountain, the wall of brawn and burly courage, is not a subtle fellow; he thinks Achilles will be impressed by an arithmetic that proves the seven women Agamemnon has promised more desirable than the one woman, Briseis, of whom Achilles has been deprived. Diomedes, vice to Achilles in terror and strength, the Greek most Trojans fear while the greatest of them is absent in his hut from war, moves everywhere in the *Iliad* with a lion's nobility and beauty; he is the profoundest gentleman of the poem, so secure in his knowledge of himself that he cannot be insulted, so free of fault that he could not, even if he would, become the hero of a tragedy. Sarpedon, son of Zeus, is so wise and precious a person, and moreover is so distinguished in his lineage, that he can twice be saved from the death that would be due any other man.

Then his goodly comrades made godlike Sarpedon to sit beneath a beauteous oak of Zeus that beareth the aegis, and forth from his thigh valiant Pelagon, that was his dear comrade, thrust the spear of ash; and his spirit failed him, and down over his eyes a mist was shed. Howbeit he revived, and the breath of the North Wind as it blew upon him made him to live again after in grievous wise he had breathed forth his spirit.

Thus in the fifth book. But in the sixteenth book, when Patroclus kills him and his body is shamefully fought over just as that of Patroclus in its own time will be, Zeus himself intervenes — against the warning of Hera — and bids Apollo save Sarpedon forever.

Nor was Apollo disobedient to his father's bidding, but went down from the hills of Ida into the dread din of battle. Forthwith then he lifted up goodly Sarpedon forth from out the range of darts, and when he had borne him far away, bathed him in the streams of the river, and anointed him with ambrosia, and clothed him about with immortal raiment, and gave him to the twin brothers, Sleep and Death, who set him speedily in the rich land of wide Lycia.

The body of Patroclus, though it cannot be restored, is no less tenderly cleansed by Achilles.

Then the fire played about the belly of the cauldron, and the water grew warm. But when the water boiled in the bright bronze, then they washed him and anointed him richly with oil, filling his wounds with ointment of nine years old; and they laid him upon his bed, and covered him with a soft linen cloth from head to foot, and thereover with a white robe. So the whole night through around Achilles, swift of foot, the Myrmidons made moan in lamentation for Patroclus.

"For to all was he ever gentle while yet he lived," said Menelaus, echoing Achilles. Patroclus is a brilliant figure, deserving of Achilles' love. And Hector is a towering figure, deserving of his hate. But Achilles himself, as Homer never forgets to show us, is the abundant, incredible genius of the poem.

Achilles is the refined gold of this world's human wealth. He is supreme in everything, for he is absolutely alive. Among Homer's men he is not only the most wrathful and savage, he is the most loving, the most beautiful, the most splendid, the most inquisitive, the tenderest in filial feeling, the strongest, the most eloquent, and in the end the most courteous. The glory of his utterance — an entirely personal utterance, piercing and revealing — is like nothing else we hear, and least like the prolixity of Nestor. For Nestor is one thing, but Achilles is many things; his contradictions, his sudden new sides turned fiercely to the light, are the source of some flaming clarity in him which almost surpasses the sun. The poem derives from him; built into it, he is visible at the end of every perspective. We know the most about him because he is reflected in the most minds: in that of Thetis who lives for no one else, in that of Patroclus who can sit so quietly while his great friend sings and plays on a silver harp, in that of Peleus his faraway father, in that of Phoenix who once in Phthia fed him morsels of choice meat, seating him on his knee and giving him wine which he sputtered. And who else is so incessantly in the thoughts of the warriors, Greek or Trojan? For he is an army in himself. He carries unique weapons, he wears at last a shield on which Hephaestus has engraved the world, and he cries out with a trumpet voice which alone turns herds of horses back. His own divine horses, Xanthus and Balius, whose grievous lot it is to live among mortals, and who are so beautiful in their grief for Patroclus, abiding like pillars on a tomb, their heads bowed to the earth, miraculously can speak. "Aye verily," says Xanthus, "yet for this time will we save thee, mighty Achilles, albeit the day of doom is nigh thee. . . . It is thine own self that art fated to be slain in fight by a god and a mortal." And Achilles answers him: "Xanthus, why dost thou prophesy my death? Thou needest not at all. Well know I even of myself that it is my fate to perish here, far from my father dear, and my mother; howbeit even so will I not cease until I have driven the Trojans to surfeit of war."

For the doom of his early death is always in Achilles' ears. Hector's last words to him are of the day "when Paris and Phoebus Apollo shall slay thee, valorous though thou art, at the Scaean gate." And Thetis darkens her first visit to him by reminding him that his span of life is brief — "thou art doomed to a speedy death and withal art compassed with sorrow above all men." He speaks of it himself when he is rejecting the gifts sent to him by Agamemnon in the ninth book; and indeed it is as often on his lips as it is on those of his mother or of Zeus. "Straightway after Hector is thine own death ready at hand," Thetis tells him when she comes again. "Straightway may I die, seeing I was not to bear aid to my comrade at his slaying," cries Achilles. "Seek not then to hold me back from battle, for all thou lovest me; thou shalt not persuade me." His love of life is as great as the amount of it which he has — no man wants less to die — but the knowledge of his doom hangs over his least gesture, deepening the colors with which his person is graced, and accentuating the line of irony which lightens each edge of the wonderful world he lives in.

The poem is his from the moment at the beginning of the eighteenth book when he is told what everybody else knows, and what he himself fears, namely that Patroclus is dead and his body dishonored. The poem has always been his, but now his world is the only one it lives in. Terribly now does he groan, and anger, "sweeter far than trickling honey, waxeth like smoke" in his breast; though the one aim he henceforth has, to kill Hector, he repeatedly insists is the aim to make strife perish and anger itself yield unto peace. His wrath against Agamemnon has been swallowed up in his grief over the best of young men; he will need to be wrathful still if Patroclus is to be avenged, but wrath now will be a ritual, ushering in the end.

The savagery of Achilles which once had slain the father and the seven brothers of Andromache now rages to its height. When his hands grow weary of dealing death in the battle of the Scamander he chooses twelve youths alive out of the river and leads them forth, "dazed like fawns," to be bound with thongs and await their burning on the pyre of Patroclus. When Hector with his last breath pleads that his body be returned to Troy for burial, the answer of Achilles is implacable and monstrous:

Implore me not, dog, by knees or parents. Would that in any wise wrath and fury might bid me carve thy flesh and myself eat it raw, because of what thou hast wrought, as surely as there lives no man that shall ward off the dogs from thy head; nay, not though they should bring hither and weigh out ransom ten-fold, aye, twenty-fold, and should promise yet more; nay, not though Priam, son of Dardanus, should bid pay thy weight in gold; not even so shall thy queenly mother lay thee on a bier and make lament for thee, the son herself did bear, but dogs and birds shall devour thee utterly.

But dogs and birds do not devour Hector, and Priam's mission will be successful.

Meanwhile the body of Patroclus is burned with a terrible magnificence, on a pyre which measures a hundred feet each way. Many sheep and kine are burned with it, their fat first gathered by Achilles' own hands and used to enfold the corpse from head to foot. He adds jars of honey and oil, four horses with high-arched necks, two of the dead prince's favorite hounds, and at last the twelve valiant sons of Troy, their throats sacrificially cut. The fire does not burn until the North Wind and the West Wind are invoked by Iris to come from Thrace and fall upon the pyre and beat upon the flame.

And the whole night long swift Achilles, taking a two-handled cup in hand, drew wine from a golden bowl and poured it upon the earth, and wetted the ground, calling ever upon the spirit of hapless Patroclus. As a father waileth for his son, a son newly wed whose death hath brought woe to his hapless parents, even so wailed Achilles for his comrade as he burned his bones, going heavily about the pyre with ceaseless groaning.

Then for the first time in many nights sweet sleep can leap upon him as he withdraws a little way from the pyre and lies down in perfect weariness, awaiting the next bright day with its funeral games.

When the games are over, the grief and the wrath of Achilles are still not cured. His companions comfort themselves with supper and sleep, but not so the son of Thetis, who for twelve nights tosses on his side, on his back, on his face, unable to forget the woes he has borne, "passing through wars of men and the grievous waves."

Then again he would arise upon his feet and roam distraught along the shore of the sea. Neither would he fail to mark the Dawn, as she shone over the sea and the sea-beaches, but would yoke beneath his car his swift horses, and bind Hector behind the chariot to drag him withal; and when he had haled him thrice about the barrow of the dead son of Menoetius, he would rest again in his hut, but would leave Hector outstretched on his face in the dust.

At last his fury becomes a scandal even among the gods. Apollo, the friend of Hector, convinces the rest that Achilles is nowise right in his mind, for his heart is still set on cruelty and he has lost all pity. The gods agree, and Thetis is sent on a third visit to her son; she tells him that heaven is angry with him, and conveys to him the will of Zeus, which is that he shall surrender the body of Hector to whatever man comes from Troy to ransom it. The body all this while has been preserved by Apollo from injury or decay; and the man who is coming is none other than Priam. Achilles, who does not know this as we do, consents — with relief, as if he had been waiting for such instructions, yet still in ignorance that it is Priam who will come.

The journey of Priam across the plain in the company of Idaeus, his old herald, and with the beautiful

Hermes for guide, is the last great event of the *Iliad*, and no other event is more memorable. The huge poem comes here to a delicate, a genre close. Priam, whom we have seen preparing at home the gear necessary for his trip — horses and a chariot for him to drive, mules and a four-wheeled wagon for Idaeus, with a wicker basket in it to contain the body of Hector — is one of Shakespeare's old men, fussily scolding like Capulet, and contemptuous of the women who would either hinder or help him. Arriving at the hut of Achilles, however, where he astonishes the hero and the friends who sit at table with him, he goes with a noble straightness to the point which will be of greatest assistance to his cause.

Remember thy father, O Achilles like to the gods, whose years are even as mine, on the grievous threshold of old age. . . . Nay, have thou awe of the gods, Achilles, and take pity on me, remembering thine own father. Lo, I am more piteous far than he, and have endured what no other mortal on the face of the earth hath yet endured, to reach forth my hand to the face of him that hath slain my sons.

To which plea Achilles, weeping for his father even while he weeps again for his friend, has no resistance to offer. Instead, he heaps courtesies upon the father of his foe as he consents to return the body of Hector. "For this present let us bethink us of supper. For even the fair-haired Niobe bethought her of meat, albeit twelve children perished in her halls, six daughters and six lusty sons." They eat and drink together, marveling at each other's greatness as they munch their mutton and lift their cups. And Achilles asks how many days he should refrain from war while Hector is being buried. Twelve, says Priam; after which "will we do battle, if so be we must."

They must. Nothing in the *Iliad* is more dreadful than this prospect, but there it is. As Priam returns across the plain, Cassandra, seeing from Pergamus what he brings, utters a shrill cry and summons the other women to raise their chorus of dirges: Andromache, who can think of nothing but the loneliness in which she will live; Hecuba, to whom Hector had been the dearest of her many children; and at last the bitter, lonely Helen, remembering that Hector had been the only Trojan who spoke no evil of her, who did not shudder at her, but was gentle and kind. These lament him in the fulness of their grief, and then nine days are consumed in building such a pyre as Patroclus had burned on; whereupon the tenth day comes with its great fire, its golden urn, and its high-heaped barrow; and whereupon with feasting the twelfth day, the day of war again, is awaited by the horse-taming Trojans.

The poem ends there, as if the last courtesy of Achilles were to say: let Hector's burning body be the image that remains. In the *Oydssey* we shall hear how his own body burned, and it was a splendid burning as the shade of Agamemnon describes it to the shade of him who was burned:

And thy mother came forth from the sea with the immortal sea-nymphs, when she heard the tidings, and a wondrous cry arose over the deep. . . . Then around thee stood the daughters of the old man of the sea wailing piteously, and they clothed thee about with immortal raiment. And the Muses, nine in all, replying to one another with sweet voices, led the dirge. . . . Thus for seventeen days alike by night and day did we bewail thee, immortal gods and mortal men, and on the eighteenth we gave thee to the fire, and many well-fatted sheep we slew around thee and sleek kine. So wast thou burned in the raiment of the gods and in abundance of unguents and sweet honey; and many Achaean warriors moved in their armor about the pyre, when thou wast burning, both footmen and charioteers, and a great din arose. But when the flame of Hephaestus had made an end of thee, in the morning we gathered thy white bones, Achilles, and laid them in unmixed wine and unguents. Thy mother had given a two-handled, golden urn, and said it was the gift of Dionysus, and the handiwork of famed Hephaestus. In this lie thy white bones, glorious Achilles, and mingled with them the bones of the dead Patroclus. . . . And over them we heaped up a great and goodly tomb, on a projecting headland by the broad Hellespont, that it might be seen from far over the sea both by men that now are and that shall be born hereafter. . . . Thus not even in death didst thou lose thy name, but ever shalt thou have fair renown among all men, Achilles.

# II · THE ODYSSEY

THE FIRST TWO SENTENCES of the *Odyssey* are enough to inform us that now we are in another world of poetry. "Tell me, O Muse, of the man of many devices, who wandered full many ways after he had sacked the sacred citadel of Troy. Many were the men whose cities he saw and whose mind he learned, aye, and many the woes he suffered in his heart upon the sea, seeking to win his own life and the return of his comrades." Many devices, many ways, many men, many cities, many minds, many woes, and upon the sea to boot — the view opens and becomes multiple. This world is wide, and there is so much to report about it that Homer cannot decide where to begin. "Of these things, goddess, daughter of Zeus, beginning where thou wilt — at some place or other — tell thou even to us."

Homer does know, of course, where such a tale should start. It is still the finest tale in print, and its author was no fumbler. It concerns itself with the final stage of Odysseus' journey home from Troy, and with his return to Ithaca in a disguise which lasts until all the necessary recognitions are accomplished, including that by the suitors who have infested his house, after which they are promptly dispatched. The beginning is in this very house, where Telemachus, the young son whom Odysseus had left there twenty years before as an infant in arms, is stung by his mother Penelope's position — and furthermore is inspired by a visit from Pallas Athene, his father's intimate deity — to set forth in his chariot so that he may find out what he can about the missing wanderer from old Nestor in Pylos and from Menelaus in the hollow land of Lacedaemon with its many ravines. Even while he is absent, learning little, Odysseus is enduring the last of his adventures on an island where he is the comfortable prisoner of the nymph Calypso; whom he leaves, only to be wrecked on the shores of Phaeacia, where he remains until for our benefit he has told the king of all his adventures to date. He gets home in advance of his son, midway through the poem; and then romance contracts into drama.

No art is lacking in Homer which is needed to tell this tale and tell it perfectly. But neither is there lacking in him a sense of the difference we must feel, now that we are free in a universe as loose as that of the *Iliad* was tight. Aristotle put the difference when he said the *Iliad* was simple and disastrous, the *Odyssey* complicated and moral. Lawrence of Arabia said the *Iliad* was huge and terrible, the *Odyssey* gay, fine, and vivid. If further epithets are in order, the following might do. The *Iliad* is tense, of great density, with no neutral territory to travel in, no free air to breathe; the *Odyssey* is relaxed and spacious, occupying as it does a porous world in which the prevailing sanity and serenity will not be disturbed or clogged by any human event.

The spirit of the *Odyssey* is something like that which breathes in the *History* of Herodotus. What the subject of Herodotus is can be debated. Is it the big story of Greece and Persia, or is it the little stories — of Gyges and Candaules' queen, of Adrastus, of Croesus and Solon, of Cyrus' youth, of Rhampsinitus, of Sataspes, of Xerxes and the five sons of Pythius, of the Spartans at Thermopylae, combing their long hair — of which the big one is stuck full, interrupting it as cloves do a ham? Or is it a third thing: the customs of distant peoples, Scythian, Ethiopian, which Herodotus pauses so frequently to describe? It is perhaps more, much more, than all that. It is perhaps the whole world as Herodotus in his curiosity now knows it, and as he certainly loves it. This world is more stationary than moving, no matter how many figures dot its foreground. It is a timeless world that keeps its own equilibrium, shining brightly clear out to its extremities; it has a vast life which is more important than the life of any one man or people, it has a fixed truth which even wars between continents may not alter. It is a universe of strangers, an immense field of leisure where time seeks its level and space its calm. It is a universe in which no conceivable thing is missing, just as it is a place where, given enough time, anything can happen. But you will not know its wonders unless you travel. If you do travel, the farther you go the more you will find — "the extreme regions of the earth are blessed" with the most gold and the greatest marvels: races of utterly bald men, people in mountains with feet like goats, countries where a half of every year is spent in sleep and the oxen walk backwards, troglodytes who feed on serpents and lizards and whose language is like the screeching of bats, or the natives of Atlas who eat no living thing and never dream. Not that the extremities are all, or marvels everything. The whole includes home, of which Herodotus is proud. But it is an immense whole, which the historian's constant effort is to keep in focus.

The world of the *Odyssey* is something like that. It is so immense and free that the reminders we are sometimes given of Agamemnon and Achilles fall strangely on our ears; those were tragic figures, and this is not a tragedy. The parallel of Agamemnon's disastrous return is maintained indeed throughout the poem. Telemachus is told by Athene, by Nestor, and by Menelaus that he may have to avenge his father as Orestes did his; and the two episodes in Hades, in the eleventh and the twenty-fourth books, are eloquent of Agamemnon's murder by his queen. But Agamemnon, for all his shade believes that "no longer is there faith in women," admits in the gloom of the underworld that Penelope is no Clytemnestra; she is the faithful wife in a story that turns out happily. So Helen, as Telemachus beholds her in Lacedaemon, is restored to her former role as the good wife of Menelaus.

Eumaeus, the old swineherd of Odysseus back in Ithaca, echoes the *Iliad* when he wishes she had perished with all her kindred; but the old man of the sea who tells Menelaus that he will spend eternity in the Elysian plain because "thou hast Helen to wife and art the husband of the daughter of Zeus" is talking with surer accent the language of the *Odyssey*. As for Achilles, we hear him wondering in Hades whether his father ever suffered dishonor as Agamemnon did, or even as Odysseus still does from the absurd suitors; and the rage he feels when he realizes his incapacity in such a case to be Orestes, or even to be Telemachus, only reminds us of furies we shall never feel here. Achilles, true to the character he had at Troy, is the unhappiest man in Hades. Odysseus hails him as the mighty ruler of the dead, but the son of Thetis answers: "Nay, seek not to speak soothingly to me of death, glorious Odysseus. I should choose, so I might live on earth, to serve as the hireling of another, of some portionless man whose livelihood was but small, rather than to be lord over all the dead."

The *Odyssey* is anything but tragedy. "I am a man of many sorrows," says Odysseus more than once; and at least once, as the raft bearing him away from Calypso is about to break up, he wishes he had died at Troy. He is moved on another occasion to deliver himself as Zeus had to the horses of Achilles: "Nothing feebler does earth nurture than man, of all things that on earth are breathing and moving," he says to Amphinomus the suitor, lifting a cup of honey-sweet wine when he has finished. But we do not forget his many devices, and we do not believe he will be put down, as indeed he never is. Even if we doubted him there is always Athene to foretell the successful outcome of his career. Penelope, praying once to Artemis, speaks of Zeus who "knows all things, both the happiness and the haplessness of mortal men." But there it is — the happiness along with the unhappiness. The two alternate in the *Odyssey*, and in the right order for our pleasure. The miseries of its people are many, but they have not the dimension of terror.

If the gods write tragedy in this world they write it as men write songs, to soothe the mind with remembered woe, and to make still further poetry possible. "There is time for sleep," says Eumaeus to the old man he does not yet know to be Odysseus, "and there is time to take joy in hearing tales. . . . We two will drink and feast in the hut, and will take delight each in the other's grievous woes, as we recall them to mind. For in after time a man finds joy even in woes, whosoever has suffered much, and wandered much." King Alcinous of Phaeacia supposes that the gods wrought so much havoc at Troy, and spun such a skein of ruin, "that there might be a song for those yet to be born." He could sit up all night, he insists, listening to the woes of Odysseus, they are so sweet to hear.

The tears of the *Odyssey* are copious beyond record, but they do not scald like the fewer and fiercer ones of the *Iliad*. Everybody weeps, and often, but it seems

easy to do so; easy, and even sweet, for these are free
dispositions, and tears are their native tongue, in which
the truth is spoken. Nobody, least of all Odysseus, can
resist a minstrel; Telemachus cannot, nor Penelope
either; tears flow like rain, wetting the beautiful sad
words which accompany the lyre. At the house of
Menelaus, when the master has ended his recital of the
uncertainties in which Odysseus must be enmeshed,
all of the company are seized with a desire to have a
good cry. "Argive Helen wept, the daughter of Zeus,
Telemachus wept, and Menelaus, son of Atreus, nor
could the son of Nestor keep his eyes tearless." In
Ithaca Telemachus weeps for his father, Penelope for
both her husband and her son, as well as for herself.
Our first sight of the hero is of a strong man weeping
on Calypso's shore: "and his eyes were never dry of
tears, and his sweet life was ebbing away, as he longed
mournfully for his return." Twice in the hall of Alcinous, listening with the others to the bard Demodocus as he sings the sufferings of Troy, Odysseus is overcome at the mention of his own name, so that he must
grasp his great purple cloak in his stout hands and draw
it down over his head to keep secret the tears he cannot
prevent. Home in Ithaca, watching the efforts of his
old hound Argos to get up and come to him, he must
turn his head and wipe his eyes. Near the end, as Eurycleia brings the women of the household in to greet
him, a sweet longing seizes him to weep and wail, "for
in his heart he knew them all." In the arms of Penelope
at last he weeps without restraint, as later in the or-

chard with his father. Once, when it was still necessary to keep his disguise with Penelope, he had with the most painful difficulty held back the tears which would have blended with hers: "his eyes stood fixed between his lids as though they were horn or iron." But such difficulty is rare in the poem. The most natural thing is what happens to Penelope on the same occasion:

He spoke, and made the many falsehoods of his tale seem like the truth, and as she listened her tears flowed and her face melted as the snow melts on the lofty mountains, the snow which the East Wind thaws when the West Wind has strewn it, and as it melts the streams of the rivers flow full: so her fair cheeks melted as she wept and mourned for her husband, who even then was sitting by her side.

Relief is regularly available to the good people of the *Odyssey*, as dew comes daily to ferns and grass.

The relief of sleep is likewise constant, bestowing upon the poem a soft atmosphere in which it easily keeps its health. This atmosphere has fairy quality, reminding us of many an ancient tale wherein a princess or an old man, a Beauty or a Rip Van Winkle, slept years away. The promise of Alcinous which Odysseus likes best is that on the morrow the Phaeacians will take him home in one of their magic ships:

Then shalt thou lie down, overcome by sleep, and they shall row thee over the calm sea until thou comest to thy country and thy house, or to whatsoever place thou wilt, aye though it be even far beyond Euboea, which those of our people who saw it, when they carried fair-haired Rhadamanthus to visit Tityus, the son of Gaea, say is the furthest of lands. Thither they went, and without toil accomplished their journey, and on the selfsame day came back home.

And the promise is true.

Then for Odysseus they spread a rug and a linen sheet on the deck of the hollow ship at the stern, that he might sleep soundly; and he too went aboard, and laid him down in silence. . . . And as soon as they leaned back, and tossed the brine with their oar-blades, sweet sleep fell upon his eyelids, an unawakening sleep, most sweet, and most like to death. . . . Now he slept in peace, forgetful of all he had suffered. . . . Then they stepped forth from the benched ship upon the land, and first they lifted Odysseus out of the hollow ship, with the linen sheet and bright rug as they were, and laid him down on the sand, still overpowered by sleep. . . . But Odysseus awoke out of his sleep in his native land.

Meanwhile Penelope's life is passed in alternate weeping and sleeping. "And she sank back and slept, and all her joints relaxed." She too finds sleep a little death. "Ah," she cries when she awakens from one long nap which Athene has blessed her with as an escape from misery, "in my utter wretchedness soft slumber enfolded me. Would that pure Artemis would even now give me so soft a death, that I might no more waste my life away with sorrow at heart, longing for the manifold excellence of my dear husband." Death in the *Odyssey* is no more stern than that. It is an enveloping cloud, beneficent, without edges.

Penelope, to be sure, has her difficulties with sleep. Sometimes it does not come, and she tosses in her chamber. And sometimes this excellent thing which "makes one forget all things, the good and the evil, when once it envelops the eyelids," does come but brings bad dreams. Increasingly as it comes, however, she loves it, so that it grows to be almost a disease with her, a drug to which she is addicted. Even when Eurycleia runs upstairs to her, laughing and stumbling and saying "Odysseus is here," Penelope tells her to go away. "Why dost thou mock me, who have a heart full of sorrow, to tell me this wild tale, and dost rouse me out of slumber, the sweet slumber that bound me and enfolded my eyelids?" Only at the end, when she knows her husband and lies by his side while he goes over his adventures since he left her twenty years ago, is she cured of her desire to absent herself from life. She listens to the last chapter of his tale.

The hardness of heart which various persons find in one another is not the caked hardness, the bitter bafflement, of Hecuba or Achilles. It is at the worst an excess of caution or suspicion, pardonable in these Ithacans who have been fooled so many times by false rumors of their lord's return, or by pretenders who have come and been exposed. "Verily," says Odysseus to Eumaeus, "thou hast in thy bosom a heart that is slow to believe." But on the whole Odysseus is pleased that this is so, because it argues fidelity in those to whom he is returning. Penelope's hopelessness is his best hope; though to Eurycleia and Telemachus it can be enraging, as when the young man, desperate because she will not believe that this is Odysseus, denounces her thus:

My mother, cruel mother, that hast an unyielding heart, why dost thou thus hold aloof from my father, and dost not sit by his side and ask and question him? No other woman would harden her heart as thou dost, and stand aloof from her husband, who after many grievous toils had come back to her in the twentieth year to his native land; but thy heart is ever harder than stone.

Even Odysseus makes use of the same terms a little later. But that is after Athene has restored his good looks, the good looks which have been Penelope's image of him all the while, and he is sure she knows him. "Be not vexed with me, Odysseus," she says. It is unnecessary, for it has suited him well that she should be so slow to believe a stranger. She has in fact been faithful to the image now restored, the image of the husband she remembers. The old beggar he had seemed to be was of course not her Odysseus. It is touching that her son and nurse have misunderstood her on this score, but it is not tragic.

Eumaeus once regrets that Odysseus had not died at Troy and thus achieved a hero's end instead of the ragged, anonymous state of one who wanders unknown in the world. But the author of the *Odyssey* prefers now to be occupied with the raveled extremity of a legend, with the tale of a return, and of a recognition. Such savagery as is here — the torture of Melanthius, the hanging of the maids, the madness of the suitors just before they die — is soon over, and it is simple as poetic justice is simple. A number of persons in the *Odyssey* lay up grief for themselves, and the grief comes; but it comes with an almost amusing promptness, a clean completeness suitable to romance which will forget that evil ever was. When at the Phaeacian games Euryalus sizes Odysseus up and says: "Thou dost not look like an athlete," he is only preparing himself for what we know must happen, namely that Odysseus will throw the discus farther than anybody.

The woes of Odysseus are numerous but serial; they are not interlocked and towered like those of Hector or Achilles. His mind is often divided in counsel, so that he must stand a while and ponder what he should do next. It is never difficult, however, to do so; the decisions of Odysseus are so brisk as almost to be instantaneous. It is as if they were forced by the certainty that the story must go the way of its foretelling. We are regularly informed that Odysseus will return, and once returned that he will execute the suitors; and if in passing we are worried about the ambush that has been prepared for Telemachus upon his arrival from Pylos and Lacedaemon, Athene takes the trouble to assure us that we need not be. A strong tide of success runs in the poem. The main direction is clear, and the decisions of Odysseus therefore cannot be hesitant or wrong. Foretelling here is not foreshortening, as it was in the fatal atmosphere of the *Iliad*. If anything, it is the opposite — the tendency of the tale is to string itself out, multiplying artificial uncertainties as it goes. Suspense is linear, it takes the form of mere delay. We are teased rather than tormented; told, simply, that we must wait a little longer. Such a function is served by Penelope's reluctance to believe; by the interpolation, just as we stop breathing to watch the recognition by Eurycleia, of the long tale of the boar hunt years ago when Autolycus was host to young Odysseus; by many hitches before the bow is tried. So irony in this narrative is of the elementary sort. It consists at the most in someone's not knowing who Odysseus is, and saying or doing things at which we shall shiver or smile. The identity of Odysseus is everything; we know it from the start, but nobody else does. Hence the complications, the discoveries, which according to Aristotle were the essence of the *Odyssey*. They are the most primitive complications possible to story.

Hence, nevertheless, their power. The irony latent in Penelope's direction to the swineherd: "Go, goodly Eumaeus, and bid the stranger come hither, that I may give him greeting, and ask him if haply he has heard of Odysseus, or has seen him with his eyes," or in her sitting then and talking with this stranger, and mourning for her husband "who even then was sitting by her side," is as sure as it is unsubtle. And the recognitions of the poem have no rival in their kind.

The *Odyssey* is a riot of recognition, and not of its hero alone. The poet makes excellent game of the discovery, first by Nestor and then by Menelaus and Helen, that the young man sitting before them with so many questions about Odysseus on his lips is none other than Telemachus, son of that same Odysseus. It is exciting to see Nestor in the amazement that falls on him when Mentor, the friend of Telemachus who has been talking at Pylos, suddenly departs in the likeness of a sea-eagle and so reveals that the boy is distinguished by the guardianship of Athene, "maid most glorious." Athene has a fine time appearing to Odysseus in new forms he must puzzle out. It is not always the hero who shines in the scenes of discovery. But his share of them is the lion's share, even to the point of his having twice the privilege of recognizing his own name and deeds in the songs Demodocus sings.

His first recognition by others occurs at the court of Alcinous, when the simple sentence, "I am Odysseus," perhaps does not surprise Alcinous himself, who has been watching the business of the singing and the purple robe, but certainly floods with light the minds of those in the court who have underestimated their stranger. So the Cyclops groans when he hears the name of the man who has blinded him. "Lo now, verily a prophecy uttered long ago is come upon me. There lived here a soothsayer, and he told me that all these things should be brought to pass in days to come, that by the hands of Odysseus I should lose my sight." Circe also has been waiting for her day in this immortal tale. "Surely thou art Odysseus, the man of ready device, who Argeïphontes of the golden wand ever said to me would come hither on his way home from Troy with his swift, black ship."

The major recognition scenes are saved, however, for the second half, at the beginning of which Odysseus comes home to Ithaca. Then, curiously enough, it is

Ithaca that must be identified to him, not he to Ithaca. For when he awakes from his deep Phaeacian sleep he does not know where he is. "The goddess had shed a mist . . . that she might render him unknown, and tell him all things, so that his wife might not know him, nor his townfolk, nor his friends, until the wooers had paid the full price of all their transgressions. Therefore all things seemed strange to their lord, the long paths, the bays offering safe anchorage, the sheer cliffs, and the luxuriant trees." The arrival of Athene to tell him that this is Ithaca, his pretense that he never heard of such a country, and her smiling delight in his effort to deceive her, make up a charming moment. But before long the serious business of getting himself known to the right persons in the right order is under way.

The first such person is Telemachus, who when his doubts are overcome flings his arms about his father and sheds tears; which start Odysseus weeping too, so that "they wailed aloud more vehemently than birds, sea-eagles, or vultures with crooked talons"; and the sun would have set on their weeping if Telemachus had not suddenly thought of a question to ask. In what manner of ship had his father come to Ithaca?

The next person — if the hound Argos may be passed over as he wags his tail and drops his ears, knowing it is Odysseus who stands there — is one whom the time has not yet come to tell, but who learns anyway. This is Eurycleia, whom in a careless moment Odysseus chooses to wash his feet. Penelope has asked the stranger if he wishes that attention, and he has said that no serving-woman of hers shall touch him "unless there is some old, true-hearted dame who has suffered in her heart as many woes as I." "I have an old dame," answers Penelope, "with a heart of understanding in her breast, who lovingly nursed and cherished my hapless husband, and took him in her arms on the day when his mother bore him. She shall wash thy feet, weak with age though she be. Come now, wise Eurycleia, arise and wash the feet of one of like age with thy master." And Eurycleia proceeds to do so, letting fall hot tears because this stranger is most like Odysseus of all men who have come to Ithaca since its master left. "So say all men," remarks Odysseus, still thinking himself safe; for although there is one sign by which she may know him, he believes he can conceal it.

So he spoke, and the old dame took the shining cauldron with water wherefrom she was about to wash his feet, and poured in cold water in plenty, and then added thereto the warm. But Odysseus sat him down away from the hearth and straightway turned himself toward the darkness, for he at once had a foreboding at heart that, as she touched him, she might note a scar, and the truth be made manifest. So she drew near and began to wash her lord, and straightway knew the scar of the wound which long ago a boar had dealt him with his white tusk, when Odysseus had gone to Parnassus to visit Autolycus and the sons of Autolycus, his mother's noble father, who excelled all men in thievery and in oaths.

Then Homer, as if he knew that one of the high moments in his poem was preparing, as indeed it is, and as of course he knows, tantalizes us with seventy lines of history about the scar, resuming only when every detail of that old day with Autolycus has been exhausted:

This scar the old dame, when she had taken the limb in the flat of her hands, knew by the touch, and she let fall the foot. Into the basin the leg fell, and the brazen vessel rang. Over it tilted, and the water was spilled upon the ground. Then upon her soul came joy and grief in one moment, and both her eyes were filled with tears and the flow of her voice was checked. But she touched the chin of Odysseus, and said:

"Verily thou art Odysseus, dear child, and I knew thee not, till I had handled all the body of my lord."

One sentence, beginning with "dear child" and ending with "my lord," is all she speaks before she turns toward Penelope, hoping she too will see. But Penelope, must not see; so Odysseus has to seize Eurycleia by the throat and draw her to him, whispering: "Mother, why wilt thou destroy me? Since thou hast found me out, and a god has put this in thy heart, be silent lest any other in the halls learn hereof."

No other scene of the series will be more exciting than this, though each one to come will have a beauty proper to its nature. The revelation to Eumaeus and Philoetius is rapid, as the situation requires. The stringing of the bow is long delayed, for we know that it is the sign by which the suitors will know Odysseus. When it does come —

And he held it in his right hand, and tried the string, which sang sweetly beneath his touch, like to a swallow in tone —

it is swift and tremendous. The excitement of that moment in the hall, if in truth it surpasses the excitement of Eurycleia's discovery, does so with the aid of the fact that the scene is central to the poem; this moment is the one toward which time has been hastening since Telemachus first felt shame because his father's honor was abused; and the moment is soon over. The persuasion of Penelope takes longer because the poem can now afford to luxuriate in the spectacle of the long-suffering wife's perplexity, and in the grave comedy of joy postponed. Even after the right appearance of Odysseus has been restored, Penelope must subject him to one more test: she orders Eurycleia to make his bed outside the bridal chamber he once had built with his own hands. His anger at this — for one post of the bed had been a rooted olive tree, and it was therefore immovable — is what she wishes to see. Only then, with a burst of entirely natural tears, does she run straight at him and fling her arms about his neck, kissing his head; and he weeps, "and from his neck she could in no wise let her white arms go." It is the gods, she cries, who have "begrudged that we two should remain with each other and enjoy our youth." But it is a goddess, the bright-eyed Athene, who prolongs the night for them so that they may first have their fill of love and then take delight in the mutual chronicle of twenty years. Hereafter there is but one more necessary scene in the list. Odysseus, finding his father in the vineyard, "digging about a plant," with a patched, foul tunic on his body and greaves of ox-hide on his shins to guard against scratches, thinks to begin with playful words, mocking the old man; but the outcome is that Laertes groans and strews dust over his head, whereupon Odysseus, his heart stirred and his nostrils shot through with pain, announces abruptly who he is. It is not enough. Laertes must have a sign. So Odysseus shows his scar; but better yet, he says to his father:

Come, I will tell thee also the trees in the well-ordered garden which once thou gavest me, and I, who was but a child, was following thee through the garden, and asking thee for this and that. It was through these very trees that we passed, and thou didst name them, and tell me each one. Pear-trees thirteen thou gavest me, and ten apple-trees, and forty fig-trees. And rows of vines too didst thou promise to give me, even as I say, fifty of them, which ripened severally at different times — and upon them are clusters of all sorts — whensoever the seasons of Zeus weighed them down from above.

After which no major recognition remains to be strung on Homer's well-woven string.

It is a string and not a structure, for the organization of the *Odyssey* is loose and free, like its refrains: "Now the sun set and all the ways grew dark"; "So the wind filled the body of the sail, and the dark wave sang loudly about the stem of the ship as she went." Its similes are fewer than those of the *Iliad*, and less powerful, because less required; though the bow that sings like a swallow could not be surpassed for its purpose. But the similes of the *Iliad* were needed to pack the tight world Homer had decided to confine us in;

or else they were breathing spaces in that world, reminding us of the greater one without. Whereas the world of the *Odyssey* is nothing but the one without. It is among other things a world of old men — Nestor, Eumaeus, Laertes, and the Old Man of the Sea — who have far memories because they have traveled much.

It is above all a bright world, open under space; and itself is full of space. Reality shines in it like mica; objects strike us because they have first been struck by the sun, as the white stones are upon which Nestor likes to go forth and sit in the early morning. The heaven of Olympus, whence Athene speeds with her flashing eyes, is a place without wind or rain, "but the air is outspread clear and cloudless, and over it hovers a radiant whiteness." The house of Menelaus, like the palace of Alcinous, has a gleam over its high roof "as of sun or moon." The epithet for Ithaca is "clear-seen." The epithet for night is "baneful," and the place where Homer's imagination least likes to dwell is the land and city of the Cimmerians, "wrapped in mist and cloud; never does the bright sun look down on them." The most grievous sin of the hero's comrades is the one they commit against Helios. And the most brilliant picture in a poem hung everywhere with pictures — for the *Odyssey* illustrates itself — is that which shows Pallas Athene preceding Odysseus and Telemachus into the hall where the weapons are, "bearing a golden lamp."

Then Telemachus suddenly spoke to his father, and said: "Father, verily this is a great marvel that my eyes behold;

certainly the walls of the house and the fair beams and cross-beams of fir and the pillars that reach on high, glow in my eyes as with the light of blazing fire. Surely some god is within."

Then Odysseus of many wiles answered him, and said:

"Hush, check thy thought, and ask no question; this, I tell thee, is the way of the gods that hold Olympus."

Distance and strangeness are the stuff of which narrative in the *Odyssey* is made. The poem lies under a sun that shines impartially on far and near. Nestor tells Telemachus that Menelaus may know something about his father because he has "but lately come from a strange land, from a folk whence no one would hope in his heart to return, whom the storms had once driven astray into a sea so great, whence the very birds do not fare in the space of a year." Strangers are the population of this world; they come and go, taking with them tales of where they have been. "There is a land called Crete," Odysseus tells Penelope, "in the midst of the wine-dark sea, a fair, rich land, begirt with water, and therein are many men, past counting, and ninety cities." It is a broad world, full of folk and fate, and the strangers who walk it are privileged persons whom it is the morality of the poem to receive with dignity in the halls they enter; though it is also the custom to shower them with questions — "Who art thou among men, and from whence? Where is thy city, and where thy parents? On what manner of ship didst thou come?" In such a world a man may move in anonymity if he pleases, but the custom is for him to reply; if his host has a good heart he loves strangers even as he fears the gods, and he will listen well. Frequently the wanderer spins yarns until he is sure of his host's heart — for safety, and perhaps for the mere fun of it. Nestor had the reputation of being so masterful and insistent a host that many a visitor to Pylos must have done as Telemachus did on his return from Lacedaemon — avoided the old man altogether, in his haste to get elsewhere. Yet certain citizens of the poem would have gone there with relish and regaled the horseman of Gerenia with mythical biographies. The poem is populated with excellent liars, of whom Athene is one, but of whom, naturally, Odysseus is king. Odysseus at a moment's notice can tell whoppers so circumstantial, so thicket-rich with detail, that only a cynic could disbelieve him. He invents families for himself, and remembers lands where he has never been unless he has been everywhere. He has the imagination of a minstrel — the person whom this society honors even more than it honors strangers. "For among all men that are upon the earth," Odysseus remarks at the court of Alcinous, "minstrels win honor and reverence, for that the Muse has taught them the paths of song." It is bad luck to kill a minstrel. Odysseus saves the one he had left at home.

It is a world on which the stars shine: "the Pleiads, and late-setting Boötes, and the Bear, which men also call the Wain, which ever circles where it is and watches Orion, and alone has no part in the baths of Ocean." But the sea which the Bear watches and never enters —

that is the element in which the poem chiefly lives, showing its back among tempestuous waves. The sea of the *Odyssey* is real to its bottom. "When the sun hath reached mid heaven," says Menelaus, "the unerring old man of the sea is wont to come forth from the brine at the breath of the West Wind, hidden by the dark ripple. And when he is come forth, he lies down to sleep in the hollow caves; and around him the seals, the brood of the fair daughter of the sea, sleep in a herd, coming forth from the grey water, and bitter is the smell they breathe of the depths of the sea." No lines could bring more water with them than these do, or more of its smell when it is old and wild.

Over such water Odysseus had come to Phaeacia from faraway Troy, through the many adventures of which he told Alcinous: those of the Cicones, the Lotus-eaters, the Cyclops, Aeolus, the Laestrygonians, Circe, Hades, the Sirens, Scylla and Charybdis, the island of Helios Hyperion, and at last Calypso's isle. Through such water Odysseus swims, wades, sails, and drifts on a raft of his own making. With it under and around him he obeys that curiosity — his ruling passion — which causes as many deaths as were ever caused by the wrath of Achilles, for it pushes him to go where his comrades cannot survive. The sea is both his savior and his foe; and it is something from which the end of the poem releases him, dedicating him henceforth to life on the land he kisses in joy at being safe.

The prophet Teiresias instructed him thus in Hades:

When thou hast slain the wooers in thy halls, then do thou go forth, taking a shapely oar, until thou comest to men that know naught of the sea and eat not of food mingled with salt, aye, and they know naught of ships with purple sails, or of shapely oars that are as wings unto ships. And I will tell thee of a sign right manifest, which will not escape thee. When another wayfarer, on meeting thee, shall say that thou hast a winnowing-fan on thy stout shoulder, then do thou fix in the earth thy shapely oar and make goodly offerings to lord Poseidon — a ram, and a bull, and a boar that mates with sows — and depart for thy home and offer sacred hecatombs to the immortal gods who hold broad heaven, to each one in due order. And death shall come to thee thyself far from the sea, a death so gentle, that shall lay thee low when thou art overcome with sleek old age, and thy people shall dwell in prosperity around thee. In this have I told thee sooth.

And Odysseus does not forget the prophecy. He repeats it to Penelope while their night is prolonged, to let her know that they will not be together always even now. But she is content if it means that his old age will be happy, an escape at last from evil. He will die so far from the sea that nobody whom he meets there will know an oar from a winnowing-fan. So be it, yet then there will be an end to evil.

The sea was foe to Odysseus in the person of Poseidon, its god, because Odysseus in blinding Polyphemus the Cyclops had blinded Poseidon's own son. The sea-god's punishment of the Phaeacians for their hospitality to the hero, and for their help to him in reaching home, springs from the same root: a friend of Odysseus must be an enemy of Polyphemus, and therefore of Poseidon. But more than that lurks in the mysterious Phaeacian background. These fairy people had once been neighbors of the Cyclopes, and like them are still in some measure children of the gods. They are a misty folk, living in a land of incredible beauty which is the last item needed to make the landscape of the *Odyssey* altogether wonderful.

As Odysseus approached this land of shadowy mountains "it shewed like unto a shield in the misty deep." Its folk were fostered of Zeus, who left them in peace "far off in the surging sea, the furthermost of men, and no other mortals have dealings with us." The Phaeacians are the ultimate strangers; they extend the beautiful world of the *Odyssey* to its limit. They care for nothing but ships, which for them are magic ships, "swift as a bird on the wing or as a thought." Their harbor is crowned with palisades; the palace of Alcinous has doors of silver and gold, and they are guarded by immortal dogs. The inhabitants of this land are favored by visits from the gods in manifest form. At sacrifices gods sit among them, feasting as they do. "Aye," says Alcinous, "and if one of us a lone wayfarer meets them, they use no concealment, for we are of near kin to them, as are the Cyclopes and the wild tribes of the Giants." The Phaeacians are Cronos-folk, of an earlier generation than mankind. No wonder they are wonderful to behold. And no wonder Poseidon punishes them for dishonoring their divine origin by the assistance they give Odysseus, who is a rank mortal if any man ever was. They are, however, the final stroke of light, and the fairest hue of distance, with which the universe of our hero paints itself.

But houses nearer home have almost an equal splendor. For the author of the *Odyssey* there is something important about any house, particularly if it is ruled by a member of that superior race, that breed of natural kings, to which Menelaus admits Telemachus and Peisistratus because they are the sons, respectively, of Odysseus and Nestor. The houses of such men, and indeed of any men that fear the gods and love strangers, are entered by the poet with awe and described with a ceremony befitting the rituals which go on there. The forms of courtesy, even the daily forms, are given full attention; there seems to be plenty of time for them in a work devoted as this one is to the task of revealing the charms of human life when it is gloriously provisioned. Such is the case not only at Phaeacia, where the reception of Odysseus is royal in its generosity — golden youths standing on pedestals in the hall, holding torches aloft to light the banqueters by night; a fair handmaiden bringing water in a gold pitcher so that the stranger may wash in a silver basin; delectable fruits brought always to his side from an orchard which never stops bearing "pear upon pear, apple upon apple, cluster upon cluster, and fig upon fig," and where the farewells as he leaves would be grateful to the most exacting god. It is the case as well in any household we are privileged to see, and certainly in that one which Penelope is keeping for Odysseus to see again. Telemachus and Peisistratus depart

from the palace of Menelaus with their chariots full of
shining gifts which match the exalted compliments
ringing in their ears. As they speed homeward over
the sand — for houses in the *Odyssey* are far apart,
and the hooves of horses have much flying to do —
they have leisure to reflect upon the splendid, spacious
world they live in.

Even Calypso in her cave, though doubtless in her
divinity she could have lived without effort, keeps excellent house. When Hermes arrived there with the
message that she must release Odysseus he found that
"a great fire was burning on the hearth, and from afar
over the isle there was a fragrance of cleft cedar and
juniper, as they burned; but she within was singing
with a sweet voice as she went to and fro before the
loom, weaving with a golden shuttle." And outside the
cave she tends a Homeric garden — rich vines fed by
four fountains, and beyond them soft meadows of vi-
olet and parsley.

We are so long in Penelope's house, once we arrive,
that we grow accustomed to its beauty and begin to
take it for granted. But it is the most interesting of all
the establishments, as of course it should be. The hall
of weapons, the mistress's high chamber, the great hall
where the suitors revel, the corridors where mendi-
cants can sit and gnaw the bones thrown at them, the
cups, the plates, the tables, the tended fires, and the
soft fleeces that line chairs — the poem lives here, as
well as in the outlying premises of the swineherd and
among the rows of trees Laertes once planted, during

eleven of its books, and makes itself at home. When the suitors are killed there is much blood to be cleaned up, and we are told how this is done. "First they bore forth the bodies of the slain and set them down beneath the portico of the well-fenced court, propping them one against the other; and Odysseus himself gave them orders and hastened on the work. Then they cleansed the beautiful high seats and the tables with water and porous sponges. But Telemachus and the neatherd and the swineherd scraped with hoes the floor of the well-built house, and the women bore the scrapings forth and threw them out of doors." No domestic detail is ignored.

The human body in this world is assumed to have great grace, and is treated with utmost affection. It is kissed all over — on the head, the shoulders, the hands, and finally where it is brightest, on "both beautiful eyes." The person of Odysseus must be beautified on numerous occasions, for his rough adventures make him a sorry sight, and as such he is not fit to be seen by the fine folk of the tale. Nausicaa of the white arms, the child princess of Phaeacia who is washing garments at the shore when Odysseus is cast up there, is given courage by Athene to look at the strange man, befouled with brine, who stares at her like a rain-beaten lion. But his attendant goddess soon makes him more presentable:

With water from the river goodly Odysseus washed from his skin the brine which clothed his back and broad shoulders, and from his head he wiped the scurf of the unresting sea. But when he had washed his whole body and anointed himself with oil, and had put on him the raiment which the unwedded maid had given him, then Athene, the daughter of Zeus, made him taller to look upon and mightier, and from his head she made the locks to flow in curls like unto the hyacinth flower. And as when a man overlays silver with gold, a cunning workman whom Hephaestus and Pallas Athene have taught all manner of craft, and full of grace is the work he produces, even so the goddess shed grace upon his head and shoulders.

A similar transformation is worked before he offers himself to the sight of Alcinous and his court; and exactly the same words are used to describe his being made ready for Penelope. In the case of Laertes, however, beautification comes after he has been made happy by the sight of Odysseus, not before. For the old man too receives the attention of Athene, growing in stature and might, so that his son, seeing him come forth from the bath, marvels at him and is glad.

The deities of the poem are seldom formidable like those of the *Iliad*. Even Poseidon, who causes Odysseus endless trouble, is not the terrible force that waited to level the wall before Troy. He is rather the god of shipwreck, presiding over accidents and preparing further toils. The Cyclopes over whom he watches wish only to be left alone, and indeed Odysseus is not attractive when he disturbs the solitude of Polyphemus, however exciting the hazards of the game played in a smoky cave where sheep and men are eaten with identical relish. Odysseus, describing the adventure to Alcinous, speaks with the condescension of a civilized man concerning this "overweening and lawless folk" who, trusting in the immortal gods, plant nothing with their hands nor plough; but all these things spring up for them without sowing or ploughing, wheat, and barley, and vines, which bear the rich clusters of wine, and the rain of Zeus gives them increase. Neither assemblies for council have they, nor appointed laws, but they dwell on the peaks of lofty mountains in hollow caves, and each one is lawgiver to his children and his wives, and they reck nothing one of another.

The Cyclopes, that is to say, dwell in primitive peace, innocent of law and war. They are earth-born, and live in simplicity.

The immortals most native to the *Odyssey* are Hermes and Athene, because they are the most beautiful. The divine messenger whom Zeus sends to Calypso goes as the poem likes all things to go, speedily, with strength and grace.

Straightway he bound beneath his feet his beautiful sandals, immortal, golden, which were wont to bear him over the waters of the sea and over the boundless land swift as the blasts of the wind. And he took the wand wherewith he lulls to sleep the eyes of whom he will, while others again he awakens even out of slumber. With this in his hand the strong Argeïphontes flew. On to Pieria he stepped from the upper air, and swooped down upon the sea, and then sped over the wave like a bird, the cormorant, which in quest of fish over the dread gulfs of the unresting sea wets its thick plumage in the brine. In such wise did Hermes ride upon the multitudinous waves.

But Athene is the divine heroine of the tale. She is its presiding genius, memorable forever.

Athene is never long absent from Odysseus' life, and
consequently from our sight. As a young maiden carrying a pitcher, as a young herdsman of sheep, as a
woman "comely and tall, and skilled in glorious handiwork," and finally as the swallow that flies up to the
roof-beam of the smoky hall in Ithaca where Odysseus
is warring with the suitors — as anything that takes
her charming fancy she comes when Odysseus needs
her; or when, as sometimes it is possible to imagine,
she desires to see this mortal for whom she has such
deathless affection. "Hard is it, goddess," he tells her
once, "for a mortal man to know thee when he meets
thee, how wise soever he be, for thou takest what shape
thou wilt." But he is only complaining of his supreme
good fortune, for she is such a companion as any man
might desire. The two of them are almost lovers. "I
cannot leave thee in thy sorrow," she says, "for thou
art soft of speech, keen of wit, and prudent." These
are the reasons she chooses to give for the delight she
takes in him — and takes particularly in his lies. When
he has told her one of them she smiles and strokes his
hand, changing herself to the form of a woman as she
says:

Cunning must he be and knavish, who would go beyond
thee in all manner of guile, aye, though it were a god that met
thee. Bold man, crafty in counsel, insatiate in deceit, not even
in thine own land, it seems, wast thou to cease from guile and
deceitful tales, which thou lovest to the bottom of thine heart.
But come, let us no longer talk of this, being both well versed
in craft. . . . Now am I come hither to weave a plan for thee.

She has loved his pretense that he is a stranger to the Ithaca whither she brought him. There was no good reason for his lie. It was merely his talent at work, and she adores his talent, as he on every occasion adores her. In the likeness of Mentes, and later on of Mentor, she has been of assistance to his son; and once she sent a phantom to his wife, so that Penelope might cease her weeping and recover the warm comfort of sleep. Now that Odysseus is home she is constantly at his side, taking clever care of him as he proceeds with his revenge. The goddess who had guided him to Phaeacia and exposed him to Nausicaa attends to each necessary detail. She assures him of success; she bears a golden lamp before him when he and Telemachus need light; she maddens the wooers and makes them miss their aim; she delays the dawn. And once she appears to him in manifest presence. Telemachus, who is with him in the swineherd's hut, does not notice her there. "But Odysseus saw her, and the hounds, and they barked not, but with whining slunk in fear to the further side of the farmstead."

The mortal she never deserts is due the preëminence his poem gives him. Odysseus is built into the *Odyssey* as the olive tree was built into his bed. Many another person is of the clearest interest. Eurycleia, the true-hearted dame who guards the treasure room and tries to keep the young master from going on his journey to Pylos, but who when he has gone is strict with Penelope lest she grieve foolishly and disturb Laertes with the news; who rejoices over the death of the suitors a little too soon to suit Odysseus, though he is more than ready to let her give him the list of the maids who must be hanged; who hovers always in the house, a servant and yet the mistress of her ancient self — Eurycleia is one of Rembrandt's women, so carved and so lighted. Nausicaa at the other extreme of life, wondering whether such a man as Odysseus — of all men — might be her husband, and when he sets sail reminding him of what he owes her, is a maiden with white arms who flashes at the center of the poem, an image never to be lost from that essential place. Telemachus, who wants so badly to be older and wiser than he is, remains boyish to the end, when he commits the error of leaving the door of the storeroom open, and apologizes for it. Odysseus magnanimously discusses things with him as man to man, but his life is yet to be. The nicest stroke lavished upon his character is that in which Homer has him refuse the gift of horses from Menelaus because there is no room for horses on rocky Ithaca. But he speaks up for his little country, saying it is "pleasanter than one that pastures horses." And Menelaus smiles, stroking the boy's hand.

Penelope is not privileged to be a heroine of tragedy; the hard heart that Telemachus laments in her is something he only thinks is there. What actually is there we discover almost as soon as the poem begins. It is a pure capacity for feeling, and for saying, or singing, what is felt. That she is wrong about the facts — Odysseus *is* coming, and Telemachus *will* return from Lacedaemon — does not qualify the force of her grief when she fears that both may be lost; it merely makes her a lyric heroine.

And on her fell a cloud of soul-consuming grief, and she had no more the heart to sit upon one of the many seats that were in the room, but down upon the threshold of her fair-wrought chamber she sank, moaning piteously, and round about her wailed her handmaids.

"Hear me, my friends, for to me the Olympian has given sorrow above all the women who were bred and born with me. For long since I lost my noble husband of the lion heart. . . . And now again my well-loved son have the storm-winds swept away from our halls without tidings, nor did I hear of his setting forth."

It is madness in the suitors to desire a woman who will never be out of love with Odysseus, or, as she says to them when she proposes the trial of the bow, with this fair house "which methinks I shall ever remember even in my dreams." She may be chargeable with lyric exaggeration when she insists: "All excellence of mine, both of beauty and of form, the immortals destroyed on the day when the Argives embarked for Ilios, and with them went my husband." Yet Athene is sufficiently aware of what twenty years can do in such a case to see that she must make Penelope's face fair with the ambrosial balm of no less a beauty than Cytherea's herself, that she must increase her stature and stateliness, and leave her whiter than new-sawn ivory. The function of Penelope is to intensify our excitement as we see Odysseus approach the climax of his home-coming, and she performs it by providing a series of

scenes in which he is so near to her, and yet so unknown, that suspense can scarcely go further. Not the
least rich of these is concerned with the dreams they
have of each other during the last night before the
suitors are slain.

No reader of the *Iliad* forgets Priam's description of
Odysseus when in the third book he discusses with
Helen the Greek warriors they can see from the walls:

Come now, tell me also of yonder man, dear child, who he
is. Shorter is he by a head than Agamemnon, son of Atreus,
but broader of shoulder and of chest to look upon. His battle-
gear lieth upon the bounteous earth, but himself he rangeth
like the bell-wether of a herd through the ranks of warriors.
Like a ram he seemeth to me, a ram of thick fleece, that paceth
through a great flock of white ewes.

Or the answer which Antenor adds to Helen's; for Antenor had once entertained both Menelaus and Odysseus when they came to Troy on an embassage concerning Helen:

Now when they mingled with the Trojans, as they were
gathered together, while men stood up Menelaus overtopped
all with his broad shoulders; howbeit when the twain were
seated Odysseus was the more royal. When they began to
weave the web of speech, Menelaus in truth spake fluently,
with few words, but very clearly. But whenever Odysseus of
many wiles arose, he would stand and look down with eyes
fixed upon the ground, and his staff he would move neither
backwards nor forwards, but would hold it stiff, like a man of
no understanding; thou wouldst have deemed him a churlish
man and a fool. But when he uttered his great voice from his

chest, and words like snowflakes on a winter's day, then could no mortal man beside vie with Odysseus.

And in the funeral games for Patroclus this burly fellow, with a torso longer than his legs, had taken many prizes — sometimes trickily, sometimes with Athene's aid. Even then he had not been young. Antilochus had marveled at his swiftness of foot in a race run with men perhaps no more than half his age. "Odysseus is of an earlier generation and of earlier men — a green old age is his, men say." That was how Antilochus explained the success of Odysseus. The immortals show special honor to older men.

But the favors of Athene are bestowed here upon a man who is neither young nor old. A son of Alcinous observes at Phaeacia: "In build, surely, he is no mean man, in thighs and calves, and in his two arms above, his stout neck, and his great might. In no wise does he lack aught of the strength of youth, but he has been broken by many troubles." And Odysseus, replying to the taunts of Euryalus, admits that he may have lost something in his passage through wars of men and the grievous waves. It is hard to see, however, what he has lost. The mortal to whom Athene is so faithful seems to have everything still, and timelessly. It is only to those at Ithaca who cannot see through the disguise she has given him that he manifests the feebleness of age. To be sure, the disguise is good. Athene shrivels his skin, she makes him bald, she clothes him in tatters, she sticks a staff in his hand, and she slings over his back a miserable wallet full of holes. And above all she makes good her final promise: "I will dim thy two eyes that were so beautiful." The brine-crusted, sea-beaten stranger washed naked on the shore of Phaeacia was less transformed than this; he still looked like a lion to the startled Nausicaa, and in her childish fancy he might some day be her husband.

The entrance of Odysseus is not until the fifth book; not, that is to say, until it has been prepared with all the skill available to Homer, which means all the skill there is. We have seen him awaited by everyone at Ithaca; we have heard him praised by Nestor and Mene-laus; we have learned that he is "great-hearted," and that as a father — three persons say this, including Athene — he is "gentle." Now on Ogygia, the island of Calypso, we find him longing for home. He admits to the immortal nymph that Penelope is less beautiful than she. "But even so I wish and long day by day to reach my home. And if again some god shall smite me on the wine-dark sea, I will endure it, having in my breast a heart that endures affliction."

The stout heart he has is altogether his, and human, just as his tongue is what a good mind makes it. For the mortal nature of which he boasts at Phaeacia shows itself in both body and mind. He is not Samson. He is spirit, too, and art personified. He is good at anything; "no man can vie with me," he tells Eumaeus, "in pil-ing well a fire, in splitting dry faggots, in carving and roasting meat, and in pouring wine." This is when he is applying to the swineherd for a position as servant to the suitors, but we do not doubt that the real Odysseus has watched every human action and can imitate it. He makes convincing gestures among the wooers in the hall, "beginning on the right, stretching out his hand on every side, as if he had been long a beggar."

To say that he is mind as well as body is not to say that he forgets his body. The man who had urged Achilles to eat before he mourned Patroclus still has an appetite. He curses this "ravening belly" which demands so much attention, but he seems not to be sorry that he is alive there also. Neither is it to say that he denies himself the pleasures of possession. In one of his lying tales about himself he says it is greed that so long delays his return from Troy. "Yea, and Odysseus would long since have been here," he tells Penelope, "only it seemed to his mind more profitable to gather wealth by roaming over the wide earth." Greed is not the word, but it is true that when he awakes at Ithaca he counts the presents Alcinous has given him, thinking the sailors may have slipped something out and gone away with it. Nothing has disappeared, and he is pleased. He is the sort of man who expresses himself in his possessions. He must have everything right — his bed was so and so, and it should still be that way. His bow with its long pedigree, once he has it in his hands, is fingered carefully: turned round and round, and tried this way and that, "lest worms might have eaten the horns." Penelope, taking it from its peg in the storeroom, had suddenly sat down with it on her knees, and wept. A thing that Odysseus owns is Odysseus.

His suspicion of the Phaeacian sailors is in character. He suspects everybody, including the gods. He is slow to believe either that his own luck is turning or that other people mean the good things they say. He has seen too many chances unwisely taken, and been too many times deceived. He moves through the final stages of recognition and revenge with a professional caution. He is no amateur in adventure, even though he is blessed with its essential spirit, the spirit of curiosity. His curiosity is always at war with his caution. There is no need for him to see what the Cyclopes are like, and his men tell him so, protesting. But there across the water, as darkness comes down, he notices smoke and hears the voices of men, sheep, and goats, and the first thing he must do next morning is to set off in that direction, though it will mean the loss of comrades who go with him. The Sirens recognize in Odysseus a victim made to order: a man not only curious, but certain to take delight in songs concerning himself. For that is what they will sing, they say, if he comes close enough to hear. It takes the strongest ropes to keep him bound upright by his mast, safe from the seduction.

Suspicion and curiosity in Odysseus are the signs of a nimble wit that explores the ground before him. A still more famous one is his guile; he is ever ready with devices which his imagination, measuring persons and predicaments, is quick and accurate to supply him with. He is at home in the entire world, for he is never lost from himself. "Thou art a knave," Calypso exclaims to him in admiration when he demands that she swear an oath not to deal doubly with him; for that is what she might indeed have done. As he sees his strategy working against the Cyclops his heart laughs within him, proud of its cunning. Polyphemus had supposed that the Odysseus destined to come and blind him would be a giant like himself, not this puny weakling who first overpowered him with wine. The greatness of Odysseus is where the Cyclops cannot see it, in his wit. It is what makes him so successful in flattery, as when he calls Nausicaa a queen. It is the chief thing that guarantees Athene's continuing love.

The song of the Sirens would have seduced his vanity, if vanity is the name for the delight he takes in himself. "My fame reaches unto heaven," he tells Alcinous; and the old beggar of Ithaca tells Penelope that her husband is "like unto the gods." The mountain-top which Polyphemus hurls after his retreating ship does not discourage him from shouting back: "Cyclops, if any one of mortal men shall ask thee about the shameful blinding of thine eye, say that Odysseus, the sacker of cities, blinded it, even the son of Laertes, whose home is in Ithaca." He cannot hear too much from Eumaeus about the Odysseus who is gone; and his challenge to Eurymachus the suitor, when Eurymachus has insulted his character and strength, loses no glory by being for the moment hypothetical:

Eurymachus, I would that we two might have a match in working, in the season of spring, when the long days come, at mowing the grass, I with a curved scythe in my hands and thou with another like it, and that the grass might be in plenty that so we might test our work, fasting till late evening. Or I would again that there were oxen to drive — the best there are, tawny and large, both well fed with grass, of like age and like power to bear the yoke, tireless in strength — and that there were a field of four acres, and the soil should yield before the plough: then shouldest thou see me, whether or no I could cut a straight furrow to the end.

If these are boasts, they are the boasts of one who is praising life. If Odysseus loves himself, he loves the moving world still more. That world, concentrated in him, is what he loves and praises.

Peisistratus touching his horses with the whip so that they speed onward, nothing loath; Demodocus sitting and singing with a cup of wine which he has been shown how to reach with his hand, for he is blind; Telemachus standing by his father's side with sword and spear, armed with gleaming bronze; Achilles in the underworld, departing with long strides over the field of asphodel, joyful because he has been told that his son is preëminent — these, with Nestor on his white stones, Nausicaa with her white arms, Menelaus under his golden roof, Eurycleia with her torches and linen, Penelope in her grave chamber, are precious persons who adorn the tale created to contain them. But Odysseus is priceless, and he is not contained. The tale is of a dark storm that gathered over Ithaca, growing in secret mass until the land could be wholly cleansed by the lightning of its lord. This lord, still free, walks in the world. There has never been another poem to match either his or that of his young comrade-in-arms Achilles.

# III · THE AENEID

VIRGIL'S MELANCHOLY EPIC of one Trojan's escape
from the burning city, of his long wanderings west-
ward, and of his building Rome, might seem to be the
purest poetry if purity in that art means a close view
of things. It does, but Virgil may not see as much as
he appears to see. He appears to see every ivory ornament, every clasp and buckle, and to hear every sigh,
every modulation in each sad voice that speaks. He
appears, even, to enter the hero's mind — concerning
which he has a great deal to say — and thus to disappear out of position altogether.

But his poem is not visible, not tangible, as Homer's
poems are, and it is not Aeneas' mind we are in. We
are in Virgil's. We are among his ideas of how a man
doomed to procreate an empire would think, feel, and
move if he could move at all under so staggering a
burden. In his hero we discover not so much a man
as a kind of man: a nation, rather, inching up to its
place in history. We discover history. Aeneas, ever
aware as he is of his doom, though he calls it his
destiny, is unable to exist in any present moment. His
image dissipates into perspective, the perspective of

Roman and human history. We have all of that in view all of the time. The closer we get to the hero's thought the clearer becomes our view of this other thing. The poem is increasingly conscious of being prophecy, the hero of being a symbol, and the poet of being physician to mankind. Homer's secret, whereby he kept a right relation between near and far, between the part and the whole, between free will and fore-knowledge, is utterly lost. It has not been found again. Virgil is the more modern poet, for history in him — history as emotion — is pure and perfect.

The *Aeneid* is lacking in the sort of life that inspires higher criticism. We do not pay it the compliment of refusing to believe that one man wrote it. It exists in literary time. Its people are not created as Achilles and Odysseus are, or as Falstaff and Hamlet are, in the first word they speak. Homer and Shakespeare seem to find their men already made, but not so Virgil, who must move slowly because he has all time to cope with as he writes. The act of creation is out of time. The date of Homer is irrelevant to our feeling that he is somehow first, that he was there before history began. Virgil produces no such illusion, nor does he wish to produce it.

He is not chosen by his subject as Homer convinces us he was. It is impossible to imagine Homer deciding to write the *Iliad*. Virgil is literary, and so is free as we know Milton and Wordsworth were — we know because they told us — to pick one subject out of many. But he is not free to be chosen. Choice of the sort he has implies an eclecticism which we do not associate with the first in any art. It implies also the absence of some whole energy which only waits to release itself until the one possible subject has appeared.

But Virgil was bound to choose a master whom he could imitate, and since his taste was right he chose Homer. For Homer then as now was greatest. With his help, and in his name, Virgil could reënforce his purpose: thread his theme with strength and wash it over with importance. If Homer's presence in the shadows only brings out Virgil's difference, throwing him and his subject into pathetic relief, it is fair to say that Virgil knows the difference too, and even seeks to accentuate it. Nobody could be more aware than he that the essence of the master is unavailable. Only the accidents can be borrowed, and transformed as best may be. Virgil already understands how to do this. In the fourth book of the *Georgics* he grandly converted Achilles and Thetis into Aristaeus and Cyrene; nor did he cease till he had given Aristaeus an adventure with Proteus like that of Menelaus in the *Odyssey*. Now Homer has his hero waiting for him, a very special Trojan who Poseidon had insisted should be saved at Troy. "For it is ordained," said the Shaker of Earth, "unto him to escape, that the race of Dardanus perish not without seed and be seen no more — of Dardanus whom the son of Cronos loved above all the children born to him from mortal women. For at length hath the son of Cronos come to hate the race of Priam; and now verily shall the mighty Aeneas be king among the Trojans, and his sons' sons that shall be born in days to come" — but not in Troy itself, whose memory the *Aeneid* will show dissolving in the eternal reality of Rome.

The opening lines of the poem suggest an order of events to come different from the order Homer followed, and it is a difference that will seem still more significant as the work grows older and wearier. In Homer war came first, and then the wanderings. But we shall hear first of Aeneas' wanderings; after which he will have to wage an exhausting war, though he is already exhausted, in order that he may found a city and become the author of the Latin race. Peace is not to be cessation from struggle, a serene decline into old age, a homecoming, and — for reward — a winnowing-fan. It will be only then that the struggle begins: the struggle to change the world into something more lawful than it has been, and to keep it changed.

In the light of this major transformation the other differences, as well as the resemblances, are minor indeed. A list of them could be as long as this book. Aeneas at Dido's court, reciting his shipwrecks between Troy and Carthage, is Odysseus at the court of Alcinous. His adventures are too few and too briefly told, and the rhetoric of their terrors is scarcely real, but the parallel will escape no one. The funeral games for Anchises are like those for Patroclus, though they are run off with less relish. The descent to Avernus in the sixth book is more elaborate than the two scenes

of the *Odyssey* in Hades, and of a richer interest, for
Virgil finds the whole of his meaning underground.
When war approaches there is a gathering of the clans
on both sides — the side of the native kings, Mezentius, Lausus, Turnus, and the rest, with swift Camilla
for support, and the side of Aeneas whose allies are
less resplendent — which of course recalls the Greek
and Trojan catalogues of the *Iliad*. As war is joined
a host of parallels appears. Pallas is Patroclus even to
the point of requiring the sacrifice of twelve enemy
youths at his bier. There are campfires by night; there
are individual combats by day, some grotesque and
some terrible, with frequent accent on the pathos of
slain warriors; the gods interfere, and Jupiter is quite
as indecisive as Zeus was; then, finally, there is the duel
between Aeneas and Turnus, suggesting if by no means
matching the one between Achilles and Hector. There
is even a cypress-tree to remind us of Homer's fig-tree;
and there is the night expedition of Nisus and Euryalus,
set in another key than that out of which the tenth
book of the *Iliad* extracts such bloody, exciting music.

There is nothing after the duel to go with Priam's
wonderful night in Achilles' hut. Nothing here is wonderful at all. That is not the word for Virgil, who must
make up for his lack of power with softer things. And
sometimes he cannot make it up. The speeches of his
warriors, as of all his people, are finished rhetoric of
the Roman sort, but there is not one note in them of
the incisive, practical force with which Homer's men
deliver themselves; unless such a note is heard in Tur-

nus, shortly before he dies. The dooms that overhang
the heroes, for such things too are borrowed from
Homer, hang there with little weight; the threatened
men are in truth not very interesting while they live.
Lausus, Pallas, Turnus, Mezentius, Arruns, Ufens —
the fame of the list is feeble if we remember Agamemnon, Achilles, Odysseus, Nestor, Diomedes, Aias, Hector, and Sarpedon. So are the ironies of Virgil feeble.
They are contrived, like his rhetoric, and have to be
pointed out. By the same token the poem derives no
such advantage as the *Iliad* does, or the *Odyssey* either,
from the fact that its end is foretold. When Homer tells
us how things will turn out our interest neither dies
nor becomes academic, for men and things in him are
individual and real, and where there is reality there is
hazard. Homer has not cut off more history than poetry can handle. Virgil has done just that, and sometimes he seems to know it. Or he may know it all of
the time, accepting it as the handicap which the pre-
dicament of his era has settled upon him. He may be
as aware as we are that the whole second half of his epic
is hyperbole — a form of evidence, attesting strain,
which in no art ever lies.

Virgil's subject is political, as Homer's was not and
doubtless could not have been. The ethical emphasis
is public, the slogans are institutional, the manners of
the life are colored by a sort of state decorum, and the
perspective through time is mainly into the future.
Homer could conceive sentiment in an army, and in
his clans there is the closest brotherhood; but the mat-

ter of his songs remained, though it did so in a large sense, personal. Virgil, in deciding to set the political above the personal, was right from every point of view save that of poetry. Rome was more important to him than any man, just as peace was more precious than all men put together. We may applaud either preference at the same time that we miss power in the poet who states it. Virgil could have had no other preferences than these, considering who he was and in what terrible times he lived; or so at any rate one is tempted to think. If criticism is to be merciless, however, it must note that the necessity was something to which Virgil sacrificed the last reach of the art he practiced.

The first ambitious simile in the *Aeneid* takes off from a term of public morality:

And as oft in some great concourse, when Sedition lifts her head and the nameless vulgar kindles to rage — when brands and stones are already flying, and fury ministers arms — if they chance to behold a man of reverend goodness and worth, on the instant all are mute; and about him they stand with listening ear, while he sways their spirit by his word and allays their passion: even so sank all that tumult of ocean, when Father Neptune looked forth on the waves, and, floating under a cloudless heaven, guided his steeds and flew onward, giving rein to his speeding car.

So the catchwords of the poem are covenant, truce, law, federation, league, order, piety, right, precedent, and justice; and the epithets of the heroes are similarly flavored — Aeneas, at all times "good," is in addition "source of the Roman line," and Ascanius is "second hope of Queenly Rome." The bees of the *Georgics* had their polity; so now have these men, and it is all they have. Decorum is their daily condition. Aeneas, wrecked with certain members of his retinue on the Libyan coast, ascends a cliff and sights three stags, followed at a suitable distance by the herd of which they are the leaders. He shoots the chieftains first, and only then the commoners. He violates no propriety even in the hunt. Virgil is careful furthermore to remark that Aeneas does not carry his own weapons; Achates hands him his bow and arrows so that with dignity he may save them all from starvation. The moment recalls its equivalent in the *Odyssey* — its equivalent, but with how much less accent on the rules of court. Odysseus, setting out for the shore near Circe's house with the intention of feeding his men, happens upon a stag.

He was coming down to the river from his pasture in the wood to drink, for the might of the sun oppressed him; and as he came out I struck him on the spine in the middle of the back, and the bronze spear passed right through him, and down he fell in the dust with a moan, and his spirit flew from him. Then I planted my foot upon him, and drew the bronze spear forth from the wound, and left it to lie there on the ground. But for myself, I plucked twigs and osiers, and weaving a rope as it were a fathom in length, well twisted from end to end, I bound together the feet of the monstrous beast, and went my way to the black ship, bearing him across my back and leaning on my spear, since in no wise could I hold him on my shoulder with one hand, for he was a very mighty beast. Down I flung him before the ship, and heartened my comrades.

There is the act itself, simple and direct in its every circumstance; and Odysseus does not have the venison conveyed away, as Aeneas presumably did, by appropriate persons. He does it himself.

The direction in which the poem points is always the future. Some Roman antiquities are touched upon, but the past is of pale importance to Virgil compared either with his own time, which to Aeneas was the future, or with some newer time not yet arrived. The fabric of the vision is prophetic. When Aeneas' departed father speaks to him from Elysium, counseling the journey which in the sixth book he will take through the deeps of Avernus, the promise is that he will thereby learn the names of his posterity and the character of the city prepared even now for his founding hand. Once he is in the underworld he is treated, at the climax of his stay, to a view of Romans not then born: to future statesmen, saviors of their city and the world. The shield which Venus has Vulcan make for Aeneas shows the future of the Empire even to the battle of Actium.

The future is as a vise in which the head of Aeneas is fixed so that he cannot look elsewhere, and least of all backward. He is reminded every minute of his destiny, nor is any effort made by god or man to recommend the prospect as agreeable. On the contrary, it is urged in terms of its supreme difficulty. The struggle to found Rome will be vast and dire. Happier days will come, but they cannot be now. And even the days to come will have their sorrow. When Aeneas spies among the unborn a shining youth with downcast eyes "and little joy in his visage," he asks of Anchises: "Who is he, my father?" And he is answered:

O my son, seek not to know the great agony of thy people! Him the fates shall but show to earth, nor suffer longer to be. . . . What moaning of men shall echo from that famed Field to Mavors' queenly city! What obsequies, O Tiber, shalt thou see when thou flowest by his new-raised grave! . . . Ay me, thou child of tears, if haply thou mayest burst the cruel barriers of fate, thou shalt be *Marcellus!*

Marcellus the nephew and adopted son of Augustus — Augustus, into whom all this future pours, and for whom, and to flatter whom, the poem is composed — had recently died; and there is a legend that Virgil read the foregoing lines aloud to the Emperor, melting him with further grief. However that may be, this is an instance of foretold sorrow; and of a tendency which grows in Virgil to anticipate current customs, current institutions, and current men as he details the ancient days of his good hero.

The world has grown irrevocably political, and the *Aeneid* is the poem which shows this happening, just as the poem that comes down from Lucretius shows the world becoming irrevocably scientific. There is no appeal from such facts, and there should be no decrying of Virgil or Lucretius for their clairvoyance. But whereas Lucretius, as will be seen, rejoices in the change, Virgil does not seem to do so. Lucretius looked for a style that would state the revolution he foresaw, and he more or less found it. Virgil, as if heartbroken by the realization that politics, however inevitable its advent, might prove an enemy to poetry, as indeed it has largely continued to be, and as Plato for one desired that it should be, relapses into a style that is less rather than more real. He is sincere, and he foresees everything; but he is soft and sad.

A political subject — in this case the great role of Rome as consolidator and pacifier of world society, and more particularly the great place of Augustus at the goal of so much progress — might seem to have demanded a forthright, confident, and masculine narrative, clearly ordered and precisely phrased. Instead of that we get in the *Aeneid* indirect lighting and misty effects. Its author's favorite adjectives are "tenuis" and "inanis." There is continual resort to the undefined — to the unspeakable, and even to the unimaginable. The scenes are invariably "tangled" or "shadowy." The prevailing hue is grey, and the time when the poet is most at home is twilight or nightfall, when things have become difficult to see in their hard, natural outlines. The result, given Virgil's genius, is a number of passages washed over with the loveliest tones the minor lyre has ever commanded.

Dim under the lone night they journeyed through the shadows, through the vacant halls of Dis and his unsubstantial kingdom — even as one who journeys in a forest under the niggard light of the faltering moon, when Jove has curtained the sky in shade, and the blackness of night bereaves Nature of her hue.

Thus, and they are justly famous, go the lines which take Aeneas and his guide underground in the sixth book; where Dido will be seen as a "dim form through the shadows," and where even among the Happy Groves the visitors will wander at large over "wide plains of mist."

Thence she seemed to hear the voice of her husband speaking and calling when night hung grey over earth; and oft on the roof the owl wailed forlorn with his sepulchral dirge and long-drawn note of melancholy.

Thus the dream of Dido on the eve of her resolution to die.

It was night, and through all the earth weary creatures, bird and beast alike, lay wrapped in deep slumber; when father Aeneas, with heart wrung by that lamentable strife, flung him down by the river's brim, under the chill cope of heaven, and allowed sleep to steal, belated, over his frame. Before him the deity of the place, Tiber of the pleasant stream, seemed, in very presence, to uplift his white head through the poplar leaves. Thin lawn draped him in mantle of grey, and shady reeds crowned his hair.

Thus — and what passage in the entire poem is more saturated with Virgil's magic? — the hero in a harsh moment near the beginning of the eighth book.

No reader of the poem forgets Palinurus the helmsman; he is the arch-inhabitant of Virgil's night, created for no other purpose, it would seem, than to be the occasion of noble nocturnes. He is the watcher of the stars as they float in the silent firmament: of Arcturus and the rainy Hyades, and the twin Bears; "and he gazed on Orion in his panoply of gold." He it is whom Sleep beguiles as he sits with his faithful hand on the rudder:

And now dewy Night had almost reached her goal in the central heavens, and, stretched by the oars along the hard benches, the seamen had surrendered their limbs to slumber's quiet influence; when Sleep, lightly gliding from the ethereal stars, parted the dusk air and clove the shades, in quest, Palinurus, of thee, and laden with fatal dreams for thy guiltless eyes! . . . And hardly had the sudden sleep touched his nerveless limbs, ere bending above he flung him sheer into the flowing waves.

Palinurus and his leader both are dwellers in a completely pretty world, one that Virgil builds not only with shadows and dim leaves of form but sometimes with the subtlest similes reachable by such art. That his similes are superfluous does not for the moment matter. They are superfluous because the style is already high and general, and does not need them. Nothing is gained by this recourse, then, to powers and forces without. Homer, in whose stories everything was particular, gained by gathering images from abroad; he amplified the spread of his vision, returning us to a great world he knew but could not otherwise use. Here, on the contrary, is all the world Virgil knows, and it is not a real world. It is made of effects and figures — even at times of Roman rhetorical figures such as Tacitus in a later day will masterfully perfect. "Deep-fixed in her breast clung his lineaments

and words." "How stout of spirit and arms!" "In one
self-same moment, let the youth desire, demand, and
seize the sword!" That might almost be Gibbon talking — Gibbon, who heard barefooted friars singing
vespers in the Temple of Jupiter as Aeneas saw scattered herds lowing in the Roman forum: one irony
was perceived after the Fall, and one before the Rise,
but the rhetoric is the same. The similes of Virgil are
merely further figures in an artificial series already long.
Yet they are everything that this circumstance can let
them be; and they are finer, it should be added, when
they decorate tableaux than when they endeavor to
invigorate action. Virgil is not a poet of action. His
style is the one contribution he could make to Euro-
pean poetry.

It is most itself when it is vague in the beautiful way
that Virgil can be vague. The description in the first
book of a harbor into which the weary comrades of
Aeneas drive their ships is highly accomplished:

There, in a deep bay, is a roadstead, which an island forms
by its jutting sides. On those sides every wave from the deep
breaks, then parts into the winding hollows: on this hand and
that are vast rocks, and twin cliffs frowning to heaven; and beneath their peaks, far and wide, the peaceful seas are silent.
From the height hangs a background of waving forests, and a
grove of dim and tangled shadows. Under the fronting crags
is a rock-hung cave — haunted by the Nymphs — and, within
it, sweet water and seats from the living rock. Here no chains
fetter the wearied ships, and no anchor with crooked fang re-
strains them. . . . Yearning for their mother-earth, the Trojans

landed: the long-hoped beach was theirs at last, and they laid their brine-drenched limbs on the sand.

It is quite as accomplished as the harbor in the *Odyssey* from which it is copied, the harbor where the Phaeacian sailors deposit Odysseus:

There is in the land of Ithaca a certain harbor of Phorcys, the old man of the sea, and at its mouth two projecting headlands sheer to seaward, but sloping down on the side toward the harbor. These keep back the great waves raised by heavy winds without, but within the benched ships lie unmoored when they have reached the point of anchorage. At the head of the harbor is a long-leafed olive-tree, and near it a pleasant, shadowy cave sacred to the nymphs that are called Naiads. Therein are mixing bowls and jars of stone, and there too the honey bees store honey. And in the cave are long looms of stone, at which the nymphs weave webs of purple dye, a wonder to behold; and therein are also ever-flowing springs. . . . Here they rowed in, knowing the place of old; and the ship ran full half her length on the shore in her swift course, at such a pace was she driven by the arms of the rowers. Then they stepped forth from the benched ship upon the land.

It is even more accomplished if accomplishment in poetry is measured by the skill with which everything is suppressed that would be interesting in prose. Homer is of the greatest because he is even more interesting than prose would be; and that is very interesting, as any reader knows. Virgil is not of the greatest because he is just a little under prose in the power he wields. He avoids prose as something that would hurt his poetry if it came too close; and it would, because his poetry could not stand the comparison. In the description of the harbor he leaves everything out that would be clear, useful, or convincing, because he has a sure sense of what for him is poetical. It is poetical for us, too; and for some it is preferable to the greatest poetry. But in none of the greatest poetry will it be found.

The style of the *Aeneid* is the most palpable thing in it. It is everywhere; or if there are stretches where it is absent, then there is nothing that takes its place. Virgil is not of that high company, the small high company of Homer, Dante, and Shakespeare, in whom there is no style. Each of the three has styles — he says the things he says in the way those things should be said in order to have their utmost force — but none of them is the victim of a limitation in language which means that certain things cannot be said at all. Those poets can and do say everything, and they are never imitated because there is nothing in the way they speak for things and men that can be imitated, unless the things and men themselves are imitated — a nonsensical condition. The words Homeric, Dantesque, Shakespearean refer to created worlds, and to the life of every sort that is lived there. The word Virgilian, like the word Miltonic, refers to a gift of language: a high gift, but not the highest, since it does not get far enough from the ground to permit a just view of the lowest things. We are always conscious of Virgil's and Milton's words, which are what their admirers must use to prove their greatness. In Homer, Dante, and Shakespeare the word tends to disappear before the thing.

The greatest poems eat their own words, they devour the shells they come in. This can be true because of the strong, even the crude, grip which their authors have on reality. The grip is too crude for prettiness, and the reality is more mysterious than dreams. Such poets are sure of their worlds, as perhaps the stylists are not. It was one stylist, Tennyson, who said of another stylist, Virgil, the best thing that has been said of him: "All the charm of all the Muses often flowering in a lonely word."

The poetry of Virgil is an applied poetry, a veneer whose business is to make things beautiful. Virgil must be beautiful or his subject dies — a sure sign of weakness. He cannot afford to be plain, ugly, and direct. Furthermore, beauty with him, as always with such poets, has to be construed as plastic or tonal beauty. The greatest poetry suggests no other art. Virgil's suggests painting and music. Homer had said this of Gorgythion, whom Teucer slew with one of his terrible arrows: "And he bowed his head to one side like a poppy that in a garden is laden with its fruit and the rains of spring; so bowed he to one side his head, laden with his helmet." It is the helmet, and the surrender of muscles in the neck, that gives point to the comparison, which is made and left to move us as it will. See how Virgil forces it in his description of Euryalus as he dies; forces it, and writes into it a pathetic music which leaves us with the flower, not the man: "And his drooping neck sank on his shoulder — as a purple flower, that the plough has severed, languishes and dies, or as poppies, weighted by random showers, bow laden heads on weary necks."

Or take the hero at Dido's hunt. It is a decorative occasion, but Aeneas himself should be less the maypole than he is:

Such as Apollo is when he deserts his wintry Lycian and the streams of Xanthus to visit his mother's Delos, and there renews the dance, while Cretan and Dryop and painted Agathyrsian revel banded about his altars; but himself he walks the peaks of Cynthus, confining with plastic hand his streaming locks in delicate leaves and entwining gold, and the quiver rattles upon his shoulder — so, with tread light as his, moved Aeneas, and beauty as glorious shone on his peerless countenance.

For the second time now Venus has beautified her son so that Dido may love him. The first time was when she materialized him from a cloud and amazed the Carthaginian queen. The spectacle Athene once had made of Odysseus so that Nausicaa and her maidens might not fear him had been splendid with grace, as we have seen. But see again how Virgil has prettified the father of Rome:

Suddenly the investing cloud disparted and was purged into the open sky, and in its place stood Aeneas, glittering in the lucent day, godlike in aspect and frame: for the mother had breathed on her son, and his locks were beautiful; he was clad in the rosy light of youth, and his eyes were lustrous and glad — as when the artist hand lends loveliness to the ivory, or when silver or Parian stone, is enchased in the yellow gold.

Homer had let Athene adorn his man with silver and gold, but he had reserved ivory for Penelope. Virgil, like most poets bent on beauty, does not know when he has all of it his subject can stand.

Aeneas does not move under his own power any more than the poem does. A reader of the *Odyssey* smiles at its hero's cosmetic ordeal as at something that does not fit his nature though it may be useful to his career. Virgil's hero, having no nature, cannot be outraged. He stands there, a patient lay figure, while Virgil puts on all the paint he pleases. Aeneas without loss, for there is nothing to lose, participates in the passive mood which makes the style of his poem the most mournful and musical of known styles.

Aeneas is regularly represented as weary, sick at heart, sluggish in spirit, and divided of mind. Homer's men were thus divided, but soon enough they told their thoughts to be still and arrived at a decision. Virgil's hero does to be sure act, but hesitation even then hangs over him; he is never without the air of one beset with the misery of a mixed imagination. Indecision is so chronic with him as to be almost beloved; it is an habitual state, it is his very own. Virgil indulges it in him by elaborating and varying its expression. "Vainly he tossed on inconstant tide, and discordant cares racked his breast with call and countercall." "Now hither, now thither, swiftly he transferred his divided mind, and swept it over all the range of thought: as when a gleam of water, tremulous in the brimming bronze, is flung back from the sun or the luster of the mirrored moon; then glances abroad over all, till mounting skyward it strikes the fretted roof high above." There, in fact, is a simile for the condition, and one so intricate, not to say so unlikely, that the condition itself takes on a sickly cast. It is not for nothing that Virgil so often represents the heart and soul of Aeneas as sick, and his entire being unnerved. Once he is spellbound, and another time he is tongue-tied. Towards the end he boasts as Hector had boasted, but there is a hollow sound to it; he has the words of the horse-tamer but not the tune. His doom is as clear as that of Achilles, though it is different; yet he never moves like a free agent as Achilles does. He recognizes that he is not "the captain of his own life"; he feels unfree, without evident relish in the things he knows he must do, even when they will issue in glory. When Penthesilea the Amazon came to the support of the Trojans, a Greek poem tells us that Achilles battled with her as if she were a man, and killed her. But she was beautiful as she lay dead, and he was filled with sudden remorse; which Thersites mocked, and at once Achilles slew Thersites. It is not suggested that Aeneas should have done anything like that, but one does miss in him a talent for unpremeditation.

His enemies in the poem call him effeminate. King Iarbas speaks with contempt of his "eunuch retinue," of his "essenced love-locks bound with turban of Lydia." Turnus addresses the Trojans as maids, not men, and his challenge to Aeneas is to a "woman-man." This is doubtless one of Virgil's ironies, suggesting either that Iarbas and Turnus are wrong or that they do not know how to estimate refinement as Rome will some day exhibit refinement in its imperial dandies. Should Virgil, however, have commended the beauty of Ascanius for any reason at all in the following style? "And lo! in their midst . . . was the Dardan boy, shining as a solitary gem shines amid the yellow gold bedecking some fair throat or brow; or as ivory gleams, set by the artist hand in boxwood or Orician terebinth — while his loose locks, gathered in a circlet of ductile gold, streamed down his neck of snow." To do so was to write beautifully but as a poet to blunder; great poetry is not preposterous in this fashion.

Virgil is more successful with his women, including his goddesses, than he ever is with men. This could be a sign of his civilization if the men came anywhere near being equal to the fatal females whom they so seldom can withstand. Such power as the poem has is in Juno, Venus, Juturna, Allecto, and Camilla, and in the three mortal women with whom the fortunes of Aeneas are linked: Dido, Lavinia, and Amata. Their power, indeed, is so disproportionate that equality disappears and civilization suffers. The only clear recollection we carry away of humanity in motion is the recollection of Camilla, who "might have flown over the topmost blades of the untouched corn, nor, flying, have scathed the tender ears; she might have sped over the mid seas, poised above the swelling wave, nor dipped her glancing feet in the flood," or of Juturna, sister to Turnus and mistress of lakes and rivers, who is honored with the finest simile in the *Aeneid:*

As a black swallow flits through the ample halls of some wealthy lord and wings her way round his stately courts, gathering her tiny crumbs of food to regale the twitterers in her nest; and now her pinions sound in the vacant colonnades, now round the water-ponds: such was Juturna, as she whirled behind her steeds through the enemy's midst, and flew over all with racing chariot, and now here, now there, displayed her brother in triumph — yet suffered him not to close in battle, but shot far away!

Alongside either of these semidivine ladies the males of the *Aeneid* are pale, sad specimens of their sex, participating as their leader does in the mood that poses so perplexing a problem.

For how, finally, is it to be explained that an epic that sets out to glorify the Capitol and crown all human life with lawful peace turns into the saddest of recorded poems? Shall Virgil be put down as a minor genius failing at a major task? Or if such an answer seems too simple, and if the genius of Virgil is something that cannot be graded off, are we to say that in the *Aeneid* a poet of unlimited powers reveals, consciously or unconsciously, the inward limits of his theme — exposes the insufficiency of Augustus, the shoddiness of Rome, the immaturity of a culture that only thinks itself the product of all history? Or the revelation might be that sophisticated epics are impossible. It might be, indeed, a disclosure of the doubt which lurks for so many civilized men at the heart of enterprise, the doubt which paralyzes effort and sours success just when it should seem sweetest. If any of these things is revealed, and revealed unconsciously, against the grain of Virgil's will, then he is indeed the sorcerer the Middle Ages said he was. He is a poet through whom the truth speaks. It is not he that utters irony; irony utters him. The author of the fourth *Eclogue*, prophesying a Messiah, would by such an account be no more than a study for the author of the *Aeneid*, prophesying universal failure, a failure that expresses itself before it knows itself, using the language of his nightingale's tongue.

He is the poet of nocturnal tears, at home with weariness and most true when most troubled. Nor are his tears the "round" ones, the "big" ones, which Homer found on the faces of his men and women. Those were distinct and visible, and they had a cause. These are hidden in the fiber of things, buried there like secret germs of misery, spreading their influence as a potion does through all of being's tissues. They are internal, ineffable; too deep for words of diagnosis or cure. They are the reference in Virgil's most famous and least translatable phrase: *Sunt lacrimae rerum et mentem mortalia tangunt.* No two versions of the phrase agree, and so it had better be left alone, with its two words, *lacrimae rerum*, weeping in their place. It is by no means strange that most of the great lines in the *Aeneid* are elegiac as this one is. When Virgil rises, he rises into lyric, while the story stops. The stories of Homer never stop to state themselves, to soar away on notes of lyric generality. They simply move on and cover the earth. Virgil is no such master of the epic art.

That may be why Virgil cannot free his hero, who walks too heavily, under too great a weight of destiny, ever to enjoy his role. He is a sleepwalker, a hypnotic subject, locked into the events that will make his life for him — a life that will mean most after he is dead. He takes no pleasure in his invasion of Italy and his slaughter of its ancient inhabitants. They live in peace, under laws which Aeneas can but disturb; he brings them present misery with their future glory. Nor do they enjoy their doom in the grim way in which tragedy can dignify and exalt its victims. The war of the second six books is a ghastly affair, unreal because unrelished. Its combatants are to the last man and woman committed to a decreed end, necessary but in its horror unrelieved. A conflict that nobody desires must somehow be got through with so that Rome may some day be — what Rome in the time of Augustus has become. Blood must be waded so that war may cease. The Nisus-Euryalus episode is copied from the tenth book of the *Iliad*, but changed into a futile, heartbreaking business; the counterparts of Odysseus and Diomedes are a man and a boy, both of whom are killed as the mission fails; and the mother of the boy cries on the battlements when the outcome is known. It is of such events that Aeneas is captain. He wins, but he is one whose duties shrivel him somewhat as Shakespeare's Brutus is shriveled by the crisis for which he is armed only with stoicism. All is duty, all is danger, all is consciousness of uncharacteristic actions waiting to be done. The speech of such a man is bound to be as impersonal as that of Aeneas is. And he is bound to cast a shadow forward over the empire his legend is intended to glorify.

The absence of epic genius in the author of the *Aeneid* may explain all this. But so may other things. So, for instance, may some special view he took of the world. And more particularly, so may some special feeling he had about the political state he most often mentions, the state of peace.

Peace is Virgil's deepest theme, but he means by it more than his art can manage. The peace he dreams of is not an improvement to be made in the world that is, but the condition of a new world to be born. Virgil, like Lucretius, has given up the world that is. He has lost confidence in its power to survive tragedy. The recent civil wars, together with the long imperial war from which they stemmed, have destroyed his nerve. The only vision of salvation possible to Virgil is the vision of a change so radical that the better world to follow will of necessity and in essence be utterly unlike this one. It will be so different that as yet it is unrecognizable; it cannot be seen ahead save vaguely. That, then, may be the reason for the lifelessness of Aeneas as he gropes his way into the future. The world for him, as for his poet, is not its own place, and indestructible. It can survive nothing more of the sort that hitherto has happened to men. It is a limp world, sapped of wrath and wit, of savagery and joy. No further chances can be taken, no further tragedy may be endured. Salvation depends henceforth upon the transformation of men into other creatures than poetry has known. History cannot afford another Achilles, or even another Odysseus. Their brawls, their wiles would shake the structure down. The tragedy of Virgil may be the history he had had to see. There was too much of it. It had left him incapable of tragedy.

It had left him capable at best of searching literature for a myth to match the quality and direction of his feeling. For it is a feeling he has about peace, an absolute feeling, and it must find an echo in some tale of absolute change, some myth of metamorphosis, which will be adequate to his desperation. The whole of his work — the *Eclogues*, the *Georgics*, and the *Aeneid*, and especially the sixth book of the *Aeneid*, the book of the other life — suggests that he found what he needed in Plato's dialogue *The Statesman*. In that dialogue the Stranger tells the Younger Socrates an important tale — important, certainly, for the Roman poet three centuries later. For it haunts his memory and informs his every thought about the world. It is Plato's rationalization of two legends: the legend of the reign of Cronos, and the legend of the earth-born folk.

Listen then. During a certain period God himself goes with the universe as guide in its revolving course, but at another epoch, when the cycles have at length reached the measure of his allotted time, he lets it go, and of its own accord it turns backward in the opposite direction, since it is a living creature and is endowed with intelligence by him who fashioned it in the beginning. . . . The universe is guided at one time by an extrinsic divine cause, acquiring the power of living again and receiving renewed immortality from the Creator, and at another time it is left to itself at such a moment that it moves backwards through countless ages.

We cannot help believing that of all the changes which take place in the heavens this reversal is the greatest and most complete. . . . Therefore we must also believe that at the same time the greatest changes come upon us who dwell within the heavens. . . . And animals cannot well endure many great and various changes at once. . . . Inevitably, then, there is at that time great destruction of animals in general, and only a small part of the human race survives; and the survivors have many experiences wonderful and strange, the greatest of which, a consequence of the reversal of everything at the time when the world begins to turn in the direction opposed to that of its present revolution, is this.

First the age of all animals, whatever it was at the moment, stood still, and every mortal creature stopped growing older in appearance and then reversed its growth and became, as it were, younger and more tender; the hoary locks of the old men grew dark, and bearded cheeks grew smooth again as their possessors reverted to their earlier ages, and the bodies of young men grew smoother and smaller day by day and night by night, until they became as new-born babes, to which they were likened in mind and body; and then at last they wasted away entirely and wholly disappeared. And the bodies of those who died by violence in those times quickly underwent the same changes, were destroyed, and disappeared in a few days. . . .

It is clear, Socrates, that being begotten of one another was no part of the natural order of that time, but the earth-born race which, according to tradition, once existed, was the race which returned at that time out of the earth; and the memory of it was preserved by our earliest ancestors, who were born in the beginning of our period and therefore were next neighbors to the end of the previous period of the world's revolution, with no interval between. For they were to us the heralds of these stories which are nowadays unduly disbelieved by many people. For you must, I think, consider what would result. It is a natural consequence of the return of the old to childhood that those who are dead and lying in the earth take shape and come to life again, since the process of birth is reversed along with the reversal of the world's revolution; for this reason they are inevitably earth-born. . . .

*Younger Socrates:* But was the life in the reign of Cronos in that previous period of revolution or in ours? For evidently the change in the course of the stars and the sun takes place in both periods.

No, the life about which you ask, when all the fruits of the earth sprang up of their own accord for men, did not belong at all to the present period of revolution, but this also belonged to the previous one. For then, in the beginning, God ruled and supervised the whole revolution, and so again, in the same way, all the parts of the universe were divided by regions among gods who ruled them, and, moreover, the animals were distributed by species and flocks among inferior deities as divine shepherds, each of whom was in all respects the independent guardian of the creatures under his own care, so that no creature was wild, nor did they eat one another, and there was no war among them, nor any strife whatsoever.

But the reason for the story of the spontaneous life of mankind is as follows: God himself was their shepherd, watching over them, just as man, being an animal of different and more divine nature than the rest, now tends the lower species of animals. And under his care there were no states, nor did men possess wives or children; for they all came to life again out of the earth, with no recollection of their former lives. So there were no states or families, but they had fruits in plenty from the trees and other plants, which the earth furnished them of its own accord, without help from agriculture. And they lived for the most part in the open air, without clothing or bedding; for the climate was tempered for their comfort, and the abundant grass that grew up out of the earth furnished them soft couches. That, Socrates, was the life of men in the reign of Cronos; but the life of the present age, which is said to be the age of Zeus, you know by your own experience. Would you be able and willing to decide which of them is the more blessed?

Certainly not.

Shall I, then, make some sort of judgment for you?

Do so, by all means.

Well, then, if the foster children of Cronos, having all this leisure and the ability to converse not only with human beings but also with beasts, made full use of all these opportunities with a view to philosophy, talking with the animals and with one another and learning from every creature that, through possession of some peculiar power, may have had in any respect beyond his fellows perceptions tending towards an increase of wisdom, it would be easy to decide that the people of those old times were immeasurably happier than those of our epoch. Or if they merely ate and drank till they were full and gossiped with each other and the animals, telling such stories as are even now told about them, in that case, too, it

would, in my opinion, be very easy to reach a decision. However, let us pass those matters by, so long as there is no one
capable of reporting to us what the desires of the people in
those days were in regard to knowledge and the employment
of speech. . . .

When the time of all those conditions was accomplished and
the change was to take place and all the earth-born race had
at length been used up, since every soul had fulfilled all its
births by falling into the earth as seed its prescribed number
of times, then the helmsman of the universe dropped the tiller
and withdrew to his place of outlook, and fate and innate
desire made the earth turn backwards. So, too, all the gods
who share, each in his own sphere, the rule of the Supreme
Spirit, promptly perceiving what was taking place, let go the
parts of the world which were under their care. And as the
universe was turned back and there came the shock of colli-
sion, as the beginning and the end rushed in opposite direc-
tions, it produced a great earthquake within itself and caused
a new destruction of all sorts of living creatures. But after
that, when a sufficient time had elapsed, there was rest now
from disturbance and confusion, calm followed the earthquakes, and the world went on its own accustomed course in
orderly fashion, exercising care and rule over itself and all
within itself, and remembering and practicing the teachings of
the Creator and Father to the extent of its power, at first more
accurately and at last more carelessly; and the reason for this
was the material element in its composition, because this element, which was inherent in the primeval nature, was infected
with great disorder before the attainment of the existing orderly
universe. For from its Composer the universe has received only
good things; but from its previous condition it retains in itself
and creates in the animals all the elements of harshness and

injustice which have their origin in the heavens. Now as long as the world was nurturing the animals within itself under the guidance of the Pilot, it produced little evil and great good; but in becoming separated from him it always got on most excellently during the time immediately after it was let go, but as time went on and it grew forgetful, the ancient condition of disorder prevailed more and more and towards the end of the time reached its height, and the universe, mingling but little good with much of the opposite sort, was in danger of destruction for itself and those within it. Therefore at that moment God, who made the order of the universe, perceived that it was in dire trouble, and fearing that it might founder in the tempest of confusion and sink in the boundless sea of diversity, he took again his place as its helmsman, reversed whatever had become unsound and unsettled in the previous period when the world was left to itself, set the world in order, restored it and made it immortal and ageless.

So now the whole tale is told; but . . . to revert to the earlier part of the story. For when the universe was turned again into the present path of generation, the age of individuals came again to a stop, and that led to new processes, the reverse of those which had gone before. For the animals which had grown so small as almost to disappear grew larger, and those newly born from the earth with hoary hair died and passed below the earth again. And all other things changed, imitating the condition of the universe and conforming to it, and so too pregnancy and birth and nurture necessarily imitated and conformed to the rest; for no living creature could any longer come into being by the union of other elements, but just as the universe was ordered to be the ruler of its own course, so in the same way the parts were ordered, so far as they could, to grow and beget and give nourishment of themselves under the same guidance.

And now we have come at last to the point for the sake of which this whole discourse was begun. For much might be said, and at great length, about the other animals, their previous forms and the causes of their several changes; but about mankind there is less to say and it is more to our purpose. For men, deprived of the care of the deity who had possessed and tended us, since most of the beasts who were by nature unfriendly had grown fierce, and they themselves were feeble and unprotected, were ravaged by the beasts and were in the first ages still without resources or skill; the food which had formerly offered itself freely had failed them, and they did not yet know how to provide for themselves, because no necessity had hitherto compelled them. On all these accounts they were in great straits; and that is the reason why the gifts of the gods that are told of in the old traditions were given us with the needful information and instruction — fire by Prometheus, the arts by Hephaestus and the goddess who is his fellow-artisan, seeds and plants by other deities. And from these has arisen all that constitutes human life, since, as I said a moment ago, the care of the gods had failed men and they had to direct their own lives and take care of themselves, like the whole universe, which we imitate and follow through all time, being born and living now in our present manner and in that other epoch in the other manner. So, then, let our tale be finished.

The tale illuminates Anchises as he stands in a green valley among the realms of joy, surveying the prisoned spirits to whom Fate owes a second body: spirits who must wait where they are in the blissful fields "till at length the hoary ages, when time's cycle is run, purge the incarnate stain. . . . All these that thou seest," says Anchises to his son, "when they have turned the wheel through a thousand years, God summons in their legions to the river of Lethe, that, with memory disenthroned, they may review the vaulted heavens and conceive desire once more to tenant the flesh." It is not the only source of light upon the sixth book of Virgil's poem, for the doctrine of transmigration throws beams in this direction, and so do other doctrines to which the poet was sensitive. But the cycle and the return — there is the form for Virgil's feeling about history, and specifically for his feeling about peace.

History for Virgil, and nothing could be more understandable than this, was the history of war and peace. His own time was a time of war; whence his imagination escaped both backward into a golden age which had known nothing but peace and forward into another such age if God and Augustus would permit it to be. He conceived of a great weight that swung, bringing now blood, now bliss; and he ached to believe that the next turn of time would bring in, and perhaps bring in forever, the cycle having then finished its function, the unspeakable bliss of peace. "The last age is come," runs the famous fourth *Eclogue,* "and the great march of the centuries begins anew. Now Saturn is king again, and a new and better race descends from on high. Our iron breed shall at last cease, and the age of gold dawn on all the world."

"There is war in all the world," cries the poet of the *Georgics.* It was otherwise when the globe lived in perpetual spring, "and the earth-born brood of men

reared its head from the stony plains." Then peace and
justice reigned, and golden Saturn lived. So the *Aeneid*
sets peace and law as the goal of its events. Jove comforts Venus, fearful for her son, with the prophecy
that Aeneas will succeed in creating the race of Romans. "For them," he adds, "I set no bounds to their
fortunes, nor any term of years: I have given them
empire without ending. . . . Then war shall be laid
aside, and the harsh world soften to peace." This last
will be when Augustus, himself born of the gods, "shall
establish again the age of gold in Latium, through the
fields where Saturn erewhile was king." Anchises is
speaking now, and saying: "Roman, be this thy care,
these thine arts, to bear dominion over the nations and
to impose the law of peace." But it is from Evander,
father of Pallas and king of the land where some day
the citadel of Rome will be, that Aeneas learns most
about the age his efforts are destined to restore:

Once these woods were tenanted by Fauns and Nymphs,
native born, and by a generation of men sprung from boles
of trees and the obdurate oak. They had neither rule of life
nor culture, nor knowledge to yoke the ox, nor to lay up stores,
nor to husband their grains; but forest boughs and the hunts-
man's rude trade yielded their sustenance. And no help came
till Saturn descended from skiey Olympus. . . . He it was gathered into a state that ungentle race, and gave them laws. Under
his sway passed those ages that men style golden: in such
serenity he ruled the nations; till with stealthy step there succeeded a degenerate time of a baser hue, and, in its train, the
frenzy of war and the lust of possession.

There the great weight swings again, and the cycle declares its course.

But it is clear that Virgil identifies the age of Saturn, which for Plato was the age of Cronos, with the reign of peace by law and government; whereas tradition had it, and the Stranger's tale very distinctly has it, that the children of Cronos or Saturn lived in peace not under their own authority, nor by arts that they had learned, but with the help of the gods, who were present among them and considered them their children. The Cyclopes of Homer, and even his Phaeacians with their superior grace, were fostered by deity; and the Cyclopes were dismissed with contempt by Odysseus because they were savages with no conception of justice. Nor did Plato leave any doubt that in those ages when the world turns backward, taking care of itself, the laws under which men live must be of their own making; the age of gold is not the age of civilization. Civilization is arduous, requiring study in those who would have it, and it does not come about by miracle. Virgil leaps at once into a near future where law is by magic, and peace by legerdemain. The Saturn who will come again is none other than Augustus. Peace in the whole world will be a Roman peace, perpetuating itself by means into which Virgil does not inquire.

The identification of Saturn and Augustus will not do; and even then it would not have done, as Virgil's doubt and sadness suggest that he knew better than anybody. It is indeed government that makes peace in a world which has been left by the gods for men to manage. But both government and peace are difficult, and reality must be their base. Homer knew the difficulty; his tragedy was real. Virgil, haunted by the difficulty, but only haunted, escapes here as elsewhere into the prettiness which for him is poetry. He sets the golden age ahead, and asks it to do what it was never intended by any myth to do. He asks it to do the work that men must do by themselves, without benefit of deity. The temptation was great, but a still greater poet would have resisted it. Virgil, giving in, may have known that he was evading the sterner way of truth by tragedy: known it, but known also that he was incapable of the harder thing. Thence, it may be, flowed his loneliness.

But his poem works its own necromancy, minor though it be, and no reader is proof against it all. The effect of the *Aeneid* has been peculiar and pervasive, as if a mysterious music issued from its sweetness, as indeed it does. The Virgil we shall meet again in Dante may not be the original Virgil, and he will exert a power over the Italian poet which he may not have dreamed would ever be his. But it will be genuine power: a touching testimony to his uniqueness.

# IV · PARADISE LOST

MILTON'S MAGNIFICENT HOPE of adding an English epic to the short list of great ones in the world, of right and successful ones, must be met by those who use his language with more than the pious hope that exactly this is what he did. It must be met with the resolution to review his poem in the ample perspective which he himself invited the world to take: the perspective supplied by Homer and Virgil. To look at *Paradise Lost* down such a vista may mean that an English reader must try to see it shorn of its famous style — famous, that is, with English readers, for its glory is not worldwide. It will be difficult to do this, but unless the attempt is made a reader can scarcely expect to acquire a view of the poem permitting him to compare it with any other epic at all; for there happens to be no English epic that is worthy to be compared with it, and so its rank, if it is to have one, must be found among the foreign poems it so consciously competes against.

So examined, it reveals that in at least one respect it is more Virgilian than Homeric. There are plenty of differences between Milton and the author of the

*Aeneid*, but it is true of both that their success is in the arts, rather than the art, of poetry. The art of poetry is an art concerning which little will ever be known except that when it is truly practiced the result is a poem whose force is simple and full. The force of *Paradise Lost* is not simple and not full, however splendid its writer's aim and however impressive the gifts he brings. Its power is not of that compact sort which exhibits itself with equal certitude in the little and the big parts of a work. The sign of a master is that each move he makes is explicit of his entire meaning; that is how he can be at once so generous and so economical, so broad and yet in any part so brief. Such mastery of the poetic art is not possessed by Milton, though he possesses many arts. Like Virgil he makes us think of music and painting, and unlike Virgil he is sculpturesque for good measure. Yet in the prime art to which he has dedicated himself he is to Shakespeare as Virgil is to Homer; he is a magician, not a maker. His style is more successful than his story.

His style will have to be talked about, but that fact itself will force him into second place. The thing we feel in him at once is a sense of strain. He must labor to keep himself — that is, his style — up to his story. There seems to be a gap between. His theme, Milton keeps saying, is somewhere above him, and he must obtain an "answerable style" with which to reach it. But in the direction of his search there can be no style that will altogether answer. Words alone can never do what Milton expected of them. His words are wonderful, but they are seldom the fitting ones, the ones which subject can absorb until only subject is seen. Milton looked in a good place for his answerable style, but he did not look in the best place, the place where subject awaited his contemplation and called upon him for formal understanding — the kind of understanding that solves structural problems before any other, and thus prepares the way for a poem in the writing of which the possibility of psychological blunders, to name no others, will cease to exist. The style of Milton alternates between the subtle and the ponderous, between that which does even better than well enough and that which does not do at all. Even his style, then, is not sure or consistent. Which goes with the fact that the force with which he feels his subject is neither simple nor full.

His subject is perhaps the last big one that poetry has found. To him it was a "higher" one than any found before, and he was entitled to the judgment. The name for it, if any other is needed than the word "disobedience" which Milton wrote into his first line, is original sin. The importance of this theme gains in the poem from its importance to him, an importance which he defined when he named it disobedience. For Milton was by nature a disobedient man, a rebel, and he was particularly competent to perceive irony in the fact that our loss of Paradise came not through our weakness but through our strength, at least as we know it now, given the Fall: through, that is to say, our love of knowledge, our pride and self-reliance, our noble interest in good and evil. Milton was a rebel and a scholar, and he was a proud, even a scornful, man.

So his story presented him with a problem, and he did not dodge it. He had to justify God's punishing us for becoming what at our best we are. He had to do this, and he did it to the limit of his ability. He made every effort to remember, believe, and prove that our original state of obedience and ignorance was better than the virtues we achieved through losing grace — the glories of our present nature, which are but as colors to white light, the prism of the Fall having created each shifting hue of our later being. Milton loved color, and as a humanist he loved knowledge, but he put forth all his powers to recommend that early state of whiteness and innocence. If his powers were not equal to the task, it may mean that no one's are. But it may also mean that his strategy was poor, and the several failures of his poem may show just wherein it was poor.

His Eden is not so interesting as it ought to be. Satan outargues God. God is a dull dictator, and the absence of character in Adam is something we notice too often. He is the hero, but Satan, because he is more attractive, has been thought to be. Milton's catalogue of the things born into the world with sin — the seasons, wind, weather, war, the rebellion of beasts, death, women, disease, and history — is a catalogue of all that poetry knows, and it kindles the reader as Eve's bower never did. Nor can Milton escape the conclusion that in the long run our experience of the Fall has built within us, if we are virtuous, another Paradise, and "happier far." These are some of the things in *Paradise Lost* that work against its author's aim. And another is its prolixity. His subject, being ancient and at heart abstract, would have benefited by the kind of brevity which Milton least of all poets can command. "And the Lord God planted a garden eastward in Eden; and there he put the man whom he had formed." "And they heard the voice of the Lord God walking in the garden in the cool of the day." Such nuggets from another source Milton magnanimously embeds in the slag of his narrative by quoting them where they will do most good. But they do not do the standing of his poem any good.

If Milton's crucial problem was one of style, it was so in a larger sense than that in which he seems to have understood the term. In the largest sense style is simply the way in which a story is told so that it can be believed as the poet wants it to be believed. Milton's job, at which he sometimes fails, is to make us believe what we see and hear. But first it is to find things for us to see and hear. His subject in itself is without a body, nor does it express itself naturally in time. His duty to it as a poet, then, is to give it body, and to set it going in time. The truth it contains has nothing to do with place or time, and could be stated — indeed has been stated — in something else than narrative altogether; for instance in such a sentence as this: Man is an imperfect and unhappy creature. But if Milton is to treat it in a poem, and if the poem is to be an epic, he must search out ways of making it material and temporal. He must arrange objects of earth in such positions that they will catch the rays of his meaning and reflect them in the reader's mind. He must select and order his symbols.

When he does not succeed at this the fault may not be wholly his own. His world was less organized in terms of meaning than was the world, for example, of Dante. He could not count so easily upon the earth to yield him reflective objects. He could not so naturally and directly use all the knowledge he had; some of his knowledge, in fact, he had or thought he had to suppress. He had to create certain of his symbols out of nothing; to pretend; to go the long way round, which is not the way of poetry at its best. His age was not an age of allegory.

But one poetic sin is chargeable to him. He is eclectic, and mixes his metaphors. He is artificial, and feigns belief. All of Raphael's long speech in the eighth book against Adam's curiosity about the stars does not conceal the fact that Milton has chosen to be archaic in his cosmology. This is because he finds it easier to make poetry out of the Ptolemaic picture than out of the picture he had in his own mind. Poetry had always been so made, and he would not desert the convention. It offered too much to him, ready made. Here Milton can be seen applying the arts of poetry rather than building a poem by the one art which can succeed, the art of being true to what one knows and sees. Milton was in love with all that was old in the many devices at his disposal. His procedure in consequence was to assemble the properties of his poem from a miscellany of sources. He did this with skill, and frequently to the end of verbal delight. But the greatest poets are not so embarrassed by riches as at times he is.

He is baroque, and describes endlessly a number of things that needed merely to be named. The poet is a namer, not a describer. The presence of description is always a sign that narrative is failing. Milton cannot do without description. He hangs banners of it all over *Paradise Lost,* and if some of these are gorgeous things no reader can forget — the burning lake, Satan huge upon it like Leviathan, the host of rebel angels thick as autumnal leaves that strow the brooks in Vallombrosa, Pandemonium that rose like an exhalation out of the earth, Hell-gates, and Adam's bower — there is always a question whether the virtue in them is relevant to the drift of the poem, and whether they do not distract as much as they delight. And in many of them Milton does not know where to stop, or how even at the start to be convincing in the simple way of poetry, the way that leaves us unaware of anything to be convinced about. In no such way does Milton deliver to us the serpent Satan became as he approached Eve:

> not with indented wave,
> Prone on the ground, as since, but on his rear,
> Circular base of rising folds, that towered
> Fold above fold, a surging maze, his head
> Crested aloft, and carbuncle his eyes;

> With verdant neck of verdant gold, erect
> Amidst his circling spires, that on the grass
> Floated redundant.

There is too much of the beast, and he is too thickly
gilded. The paradise in which this serpent finds the
first man and woman is sweeter to behold, yet there
again the effect is a piled one; ambitious epithets refer
to what we should see, but they do not show it:

> Thus was this place,
> A happy rural seat of various view:
> Groves whose rich trees wept odorous gums and balm;
> Others whose fruit, burnished with golden rind,
> Hung amiable — Hesperian fables true,
> If true, here only — and of delicious taste.
> Betwixt them lawns, or level downs, and flocks
> Grazing the tender herb, were interposed,
> Or palmy hillock; or the flowery lap
> Of some irriguous valley spread her store,
> Flowers of all hue, and without thorn the rose.

The terms keep on assembling, yet the image is never
clear. The garden is a gathered thing, depending on
our knowledge of the stock from which it comes —
the rich Latin adjectives, and later on in the same passage a series of other gardens famous in poetry, gardens
than which this one is more beautiful: the fair field of
Enna, the sweet grove of Daphne, and half a dozen
more that lie in the deep chest of Milton's memory.
The direction of such poetry is outward and away;
our attention is dispersed, not concentrated.

This is because the best that Milton can do toward rendering his subject mobile and visible is to heap upon it the many things — the too many things — that move in his mind as he recalls the poetries he knows. They are too many only because they are mixed. There cannot be too much of a good thing, but there can be too many good things if they are good in other connections than the one at hand. When Milton cannot find the poetry that should be in his subject he imports it from far places. The celebrated passages in which he harmonizes geographical names —

Mombaza, and Quiloa, and Melind —

are in the ancient tradition of Homer and Aeschylus, but the places they name are not of practical, of narrative importance. It is only the haze of their distance, the honey of their sound, that matters with us.

So with Milton's devices to express the inexpressible. He decides too soon that the things he must tell us about are things that cannot be seen. He slips too easily into darkness visible, the palpable obscure, a vast vacuity, and confusion worse confounded; such phrases deserve their reputation, for their ingenuity is great, but it is not an ingenuity that has given us things to keep. It has given us swelling words, a second-best possession.

He is nowhere more wonderful with words than when he is describing the flight of a devil or an angel through measureless regions. Here is Satan on his way up to earth:

Sometimes
He scours the right hand coast, sometimes the left;
Now shaves with level wing the deep, then soars
Up to the fiery concave towering high.
As when far off at sea a fleet descried
Hangs in the clouds, by aequinoctial winds
Close sailing from Bengala, or the isles
Of Ternate and Tidore, whence merchants bring
Their spicy drugs; they on the trading flood,
Through the wide Ethiopian to the Cape,
Ply stemming nightly toward the pole: so seemed
Far off the flying Fiend.

And here is Raphael descending to the same objective:

Down thither prone in flight
He speeds, and through the vast ethereal sky
Sails between worlds and worlds.

Yet the virtuosity of these lines is in the service of an idea which has less value than Milton thinks. It is the idea that the world of his poem in order to be important must be big. He has strained for size, but size is of no advantage to his theme. His universe is huger than Homer's was, or Virgil's; indeed, being Christian, it is infinite. Then he would have done better, instead of trying for vastness, to give his world no size at all. The more bigness he suggests the less reality he achieves of the sort that would count with respect to the abyss he considers. He should have stared still longer into this abyss, till he grew mute. He cannot handle either the space or the time he creates to convey his truth. He had to create them, but as they stand in the poem they have too much the look of geography and history. God has a career, and heaven its annals. And the landscape is literal gold or clay.

Milton's way of using other poets is not the master's way. Master poets help one another, but only to the end that each seems more himself; he is better for the company he keeps, but one does not see what has been borrowed. Milton's conception of his persons and events is not original enough to be firm against the temptation to bring over intact the properties of other persons, other events, which had been well used in their place but which are confusing here because they do not fit. The stock things he imports from Homer — the catalogue of rebel angels, the foretold issues, the individual combats which decorate the war in heaven, the campfires of Michael and his host — bolster his fable but do not authenticate it. Even the Zeus of the *Iliad* contaminates this God — who thunders and lightens from a throne in the clouds, shakes the universe with the oaths he utters, and hangs forth golden scales in which a descending weight declares the defeat of Satan.

Milton should forget Zeus in the latitude his poem inhabits, and yet he cannot. Nor can he let a hundred other pagan deities go — deities whom he had banished in his ode *On the Morning of Christ's Nativity*, but whom he brings back by one device or another until they throng the dusky avenues of *Paradise Lost*, glittering illicitly, decorating a scene which Milton does not know otherwise how to prevent from being bare. The most beautiful of these is Hephaestus, the architect of Pandemonium:

> Nor was his name unheard or unadored
> In ancient Greece; and in Ausonian land
> Men called him Mulciber; and how he fell
> From Heaven they fabled, thrown by angry Jove
> Sheer o'er the crystal battlements: from morn
> To noon he fell, from noon to dewy eve,
> A summer's day, and with the setting sun
> Dropt from the zenith, like a falling star,
> On Lemnos, the Aegean isle.

The verse, communicating as it does that famous fall, is more to be admired than the decision to save an irrelevant legend from oblivion.

Milton should mean what he says at the beginning of the ninth book when he dismisses martial exploits as unfit matter for his song. His poem through long stretches is military, and in the very accent of the tradition to which he declares himself superior. His argument is "higher" than the wrath of Achilles or the rage of Turnus; "wars," he says, "hitherto the only argument heroic deemed," are less so than the spiritual subject he pursues. We can assent to this, but then we must be surprised to find that Milton's God, when he is not like Zeus, is something like Charlemagne — a medieval emperor — and that Christ at his right hand is a proud and scornful knight even to the "tinsel trappings" Milton has denounced. The angels are more knights in remembered armor; and one whole book of the poem, the sixth, is full of a war on the plains of eternity, with chariots and cannon in it, and banners and everything, which no recorded reader has failed to find outlandish, either for its intrusion or for its excess. Milton was correct in his suspicion of the martial idiom, but when he had to fill his poem with particulars he could devise no other idiom to take its place.

So with his omens, his hero's visions of the future, and his Virgilian strain of hyperbole. We know where they come from, and note that they were fitter where they were found. The Limbo of Vanity, from Ariosto, is still the toyshop that it was in *Orlando Furioso;* but there is no room here for a toyshop. Milton simply cannot do without some metamorphoses in the manner of Ovid. Here for example is Satan turning into a snake:

> His visage drawn he felt to sharp and spare,
> His arms clung to his ribs, his legs entwining
> Each other, till, supplanted, down he fell,
> A monstrous serpent on his belly prone.

The details are of anatomical interest, but Ovid's artifices in this kind, while charming enough in the brittle universe he haunted, are an outrage in this one, as is the literal realization which Milton, still in the grip of Ovid, gives to the ancient metaphor of ashes in the mouth. The devils, all turned serpents now,

> fondly thinking to allay
> Their appetite with gust, instead of fruit
> Chewed bitter ashes, which the offended taste

With spattering noise rejected. Oft they assayed,
Hunger and thirst constraining; drugged as oft,
With hatefullest disrelish writhed their jaws
With soot and cinders filled.

When Milton borrows he grows greedy, and lugs off
more than he will profit by.

A line in the fifth book suggests that Milton saw the
problem of symbols in something like its right proportions. Raphael is explaining to Adam why it is so difficult to tell him of things that have happened in heaven:
they happened out of time and place, and indeed they
never happened at all. The human intellect is so con-
ditioned that translation becomes necessary.

> For how shall I relate
> To human sense the invisible exploits
> Of warring Spirits? how, without remorse,
> The ruin of so many, glorious once
> And perfect while they stood? . . . yet for thy good
> This is dispensed; and what surmounts the reach
> Of human sense I shall delineate so,
> By likening spiritual to corporal forms,
> As may express them best.

It is a matter, says Raphael elsewhere, of "measuring
things in Heaven by things on Earth." The immediate
acts of God, "more swift than time or motion,"

> to human ears
> Cannot without process of speech be told.

The whole of Raphael's narrative, he is saying, is a
metaphor. Created objects must be used to describe an

event that took place before creation; words must be forced to do work that no words could do. Milton's statement of the problem is clear, but this does not mean that he knew how to solve it. In the precise form it took for Milton, no one does. Milton was attempting the impossible — a huge mistake in art. And his hugest mistake was to have a heaven at all: one that he must describe. The God of this heaven is by definition one who does not think or speak. Milton committed the blunder of making him a theologian.

Such blunders are not balanced in any final opinion we form of the poem by the presence in it of such lyric masterpieces as adorn the openings of the third, seventh, and ninth books. Those are indeed flawless masterpieces, and English poetry would be weaker without them. Their subject is Milton himself, and it was a subject of which he was master. But an epic poem cannot be about its author. It must be about a world that he has made. Milton has not known how to make a world and keep it made. He has not solved, for instance, the problem of how to suggest power in the God of his world. This is partly, as has been said, because he has not freed God from time: we see him as cause, which convinces us less than the effects would — that is, the objects of earth — if we were permitted to review them as we are by Dante, who has only to name their maker and at once they are enhanced. Not their maker, whom Dante does not think he has to enhance. Milton is constantly afraid that we shall forget how great and good God is; so he tells us, and even has God tell us. But with every telling God shrinks, as when for example he remarks to Christ in the seventh book that his goodness is "free to act or not." He endeavors to be intelligible, and to justify himself. There is actually a touch of petulance in the proof he offers Christ in the third book that those will be wrong who say he should have prevented Adam's error:

> So will fall
> He and his faithless progeny. Whose fault?
> Whose but his own? Ingrate, he had of me
> All he could have; I made him just and right,
> Sufficient to have stood, though free to fall.

He is not obliged to prevent it any more than he was obliged to prevent the rebellion of the angels:

> They themselves decreed
> Their own revolt, not I. If I foreknew,
> Foreknowledge had no influence on their fault,
> Which had no less proved certain unforeseen.
> So without least impulse or shadow of fate,
> Or aught by me immutably foreseen,
> They trespass, authors to themselves in all.

This is what a theologian should say about God, but not what God should say about himself. God is not a theologian, for he is not a man of words. He is one Word, and a poem which contains him can no more than hint the composition of that Word. But Milton's God drones on, ever in worse prose and ever with less power. It is the natural consequence, no doubt, of a conception which allowed him in the first place to be a fighting emperor in heaven, and which in the eighth book allows him to answer Adam's appeal for a companion in Paradise with demonstrations that he in eternity lives alone and likes it.

His lieutenant-Son, who drives a chariot over the necks of vanquished angels and declares in exultation that all he knows of hate he has learned from his Father, is a flat failure in so far as this is the only image of him Milton can give us. But Christ is an abysmal failure in the role of Redeemer. His Father, asking in heaven for a volunteer who shall consent to live on earth awhile and die to save mankind, hears no voice at first, and there is danger that the Redemption will never occur. The Son of God, however, offers himself in these words:

> Behold *me*, then: me for him, life for life,
> I offer; on me let thine anger fall;
> Account me Man. I for his sake will leave
> Thy bosom, and this glory next to thee
> Freely put off, and for him lastly die
> Well pleased; on me let Death wreak all his rage.
> Under his gloomy power I shall not long
> Lie vanquished. Thou hast given me to possess
> Life in myself for ever; by thee I live;
> Though now to Death I yield, and am his due,
> All that of me can die, yet, that debt paid,
> Thou wilt not leave me in the loathesome grave
> His prey, nor suffer my unspotted soul
> For ever with corruption there to dwell;
> But I shall rise victorious, and subdue
> My vanquisher, spoiled of his vaunted spoil.

The New Testament, taking the story at its other end, the end we can see on earth, derives its success from that very circumstance. We are asked to believe that its hero, who looks like a man, is nevertheless God, and we can do so if we will. But nothing can make us believe that this Son will feel his sacrifice. He may indeed be God, but the other half of him that will be man, the half of him from which poetry might be made, is missing. The Passion is inconceivable in a person who says so readily that it will be but a moment in his eternal life.

There is Milton blundering again with time — seizing it by the wrong end, the end that cannot move. He does so with an obtuseness scarcely to be matched in all poetry, unless it is matched by himself in *Paradise Regained*, where instead of Christ's temptation by stone and bread (an unannounced temptation that we can imagine succeeding, though in the New Testament it does not), we are told of a banquet so baroque — all game, all fowl, all pastry, all fish and shellfish, all regal on the board, and all odorous — that anybody would recognize it as what it is, Temptation its very self.

No challenge to an epic poet is sterner than that which is posed by the celestial persons and events he elects to handle. He cannot avoid them if his poem is to have importance. But he must not ruin their potency. Milton twice mentions Tobit, to whom, and to his son Tobias, Raphael once appeared. But *The Book of Tobit* was perfect in its management of the tale.

Only at its end does the stranger who has been help-
ing the mortal pair say the simple words: "I am Raphael." No three words in story are better than these
three, coming when they do. The point is that they
come when they should. Milton evidently admired the
tale, but he never learned what it could teach him.

His failure with Adam and Eve before the Fall is a
psychological failure, and it results from his decision
to be psychological with them at all. Psychology itself
is a consequence of the Fall — deplorable or delight-
ful according as we choose to view it. For Homer and
Shakespeare it is what makes the outer wilderness their
characters inhabit the fair, foul place it is. For Milton
it is a handicap in Paradise, where our first parents
have nothing to do but smile and prune. The fact is
that we cannot imagine the first man and woman if we
try to imagine them as feeling and thinking. They have
no past, so we cannot conceive their present. We could
accept them in a state that was altogether different from
ours — a metaphysical state at one extreme, with un-
spoken thoughts branching deep in them like subterranean brooks, or at the other extreme a molluscoid
state, wherein they breathed the truth with bivalvular
ease and peace — but we do not know how to understand them when they can speak like us yet have nothing to say. Their work is something they must make
for themselves — a little manuring, a little lopping of
twigs so that alleys and arbors may appear — and it
leaves us yawning; as does their talk of recreation
where all indeed is recreation, and as does their love-

making, which in the nature of things neither Milton nor we should attempt to conceive. Once they eat of the forbidden fruit, and shame comes like a dark wind into the world, their mutual recriminations and their cries of mortal pain have power to convince us, and that is what they do. From the end of the ninth book on, the story solidifies itself into one we can accept. Before that it fails as the impossible must always fail. Before that it makes the blunder so common with Milton, the blunder of trying to make us see what cannot be seen, or what at any rate can be seen only in a flash of metaphor. The rib of which Eve was made is credible in Genesis because it is nothing but a rib, a single word in a fable. Milton, of course, brings us closer to it than that, and adds some fatal details. Adam is recalling how as he slept in a trance the Shape of God

> opened my left side, and took
> From thence a rib, with cordial spirits warm,
> And life-blood streaming fresh; wide was the wound,
> But suddenly with flesh filled up and healed.

This is butcher's meat, and we shall never believe that our first mother was so made.

Fatal is the word for many a length to which Milton lets his imagination, unregulated as it is by a right conception of its task, labor on its way. The work he wastes, for instance, on the things eaten by Adam and Eve, and even by the angels, is a pity to behold. Milton cannot keep away from the unfortunate subject of food, which he inveterately fumbles. When Raphael is a guest in Paradise, and is invited to eat, we are told that they all postpone the pleasure because discourse is a still higher pleasure; and Milton thinks he must insert the parenthesis, "no fear lest dinner cool." The diet of Paradise was exclusively a salad diet. Raphael, furthermore, explains to Adam and Eve why he also is possessed of an appetite — different from theirs, to be sure, yet still an appetite. Heavenly creatures too, he says, "concoct, digest, assimilate." Even the Sun, that gives its light away, "receives alimental recompense" from the mists that rise to refill it, "and at even sups with the Ocean."

> Time may come when Men
> With Angels may participate, and find
> No inconvenient diet, nor too light fare

in whatever it is that "intelligential substances" eat, Raphael assures his host and hostess. As for here and now at this board, "think not I shall be nice," he says; and he falls to

> with keen dispatch
> Of real hunger, and concoctive heat
> To transubstantiate.

Failure in poetic tact has never gone farther than that.

Tact is a secondary virtue, but it is one without which we shall not survive, and this is especially true in the art of poetry, where as tactics it supplies the writer with knowledge of what he can or cannot do if he is to be taken at his word. Milton's lyric tact is impeccable, but in narrative he can go egregiously wrong.

He never knows what not to explain, what not to fill in. He has to tell us that the harps of heaven are always in tune; that spirits, being of "liquid texture," cannot suffer internal injuries because they are without "entrails, heart or head, liver or reins"; that the good angels who are the targets of Satan's artillery could have kept their feet when they felt the impact of the "iron globes" had it not been that they were weighed down with armor, and hence incapable of dodging — or, as Milton puts it, of "evading swift by quick contraction and remove." His ironies are elephantine, like his occasional excursions into humor; they are like his own famous elephant in Eden, who, to amuse Adam and Eve,

> used all his might, and wreathed
> His lithe proboscis.

He is nowhere more ponderous, perhaps, than when his logic is superfluous, when he is systematic without cause; as when Moloch, presenting the case for further campaigns against heaven, tells the fallen angels that they have nothing to lose even if they are destroyed:

> More destroyed than thus,
> We should be quite abolished, and expire.
> What fear we then?

All such things in *Paradise Lost* are of a piece with its diction, which at its best is wonderful and at its worst is woeful, but which everywhere is starched with latinity, as if Milton did not trust his own language, falling into which might mean falling from the high horse of his style. The fuse of the infernal cannon which Satan directs at his angelic foe is an "incentive reed, pernicious with one touch of fire"; and the fire, once kindled, is "dilated and infuriate." When Raphael arrives at grass and trees in his account of the Creation, he is careful not to ignore "the humble shrub, and bush with frizzled hair implicit." This absurdity may be balanced by the grandeur in the first book of Satan's headlong fall

> With hideous ruin and combustion, down
> To bottomless perdition, there to dwell
> In adamantine chains and penal fire.

But it is an absurdity, and the balance is no more than even. For everything Milton gives he takes something away. His poem only half lives, because he is only half sure of what he understands and sees.

He would have done better to sacrifice his passion for music and description, for adornment and device, and to settle down to the bare argument, the unfigured statement, at which he is so proficient. The best things in his poem are not splendid; or, if they are splendid, it is with an intellectual light he knows how to control. Satan is his one master in the style he should have been content with everywhere.

> Farewell, happy fields,
> Where joy forever dwells! Hail, horrors, hail,
> Infernal World! and thou, profoundest Hell,
> Receive thy new possessor — one who brings
> A mind not to be changed by place or time.

> The mind is its own place, and in itself
> Can make a Heaven of Hell, a Hell of Heaven.
> What matter where, if I be still the same,
> And what I should be, all but less than he
> Whom thunder hath made greater? Here at least
> We shall be free; the Almighty hath not built
> Here for his envy, will not drive us hence:
> Here we may reign secure; and, in my choice,
> To reign is worth ambition, though in Hell:
> Better to reign in Hell than serve in Heaven.

Nothing could be better than that, and nothing is. Nor does anything in the poem surpass Satan's final speech to Eve concerning the tree from which she has been forbidden to eat:

> If what is evil
> Be real, why not known, since easier shunned?
> God, therefore, cannot hurt ye, and be just;
> Not just, not God; not feared then, nor obeyed:
> Your fear of death itself removes the fear. . . .
> What can your knowledge hurt him, or this Tree
> Impart against his will, if all be his?
> Or is it envy? and can envy dwell
> In Heavenly breasts? These, these and many more
> Causes import your need of this fair Fruit.
> Goddess humane, reach, then, and freely taste!

The only trouble is that nobody, not even God, shares Satan's mastery with him. Satan speaks out of this life, in English, and much of the time in potent monosyllables. The life beyond may be something that Milton considers it his duty to see, but the celestial Latin which delivers it to us is a sign that he does not. So is the uncertainty of its form, and so is the imperfection of Milton's taste as he decides what he shall put into his picture of it, into his account of what was said and done there. His greatest mistake was his first one. He did not clear his mind of what it did not believe.

His success in the world beyond, when by accident success is his, is by magic, not by making, in the same way that Virgil's was. And his magic is fine. The patterns of dark and light, of down and up; the pendent earth at the end of the second book,

> in bigness as a star
> Of smallest magnitude close by the moon;

the palaces submerged by the Flood, late the scene of luxury but now a place where "sea-monsters whelped and stabled"; the newly created eagles and storks which

> wedge their way,
> Intelligent of seasons, and set forth
> Their aerie caravan, high over seas
> Flying, and over lands, with mutual wing
> Easing their flight: so steers the prudent crane
> Her annual voyage, borne on winds: the air
> Floats as they pass, fanned with unnumbered plumes;

the glorious shape of Raphael that for Adam

> Comes this way moving; seems another morn
> Risen on mid-noon;

the hymns concerning himself, unchanged in voice and strength "on evil days though fallen" — such things have their glory, and it is not to be forgotten. Nor is Milton without epic power. Nor does he fail to insist with God that Adam, for all he will learn outside the gates of Paradise, was better off within them:

> Happier had it sufficed him to have known
> Good by itself and evil not at all.

*Paradise Lost* is as near to greatness as a poem without simple vision can go. Since its vision is not simple, however, or its author's mind made up, as an epic it suffers serious handicap. It comes last in the great list, walking lame.

# V · CONCERNING THE NATURE OF THINGS

*De Rerum Natura.* Not the tears of things, as with Virgil, but their nature is the subject that sends Lucretius in search of aid from Calliope, who for him is the "ingenious" Muse. He has no story to tell, no tale within whose folds his subject will more or less lie hidden. He begs us to look upon his subject bare, for itself is the story of all that happens; it explains away other stories, and exposes the illusions which made them seem important; it is all we need to know about whatever can and does occur in a world containing nature and ourselves. It is a story to end story. It is a demonstration, if we will accept it, that tragedy cannot be. It has no hero unless the author is one — a tragic hero, too, considering the intensity of his belief that he at last, and he alone, has hold of the world's secret. But that is still another story, and Lucretius gives no sign of knowing that he tells it.

No poem is more deeply, more madly, penetrated by paradox. No sooner are two of its contradictions suggested than two others suggest themselves. The *De Rerum Natura* is a passionate attack upon passion. And it is a poem whose purpose is to kill poetry.

Feverish with the power of his own feeling, Lucretius hunts through the world he knows for an added power, the power of the poet whom no mortal may resist. For the poetry he must kill is a gigantic thing, and it will take a gigantic force to remove it. So Lucretius invokes every sort of aid from goddesses and muses, and studies the sorcery of every predecessor in his art, with a view to gathering maximum strength for his assault on song, on story, and on the soul. Milton reënforced *Paradise Lost* with all the poetry he could import from the past, but his motive was less strange; he only wanted to beautify a truth which he could not trust without such help to seem substantial. Lucretius has no doubt about his truth, which for him is most substantial when most naked. But he does not trust men to love its nakedness as he does. They must be seduced to enter his subject. Once in, they are bound, he believes, to feel the force of its truth. The question is how to get them in. The answer is, by poetry.

> For as physicians, when they seek to give
> Young boys the nauseous wormwood, first do touch
> The brim around the cup with the sweet juice
> And yellow of the honey, in order that
> The thoughtless age of boyhood be cajoled

As far as the lips, and meanwhile swallow down
The wormwood's bitter draught, and, though befooled,
Be yet not merely duped, but rather thus
Grow strong again with recreated health:
So now I too (since this my doctrine seems
In general somewhat woeful unto those
Who've had it not in hand, and since the crowd
Starts back from it in horror) have desired
To expound our doctrine unto thee in song
Soft-speaking and Pierian, and, as 'twere,
To touch it with sweet honey of the Muse —
If by such method haply I might hold
The mind of thee upon these lines of ours,
Till thou dost learn the nature of all things
And understandest their utility.

Hence his search, like Milton's, for a style suitable to the elucidation of "things unattempted yet in prose or rhyme." Those are Milton's words, but Lucretius uses similar ones.

I wander far afield, thriving in sturdy thought,
Through unpathed haunts of the Pierides,
Trodden by step of none before. I joy
To come on undefilèd fountains there,
To drain them deep; I joy to pluck new flowers,
To seek for this my head a signal crown
From regions where the Muses never yet
Have garlanded the temples of a man.

The search is arduous, he says. He lives laborious days, as Milton did, and keeps awake through clear nights, wrestling with the problem of language here in this region of thought — it is the region we call science — where there is no language, for the Romans were not scientists.

> I know how hard it is in Latian verse
> To tell the dark discoveries of the Greeks,
> Chiefly because our pauper-speech must find
> Strange terms to fit the strangeness of the thing.

But he is not daunted, and somehow he arrives where he wishes to be: "beyond the flaming ramparts of the world," in contemplation of "the core of being at the center hid."

The great poet in Lucretius is the man who thus arrives in the total darkness he desires, a darkness so deep and far away that nothing is remembered there of hope or fear, of love or religion, of tragic failure or tragic success. Nothing is there, he insists, except serenity, which he would share with us. It is a place beyond poetry as we have known poetry. We have known only the sort of honeyed song he uses to invite us in. Here now is the wormwood of his truth, and just as that is a bitter thing to see and accept, so henceforth his singing need seek no more to be agreeable. And it is not agreeable. The bulk of the *De Rerum Natura* is angular and harsh. But that is where the poetry is. The delicious proems which begin the several books are rightly celebrated. No one, however, has taken the measure of Lucretius who has not watched him using all of the knowledge he has, regardless of

whether it hates or loves the verse he wraps it in; who
has not listened to the lofty and stubborn rage of his
eloquence as he sweats his way through resistant sub-
divisions of his theme; who has not felt in him the
fire which a fierce sense of vocation — the call to sing
what no one else will even say — keeps kindled in him
as he writes. He may be mad to think these things, or
to think that they are the only things possible to be
thought. But that is another matter. As a philosophical
poet, or if you please as a scientific poet, he has no
equal upon the earth he anatomized.

All good poems are in some sense philosophical —
they are able to mean what they say — but few of them
are direct and categorical as the *De Rerum Natura* is.
Lucretius is didactic to the core, and — except in the
proems — never anything but didactic. He knows the
truth, the one truth; it is simple and solid, even though
instruction is necessary before we see it; and he will
speak it, supplying the instruction as he goes. No story
could suggest this truth as the sweetness of roses is
suggested by their scent. Morality for him is not to be
obliquely learned. It is to be stated. The truth for him
is something that stands under other things and makes
them what they are, or rather explains their being what
they are and nothing else. And since it makes so much
difference whether we possess this truth or do not possess it, he will lay it on with all the passion and all the
learning he commands. He is proud to be didactic, for
he is saving mankind from the curse of emotion. He is
willing to be technical, for the vision he invites us to

share has no content unless it is supported with a cosmology, a physics, a psychology, and a theory of universal history. He is content if we call him fanatical, and if sometimes we find him obscure; the obscurity at least goes with the difficulty, and it may impress us. But there is a further thing he wants us never to doubt, and that is the excitement he himself feels as he contemplates the core of being. It is a dark core, and colorless, and poetry has not been there before. But if poetry means what it says when it says it is interested in truth — why, here is the truth itself, and poetry need search no farther. This is what it has been looking for. Now it can be silent.

Again it is necessary to say that Lucretius makes his poem out of the death of poetries — of fear, of love, of superstition, of error, of myth, of custom, of tale and tradition — and that nothing leaves him more ecstatic than the bleakness he discovers, the hues he sees dissolving. The perfect hue for him is now the cold grey he finds in his atoms. The perfect mystery is the lack of mystery underlying death and change, birth and corruption, loveliness and decay. The perfect song is the silence of what is because it is. The clamor of tragedy comes no longer to his ears: the cries of heroes lost between irreconcilable necessities. There is only one necessity, that things should be what they are. This new doctrine dates all tales of woe. Lucretius hails Homer as the king of poets, but Homer for him is only a ghost who came to Ennius and unfolded "the source of Nature" — the last thing the living Homer would have claimed he could do. For Homer lived in the world of suffering men. There was no new truth for him, and no truth at all except that which appeared on the surface of things done. He walked the familiar world, understanding it better than most men do but asking for no other.

Lucretius rejects appearances as he rejects the appeals tragedy makes to our pity and fear. Tragedy for him is not to be understood; it is to be avoided. The sweetest thing is to watch from dry land others who are drowning, to look upon a battle in which one has no part, to hold the high serene plateaus whence the miseries and mistakes of ambition may be inspected in peace:

> O wretched minds of men! O blinded hearts!
> In how great perils, in what darks of life
> Are spent the human years, however brief!

Tragedy is not to be conquered as poetry can conquer it, by telling great stories of men who have dared the dark, who have reached for what they could not have, who have accepted terror; by telling such stories, and by purging us of our ignorance concerning death and fate. Tragedy is to be dodged, to be burrowed away from in the core of being at the center hid. Terror is to be argued out of breath. And if Lucretius himself seems to walk in darkness, raging, if the most terrible thing to him is terror, that need not concern us now.

His belief is famous and familiar by this time, for it

is built into most of our literature and our thought. The name of his vision is materialism — there is nothing but matter and void, and all things have in the end a single substance, an irreducible body which if we look sharp enough may be found from form to form. Forms change and things are born or die, are made or unmade, but the atom, deathless and indivisible, goes on forever. Nothing comes from nothing — there was no creation — and nothing goes to nothing. Death is merely the disappearance of what could once be seen. What is never seen, but unalterably is, is the primal bodies out of which ourselves and the things we live among are made. Of any given object or occurrence there is only one explanation to be sought. It is the material explanation. All others are fables, hoaxes, or child's play, or the sinister inventions of priests. The child — and this signifies many a man — fears that meaning or intention lurks behind thunder. But no meaning lurks there, and no mind. There is only matter, which for our comfort we had better understand. And for a single thing there can be no more than a single cause. We may be uncertain which this is, and tentatively name several; but only one of them will turn out to be true. Matter, furthermore, is constant; the seeds of things are fixed and there can be no monsters. Mind and soul are matter too. And death, even our own, is not to be feared, since nothing waits for us beyond it. Indeed there is nothing to be feared, though men persist in acting as if the contrary were the case. Lucretius will cure them.

> This terror, then, this darkness of the mind,
> Not sunrise with its flaring spokes of light,
> Nor glittering arrows of morning can disperse,
> But only Nature's aspect and her law.

The common source of fear and ignorance is religion, which imputes mind to what can only be matter. There is something unseen, but it is not the will of a god. It is what the scientist must try to see, as Epicurus, the master of Lucretius, first saw it in Greece.

> Whilst human kind
> Throughout the lands lay miserably crushed
> Before all eyes beneath Religion — who
> Would show her head along the region skies,
> Glowering on mortals with her hideous face —
> A Greek it was who first opposing dared
> Raise mortal eyes that terror to withstand. . . .
> And thus his will and hardy wisdom won;
> And forward thus he fared afar, beyond
> The flaming ramparts of the world, until
> He wandered the immeasurable All.
> Whence he to us, a conqueror, reports
> What things can rise to being, what cannot,
> And by what law to each its scope prescribed,
> Its boundary stone that clings so deep in time.
> Wherefore religion now is under foot,
> And us his victory now exalts to heaven.

There are gods, but Lucretius' name for them is the Calm Ones. They may be safely believed in by one who thinks of them as remote epicureans, immortal like the space they inhabit, a space unvisited by rain,

wind, or snow. They take no care of us, and we are
to have no fear of them. They did not make us or our
world. They simply hang somewhere in a universe of
their own, beautiful creatures concerning whom we
are permitted to have beautiful dreams — but when in
our dreams they seem to have locomotion or will, we
are not to awake and say that they have influence over
us. This is what the priests have taught us, with too
much success. The priests even see to it, if they can,
that we believe their impossible myth of a creation
whose end, whose final cause, was human life.

No god, says Lucretius, would have made a world
that looks as accidental as this one, or is so imperfect;
and the argument by design can always be refuted by
reversing the order in which the evidence is seen. Eyes
were not made for seeing, or tongues for speech; once
those organs were begotten by chance, their birth en-
gendered their use, slowly, as our intelligence grew.
No, nature is self-made, self-tended, and remembers
the touch of no divine artificer; nor do we have recol-
lections of immortality, though some philosophers
fable that we do. It is an agreeable exercise of the fancy
to associate grain with Ceres, wine with Bacchus, and
the ocean with lord Neptune, and to call the earth the
Mother of all the Gods. But beyond that we should be
careful not to go, tainting our souls with the foul fears
of religion. So we may utter the name Prometheus,
provided we do not credit the tale that he it was who
gave us the idea of fire. Of course we got it from
the lightning. The wonders of the world — thunder,

whirlpools, rainbows, volcanoes, earthquakes, and pestilences — subject our serenity to the sternest test, tempting us as they do to propitiate the wild anger of distant deities. The deities are distant but not wild, and they do not know that it is thundering along the Adriatic.

Thus Lucretius on religion as he prepares to state his own. For it has always been recognized that he too had his faith. No man's was purer or more resolute. Epicurus is his god and father, and Nature is the scripture in which he daily reads. He has all the marks of the believer — the zeal to convert us, the skill to discover evidences in every cranny of creation, and the sense that he has been liberated into something greater than himself. "Eternal time and not the single hour" is the object of his devotions; he is dedicated to the All, which swallows up and soothes his cares, his self-anxieties. Pride perishes in the total vision. For he has learned

> To look on all things with a master eye
> And mind at peace.

This sounds very much like the things said by holy contemplatives in any order, East or West. And once, though what Lucretius says must be read in reverse to get the effect, we find him in the role of Job:

> Who hath the power (I ask), who hath the power
> To rule the sum of the immeasurable,
> To hold with steady hand the giant reins
> Of the unfathomed deep? Who hath the power

At once to roll a multitude of skies,
At once to heat with fires ethereal all
The fruitful lands of multitudes of worlds,
To be at all times in all places near,
To stablish darkness by his clouds, to shake
The serene places of the sky with sound,
And hurl his lightnings — ha, and whelm how oft
In ruins his own temples, and to rave,
Retiring to the wildernesses, there
At practice with that thunderbolt of his,
Which yet how often shoots the guilty by,
And slays the honorable blameless ones!

The answer for Job — and to him, from the whirlwind — had been God: who, indeed, but God can
work such wonders? The answer for Lucretius is Nobody, but his excitement is the same. The world he
sees running by itself — running down, and then returning to its strength — inspires him also to prophetic
speech: the world, and the blind laws he has deciphered
from its surfaces, concealing as they do the awful cun-
nings of matter and chance.

For him, as truly as for any Christian believer, faith
is the evidence of things not seen. He must always be
telling us that the dark principle of his world is invisible. Its elements, "secret and viewless, lurk beneath,
behind." They are far beyond the range of the senses.
More than once he develops a figure for the search he
makes among the mysteries of matter. His mind is like
a hound's nose, sagacious and keen-scented, and so
must be the mind of any disciple.

· 159 ·

Thus thou thyself in themes like these alone
Can hunt from thought to thought, and keenly wind
Along even onward to the secret places
And drag out truth.

Truth for him is a hidden thing, not palpable except
to the searching reason. It is even a thing that laughs
at our vain attempts to understand it all; and at our
errors — well, the germs of things will

laugh aloud, like men,
Shaken asunder by a spasm of mirth,
Or moisten with salty tear-drops cheeks and chins.

Lucretius must be as subtle as any theologian in his
analysis of the deep, secretive stuff he finds in things.
The theologian has a thousand problems to solve before he can establish the creation. Lucretius has as
many to solve before he can complete the story of how
things came into being gradually, by evolution. He
cannot know all of the details, but his faith is sufficient
to convince him that if all of the details were known
the record would be equivalent to the one his ingenuity invents. He kindles as he invents, becoming the
best poet he is capable of being in the process of his
demonstration that nothing is new or strange — each
thing has had its natural development. Man is what
time has made him. Marriage, law, mercy, fire, education, language, tools, war, agriculture, music, letters,
the sense of history, and religion — yes, even religion
— all happened in their turn, and are plausible if we
look no farther than themselves in our effort to under-

stand them. The science of sciences is anthropology, because it saves us from the superstition that anything we have or are is a gift, a perilous gift that must be paid for, from the capricious gods. There is no miracle about our minds. They were not created. They simply became, as all things in the realm of matter do.

Lucretius has not gone far in his poem before he warns us that the most difficult thing he will ask us to do is

> to see with reasonable eyes
> Of what the mind, of what the soul is made.

He will not undertake to say of what reason is made. He could if he had to, he surely believes; but he goes nimbly on to dispose of the two terms that most intimidate us, the two regions where a suspicion of divinity lurks longest in those who would make themselves free.

> First, then, I say, the mind which oft we call
> The intellect, wherein is seated life's
> Counsel and regimen, is part no less
> Of man than hand and foot and eyes are parts
> Of one whole breathing creature.

And so for the soul:

> Therefore a vital heat and wind there is
> Within the very body, which at death
> Deserts our frames.

*Animus* and *Anima* — both are corporeal, and in a sense they have a single nature. There is no mystery

in them except the superfineness of their particles —
"most round, most tiny."

> Thus soul entire must be of smallmost seeds,
> Twined through the veins, the vitals, and the thews,
> Seeing that, when 'tis from whole body gone,
> The outward figuration of the limbs
> Is unimpaired and weight fails not a whit.

This mystery does in truth fascinate the poet, who expends a subtlety upon it that may remind us of angels and needles. The exercise of inventing an evolution for humankind was child's play compared with the steps that must be hewed through darkness before we can see how it is that the mind perceives what it perceives. It has a triple nature — it is breath, heat, and air — but on top of that there is a fourth principle for which Lucretius admits he cannot find a name, a fourth essence which nevertheless must somehow be conceived.

> For lurks this essence far and deep and under,
> Nor in our body is aught more shut from view,
> And 'tis the very soul of all the soul.

Beginning thus, he goes on with the excellent mind he has to prove that there is no mind — or rather, to explain mind as mechanics. The better the mind that does this, the falser the demonstration. For what Lucretius asks us to believe is no easier to believe than that the mind is a miracle. And it takes longer to say.

The mechanisms he creates, here as everywhere in the *De Rerum Natura*, are of necessity cumbersome. If the world had to explain itself it would grow tired of doing so, and relapse into its old way of simply and successfully being. In Lucretius the world is explaining itself, and it exhausts both itself and us. The most familiar things require the most roundabout exegesis. Walking, sleeping, seeing, grow into mysteries we did not know they were. Particularly seeing. All senses are forms of the sense of touch — naturally, since they are forms, as everything is, of contact between atom and atom. Sight is a miracle by any account, but the miracle here is the throng of images that fills the air as men see buildings, mountains, mirrors, and one another. What happens, Lucretius has to say, when a thing is seen is that a film departs from it and flies until it touches the seeing organ.

> Now these same films I name are borne about
> And tossed and scattered into regions all.
> But since we do perceive alone through eyes,
> It follows hence that whitherso we turn
> Our sight, all things do strike against it there
> With form and hue. And just how far from us
> Each thing may be away, the image yields
> To us the power to see and chance to tell:
> For when 'tis sent, at once it shoves ahead
> And drives along the air that's in the space
> Betwixt it and our eyes. And thus this air
> All glides athrough our eyeballs, and, as 'twere,
> Brushes athrough our pupils and thuswise
> Passes across.

The world rustles as we read, filling itself with snake skins and locust shells that get in the way of our seeing

the act of seeing. But Lucretius does not weary or repent. His courage is unkillable, as is the stubbornness
with which he accepts every challenge the customary
world offers him. The customary world? It is more
than we think it is, he says. It is wonderful in its hidden
ways. It is a measureless machine among whose wheels
we wander — measureless, yet he will measure it too,
or prove that it could be measured if we had all the
rules. The most ethereal of sciences, the science that
tells us how nothing is what it seems — that tables
have no edges, that bodies are mostly void, that the
patient block of wood is a whirling universe of forces
disposed in secret patterns, that feathers fall with can-
nonballs — the science of physics never daunts Lucretius.

For he is confident that the world it explores is after
all a uniform and constant place, a place wherein each
given thing is what it must be and no more. The
faithfulness of things to their own form is his perpetual
comfort. Spring after spring the birds come back in
their old colors, wearing the same spots and streaks.
The leaf of an oak tree grows to a certain size and
shape, then stops. Cows bear nothing but calves, and
horses colts. The cat is the same on any continent, in
any century. Matter is immutable, and with it form.

> For change of anything from out its bounds
> Means instant death of that which was before.

The scope of each thing that is has been prescribed
by the nature of the primal bodies which compose it;

its boundary stone is fixed deep in time. No intelligence in the world is free to upset and alter species, though it is true that by themselves species may advance or disappear. Even then, nothing can be said to leap into existence or out of it. Change occurs by inexorable and limited process. The germs of things are buried as deep as tears are for Virgil: buried, and not to be removed or minimized.

Individuals decay and change. Form is long, but life is short. Lucretius is more than aware of this; he is ecstatic about it. Dissolution is a fact in which he rejoices — because it is a fact, and because it is the occasion for most of our mistaken woes. We make the mistake of fearing nothing. Death is nothing. It is even a privilege, for it returns us to the vastness of which we had scarcely known how small a part we were. Lucretius takes the grim delight that children can take, and some scientists, in the inconceivable coldness of the spaces between the stars, in the awful impersonality of this world. The great conclusion of his third book leaves out no argument against the fear of death. And the conclusion of his fourth book, against the erroneous torments of love, is equally thorough. The torments of love are erroneous because they are based upon the illusion that woman is more than matter; that matter can unite with matter; and that Lydia is unique. The philosopher will not suffer from the absence or the coldness of what is not. Both passages are terrible in their truth, and for their untruth to any world in which tragedy is real.

The one passion Lucretius does not explain away, does not undermine with analysis, is his own. It is the passion to convince. It may even be the passion to believe the dogma he would make convincing, for doubt is often the source of excitement such as his. But at any rate the teacher and the preacher in him never flag. It does not seem to concern Lucretius that his very premises prevent the consummation he desires, namely that we too shall believe. Among many fallacies he commits — for he is too ready to say "thus," he impatiently begs questions, he assumes without argument that we should have faith in matter rather than in soul, he descends to tautology, he belabors us with melodramatic instances, he in a word invents to convince — there is one fallacy that is fatal: he expects us to change our minds when he has proved that we have none. Having reduced all to necessity, he asks us to be free — to decide that we believe what only our atoms could believe, our atoms which surely are too deep within us to be consulted. If all is Nature, including the minds we carry in us, how could any mind think an unnatural thought, how could any man have what Lucretius calls illusion, or if he did have illusion, correct it? Illusion too must have its particles, tiny and crooked and obscure.

Lucretius is not the first or the last naturalist who has tried to sweat an ethic out of necessity. All naturalists, indeed, are didactic; we must go with them or there will be no world. But Lucretius outsweats his fellows. The swerve of the atoms as they fall through

universal void — this principle which he has invented
in order to explain the coming and going of forms, the
combining and parting of primal bodies — is switched
now to a new function in the poem. It explains, he
hopes, our free will, and leaves us room in which to
decide that we believe him rather than some lover,
some priest, some other poet. But it does no such
thing. Lucretius may or may not understand how illicit
six of his lines are:

> But that mind's mind itself in all it does
> Hath not a fixed necessity within,
> Nor is not, like a conquered thing, compelled
> To bear and suffer — this state comes to man
> From that slight swervement of the elements
> In no fixed line of space, in no fixed time.

Since they are necessary so that he may go on, he does
go on, delivering epicurean homilies whenever the occasion suits. And he delivers them with wondrous
urgency: it is wrong to desire, it is folly to hope, it is
madness to think we may possess. Nor are they easy
to resist, since the most familiar of all truths is in them,
namely that man wants but little, nor that little long.
But a reader whom Lucretius has really convinced in
the beginning will now be at a loss to comprehend
how he, rather than his atoms, shall swerve. Lucretius
has not told him, for nothing in his system permits
him to do so.

The heat he generates as he exhorts us to be cool is
comparable with the pitch to which he raises his voice

as he insists that he will soothe the torments of our mind, will reassure and cure us with sound knowledge. Sound knowledge is pacifying and tranquilizing, for it is knowledge of the fact that nothing is what it seems: the elements of every object are insensate, so that if we are in danger from any source there is no hostility behind the danger. We shall be destroyed, but nothing seeks to destroy us. Nature is not a person. The very hugeness of creation can be a comfort to us if we will. So Lucretius soothes us, and his is one of the ways in which this can be done. But as the poem grows older it grows hoarser, and there is at last a perversity in the means the poet seizes to console us. The terrifying spectacles he rears — of flood, of annihilation, of "wrack and wreckage" everywhere — suggest too much. Consolation now is by cataclysm, and comfort by all that is most horrible. We may love Nature the more for what we learn it can do to us, but it is a queer love we must have if it matches his. His eloquence, nowhere more mighty than here, is poetry's heroic remedy. The *De Rerum Natura* as we have it ends with a description of the great plague at Athens, the climax of many monstrous happenings which we must somehow love. Reassurance can no farther go.

The crowning paradox of the poem has by this time all but stated itself. There is no calmness in this priest of calm. The perfect epicurean, if such a man is possible, would remain silent in his garden, pitying our fears and desires; but here is Lucretius in the thick of things, wrestling with them for our sake. He has rushed out to save us from ourselves, and in order to do so he wades through more terror than we had ever known was in us. And in a wild way he is happy, for this is where he wants to be. His business is to explain away the world, but the world fascinates him as it has fascinated few men. It is all one, all matter — so he declares, but the world he makes us recognize is compounded of multiple wonders, and it is everywhere glorified by his own powerful feeling. It is the kind of feeling that justifies the most extravagant metaphors; they do not seem at last extravagant, and they may not seem even to be metaphors. Their maker, utterly earnest, is humorless too — sarcasm with him is never playful, it is a body blow, beating the doubter down. So beat the bodies of the world one on the other; in the language of Lucretius they clash, they grip, they crush, they leap, they bound, they toss, they tangle, they embrace, they lunge apart again, they swarm — only violent verbs will do for the account he must render of life at its whirling center.

As for appearances — the accident of cloud and lightning, the behavior of beasts, the oddity of human love — Lucretius, who by logic should disdain them, is infatuated by them all. The vigor with which he renders the doings of earth is surpassed not even by Homer. The cow seeking her lost calf, the shadows on the mountains, the nebular origin of worlds, the panoply of heaven by night ("Now let us sing what makes the stars to move"), the sylvan splendor of the golden age — these, and hundreds of like things in the *De*

*Rerum Natura,* leave us with no doubt that Lucretius has looked upon the very world we live in, and has had more luck than we in realizing its importance. All is vivid to Lucretius, all is precious.

His method of argument, like that of Epicurus his master, is the method of analogy. Since the things he would discuss are invisible, he must substitute visible things so that we may seem to see with the eye as well as with the mind. The atoms are beyond our reach, but if we could penetrate to them we would discover that they are something like the sheep in a flock, the soldiers in an army, the motes in a sunbeam. The void is never to be encountered by any sense, but it helps to remember that water seeps through limestone and voices can be heard on the other side of walls. The conception of an atom's smallness is assisted by the image of stone steps worn away, of rings becoming thinner on fingers, of plowshares losing weight, of color in linen disappearing as the threads are picked apart. So on and on, richly, without ceasing.

The analogies of Lucretius are famous, and some of them are more useful to his argument than others. But it is not their ingenuity, or their legitimacy, that explains their peculiar splendor. Their meaning in the poem is rather that they betray the poet's true interest in those things — all things — whose nature he seemed to be saying was more important than themselves. It is themselves that poetry must deal with in the end. So Lucretius, dealing with them as he does, is in the end a poet. Whatever his motive, whatever his faith, he sees what all men see. The intensity, the accuracy of his gaze is due no doubt to the sincerity of his desire that he should see through what most mortals, foolish and fearful, merely look at. But things seen through are well seen, as Socrates and the saints attest.

# VI · THE DIVINE COMEDY

THE FULL WEIGHT of Homer's wisdom was delivered in stories of particular persons who did what they did in particular times and places. For Virgil a story was not enough; there had to be an idea, too, and a view of human history. But all of that together did not add up to the one thing, or the two things, Homer sang. Neither was Milton content with the brief, tremendous myth he started with; he loaded it with inventions, and in these inventions it lost some of its original force. Lucretius, superior to story, addressed himself to things; he tried to say what they were made of, and to fix truth so that it would never move again. He was a noble poet, but the truth still moves, still seeks its natural pace, which is that of narrative.

The vast and delicate poem of Dante does not readily answer a question put to it by the context of its peers. Which comes first in its author's being, the philosopher or the poet? The answer in fact is never given, for Dante is that unique thing, a successful philosophical poet: his story, for he tells one, cannot be separated from the thing it means. In this respect he is the peer of Homer and of Hamlet's historian, though his procedure is different from either of theirs. The journey his narrative takes is through the entire universe, and that universe is stationary; its parts wait for him to pass, learning their nature as he goes. But he does go; a journey is taken. Our belief in his story is simultaneous with our interest in what it signifies.

The *Divine Comedy* has to be sure absorbed a philosophy, and it is the most complex, not to say the most intimidating one, that poetry anywhere contains. Furthermore it is Dante's most serious conscious concern. The "sacred poem to which both heaven and earth so have set hand that it hath made me lean through many a year" is sacred to him because of the faith it explores. And the exploration is through regions where no other poet has been. "The water which I take was never coursed before." Things unattempted yet in prose or rhyme — by now it is a familiar warning, and we shall be kept off if our curiosity is not great or pure. Its author is an intensely personal and passionate man who would rather be understood than admired. He believes the story he tells — of his own journey, with Virgil and Beatrice for guides, through Hell, Purgatory, and Heaven — as genius believes things, with simplicity; and he tells it as genius tells things, without obscurity or reservation. Without obscurity, though with difficulties proper to the theme. For the journey is through knowledge, and knowing is often hard.

The initial canto, so famous and so spare, announces every quality of the poem to come.

> In the middle of the journey of our life I
> came to myself in a dark wood where the
> straight way was lost.

The journey is more than a casual expedition; it is Dante's life, and in addition to that it is our life, midway in which a darkness may come down, and direction be lost. The darkness is real, and therefore terrible.

> Ah! how hard a thing it is to tell what a
> wild, and rough, and stubborn wood this was,
> which in my thought renews the fear!
> So bitter is it, that scarcely more is death. . . .

Yet out of the terror will come knowledge — of what caused the darkness, and of better light beyond. So Dante will tell of both the darkness and the light.

A hill he comes to, with the sun shining on its summit, seems to offer escape from the obscure wood, and he thinks to ascend it. But three beasts prevent him, and he is in despair until there appears before him one who seems "hoarse from long silence" — a shade, not a man, though he was once a man.

> A poet I was; and sang of that just son
> of Anchises who came from Troy after
> proud Ilium was burnt.

It is Virgil — "O glory," cries Dante, "and light of other poets! . . . Thou art my master and my author. . . . See the beast from which I turned back; help me from her, thou famous sage."

"Thou must take another road," Virgil answers, "if thou desirest to escape from this wild place. . . . Wherefore I think and discern this for thy best, that thou follow me; and I will be thy guide, and lead thee hence through an eternal place, where thou shalt hear the hopeless shrieks, shalt see the ancient spirits in pain, so that each calls for a second death; and then thou shalt see those who are contented in the fire; for they hope to come, whensoever it be, amongst the blessed; then to these, if thou desirest to ascend, there shall be a spirit worthier than I to guide thee; with her will I leave thee at my parting. For that Emperor who reigns above, because I was rebellious to his law, wills not that I come into his city."

Dante, in other words, is not to save himself, but has like any man to be saved; has to go the long way round — the longest way, through all three parts of existence; and Virgil, because he lived before Christ, can go with him only through Purgatory, the second part. After that Beatrice will be his guide; neither poetry nor philosophy, but grace, must be the final means to bliss. The three beasts, a leopard, a lion, and a she-wolf, are the reasons within himself, the natural reasons, why assistance will be necessary from without. They have been said to stand for worldly pleasure, ambition, and avarice, as Virgil has been said to stand for worldly wisdom. In any case they necessitate the journey, and the poem. Dante beseeches Virgil, "by that God whom thou knowest not," to lead the way.

Then he moved; and I kept on behind him.

As swiftly as that, and as certainly, Dante plunges us into the midst of his many meanings. His many meanings are one at last, but the truth that runs through his poem has countless tributaries, the voice it speaks with is echoed from numerous mountains. There are occasional entanglements and ingenuities; the three beasts, for instance, manifest their meaning less clearly than does the "way" that Dante takes. Their trouble, strangely enough, is that they seem to have only one meaning; whereas the "way" is at least a double thing: it is a road and it is the direction life follows. Dante is most at home when more than one meaning sleeps in his words. He is entirely at home when his meanings are mutual; and when, as in this initial canto, they meet in the quiet of understatement, the courtesy of recognition, to give his story the importance it must have if it is to be the story of how all truth, tried in fire, becomes known.

Dante comes as near perfection in allegory as any poet has come. Allegory for him is not a trick. It is the truest language of a world the whole of which is organized in terms of meaning. No part of existence is neutral to Dante's purpose. He can use every piece of his experience, every item of his knowledge, in the service of a vision which his poem will fit. All of his loves and hates, all of the life he has seen and the books he has read, all that he thinks and feels he can bring somehow into a focus which renders the *Divine Comedy* both as simple as a parable and as formidable as a treatise. This is because allegory for him is more than pretending that one thing means another, more than concealing this behind that. Indeed it is more; it is the expression, the one direct and natural expression, of a multiple reality which he knows how to take for granted. The world is all about him all of the time: close about, exerting the pressure of its truth, each fragment of it waiting in its place to be noticed and to testify.

To say that Dante is good at allegory is to say that no one of his meanings, or kinds of meaning, tends to be more important than another. His details have in the end an equal depth. There is no philosophy "in" his poetry of which the poetry is the disguise or the container. His poetry is his philosophy, his philosophy is his poetry. It has been said that "a good allegory is clearer than any explanation of it would be." So with Dante's, which it is a greater pleasure to praise than to expound. It is a pleasure to praise it because it deals with the things men know. No fact is alien to it, for it writes itself in every part of the universe, and finds even the false gods edifying. The horrible giants who stand half-buried at the edge of Hell's deepest pit were hated in the old world too; Jove, says Dante, still threatens them from heaven when he thunders.

Dante does not prove his world; he reveals, he exposes it. He explores it systematically, transforming its matter as its inmost structure grows ever more intelligible. Nor does this operation seem to be a series of verbal acts. The poetry of the *Divine Comedy* is in

its words, of course, but still more it is in the arrangement of its things. Each of them derives its chief beauty
and force from the position it is given. The great work
is done silently, and finished sometimes before we
know it was begun. When Virgil bids farewell to
Dante near the summit of Purgatory, saying that wit
and art, so necessary in the narrow ways, can take him
no farther now, since his own pleasure must guide
him through Paradise, he concludes:

> No more expect my word, nor my sign. Free, up-
> right, and whole is thy will, and 'twere a fault
> not to act according to its prompting; wherefore
> I do crown and mitre thee over thyself.

Dante, recovered from Adam's fall, and therefore safely
trusted with his freedom, is henceforth king and bishop
of himself. The conception is daring, and we are
tempted to call Dante vain, doubting that he or any
man deserves the honor to be so addressed. But at
once our long memory rebukes us. How has Dante
earned this? Why, by writing the poem! He is placed
here, and so can listen to these words, because his
thought has taken him thus far; and incidentally it is
he who has created this Virgil of whose good word
we are so jealous.

Many another time the allegory collects itself in such
fashion and strikes with all its force. Dante, learning
in Paradise that to see truth in its own light is to love
it and rejoice, does not master the lesson by memoriz-
ing phrases; he blinks with ever-increasing wonder as

he moves among luminous spheres whose happy selves express their love not so much by singing as by whirling and glowing. But we also are there; we hear what he hears, see what he sees, and comprehend the fourfold simplicity of truth, light, love, and joy at the same minute that his poem does. It was different in Hell, when the angel came — from this same Paradise, but then it was remote and only imagined — to assure the entry of Dante and Virgil into the doleful City of Dis. He came over the stinking marsh that surrounded the city as a hurricane comes, stripping the trees and making the wild beasts flee; a thousand ruined spirits ran from him like frogs, and squatted on the bottom. Full of indignation, waving the gross air from his countenance with his left hand, he arrived and dispersed the uncivil shades who had denied the poets entrance. "Then he returned by the filthy way, and spake no word to us; but looked like one whom other care urges and incites than that of those who stand before him." Each of the three effects is proper to its place, and is great because it is proper. The angel, hating to be visible, will return and be again a wheel of light; and Dante, justified by his studies until he is free to think of the highest, the most abstract things, will see him there with the same eyes that see so easily now — so easily that we do not say: No man has ever been where such things are beheld.

An excellent measure of Dante's achievement in allegory might be taken by one who imagined the *Divine Comedy* not yet written, and who thus was free, as

Dante must have been, to ask whether its contents were to be said or were to be told. The two forms of communication rarely coincide. In the *Divine Comedy* they do so with unique precision — but how, in what original moment, did its author come upon the means? There is no more searching question that criticism can ask, or that a poet can ask of himself, assuming in him a capacity for being completely serious.

Dante's answer, of course, was that his poem must both say and tell, and that the two languages must be somehow one language; allegory meant this much to him at least, quite naturally, by the custom of his age. But how? The answer, in so far as there can be any, is to be found in Dante's seriousness: in his power to believe that it is of life-and-death importance whether or not the soul understands the universe in which it has been placed. His subject is the soul's understanding. And his story is the progress of that understanding. For the soul to explore the riches of being, and to define its ultimate nature, time is required. Progress, in other words, implies time. It even implies space. So the *Divine Comedy* must be among other things a narrative, it must describe a journey taken by the soul through days and places as existence is explored. Dante does not forget that the primary tense of poetry is the past tense.

But Dante's concern is also with the understanding to be had. The end of the poem cannot be the same as its beginning — darkness and ignorance must yield to light — yet the poet must know the end at the beginning. Even if the action is to draw a perfect circle, that circle must indeed be drawn — it cannot be printed all at once. Yet the poet must know the meaning of his story, which as meaning exists in eternity, before he has written a word. Dante, that is to say, is as much interested in the truth being sought as in the person — himself — who seeks it. His problem is therefore double: to tell his story well, and to make sure that it has the right meaning. He must know all before he starts, but he must conceal his knowledge, saving its essence till the end. His knowledge must order every step the journey takes at the same time that his imagination maintains the tensions of suspense, the excitements of learning. The relations which in his final vision he will possess as if they were one indivisible thing he must keep meanwhile so separate from one another that they can seem to tremble with unfinished life. On no page before the last may we be permitted to feel that we are There, yet on any page we must be both satisfied with what we know and studious to know more. Dante wants neither to deliver a sermon nor to tell a tale; he wants to be, if this is possible, at once didactic and diverting.

His success, for in his case the possibility was real, is perhaps not different from the success of any great poet. Any great poet is in a sense beyond criticism for the simple reason that he has written a successful story. Such a story is conceived out of time, but it is told in time. And the fact that it is easy to understand does not mean that it will be easy to discuss. Criticism is most at home with failure. In the presence of success it may be as dumb as the least instructed reader — more so, even, since many a reader understands by instinct how to receive what the poet by art knew how to prepare. Faced with the *Divine Comedy*, criticism can do little more than admire the patience with which its poet, who creates in time what he has conceived in eternity, holds himself back from saying all that he will ever mean. The poem must do that in its own time, through one detail after another. As for us who read, whether we are critics or not, we must do with each detail in its place, noting if we can how it is anchored to every other detail, but content if no connecting line appears. For a great poem conceals its structure; it talks not about itself but about its subject. About itself it is silent, and criticism invades that silence at its peril. The dare must perhaps be taken. The parts of a whole which is so simple that it seems to have no parts must nevertheless be named. But no list of parts will be equivalent to what the poet left behind him to be read.

The *Divine Comedy*, then, is both narration and analysis; it moves, but toward a truth that stands still. Its stages are at once sequential and simultaneous. Man learns one thing after another, but all the things he learns are one from the beginning; they are true at the same time, however prior or posterior may be his process. This is the fact with which Dante wrestles as he seeks to express the uncreated in terms of the created — and never blundering, as Milton does, by falling into the idiom of history. He never forgets that the created and the uncreated we have always with us, here and everywhere. He does not strive to make his universe look either very big or very old. It is what it is when we find it. The difficulty of finding it is what he most remembers.

> O Muses, O high Genius, now help me! O
> Memory, that hast inscribed what I saw,
> here will be shewn thy nobleness.

The difficulty of finding the truth is for Dante the same thing as the difficulty of writing his poem. "Who is that, who, without death, goes through the kingdom of the dead?" It was thus that the rebellious spirits challenged Dante at the entrance to the City of Dis. And in a sense they were right. For Dante's journey outrages nature. It is natural to desire this much knowledge, but it is unnatural to have it. The remotest objects are the most resentful of the mind's intrusion. Abstraction, the deepest secret, fights us off. Our only armor is a disinterested desire to know, a spirit pure in heart and pure in study. It was because Virgil could certify such a spirit in Dante that the angel came and opened those inhospitable gates.

Dante's allegory at its best, which means most of the time, declares itself in silence: one thing is another, and that is all, except that it is itself too. The mutual meanings are as immediate, and as noiseless, as com-

munication among mirrors. The result of this is that
he does not have to call our attention to what he is
doing; the poem is doing it as we read and understand.
But his allegory is not always at its best. Upon occasion Dante must pause and point; his cunning has not
been adequate to his plan.

Such an occasion mars, though it does not make un-
interesting, the episode before the walls of Dis. Above
those walls have suddenly appeared three hellish Furies, and they have threatened to summon Medusa,
"that we may change him into stone." But Virgil will
summon the angel, and with that aid the poets may
go on. This is where Dante doubts that we shall understand — doubts, in other words, that he has contrived
his poem with sufficient skill, as indeed he has not.
For he must say:

> O ye who have sane intellects, mark the doc-
> trine which conceals itself beneath the
> veil of the strange verses!

"Doctrine" is the word of weakness here. We are to
gather, perhaps with a scholar's help, that "a bad con-
science (the Furies) and stern obduracy which turns
the heart to stone (Medusa) are impediments that ob-
struct the path of every sinner intent on salvation.
Reason (Virgil) may do much to obviate these evil in-
fluences; but divine aid (the angel) is necessary to dis-
sipate them altogether." So once in Purgatory Dante
must break off his narrative to remark:

> Reader, here sharpen well thine eyes to the
> truth, for the veil now is indeed so thin,
> that of a surety to pass within is easy.

If "doctrine" is not a confession of failure, then "veil,"
twice used, must certainly be. In a perfect allegory,
which doubtless will never exist, neither word would
be needed. Doctrine would be implicit everywhere, no
veil would have to be withdrawn.

Another form that failure takes is the lecture. Teaching is not done best in lectures, but there are times
when Dante has no other resource. Virgil lectures in
Hell upon the classification of sins, and in Purgatory
upon gravitation, which as attraction is also love, the
force which keeps the universe organized about its
center. The position of this second lecture — at the
exact center of the poem — is itself an allegorical stroke
of the finest force. But the lecture, or the necessity for
it, shows again that the system has for a moment broken
down. How the breakdown could have been avoided
no one knows, since Dante did not. If he could have
avoided it he surely would have. Doubtless there was
no way; doubtless the world is not that kind to man,
that transparent at its center. At any rate Dante went
on with his lectures. Virgil must explain the topog-
raphy of Purgatory, and Beatrice must discourse
concerning many things which no images can be
summoned to convey.

A minor form of failure, though it is positive too,
is the homily to the reader, the direct preachment, as

when Dante, following Virgil's glance in Purgatory, sees the proud approaching, bent double under immense burdens of stone, and bursts forth thus:

> O ye proud Christians, wretched and weary,
>   who, sick in mental vision, put trust in
>   backward steps,
> perceive ye not that ye are worms, born to
>   form the angelic butterfly that flieth to
>   judgment without defence?
> Why doth your mind soar so high, since ye
>   are as 'twere imperfect insects, even as
>   the grub in which full form is wanting?

The message may be true, but the form of it, given a surrounding allegory which for the most part makes any message superfluous, is shocking. So are the other devices to which Dante now and again descends in order to secure the emphasis he has not known how to maneuver into expressing itself.

None of these failures, however, is more than momentary. And all of them together are cancelled in Dante's final effect by the host of superb figures— little allegories inside the great one — with which his poem swarms. The whole world of the poem is one metaphor, but this does not prevent the existence of many within that one. The similes of Dante are as important to his purpose as Homer's were to his, though they are seldom so elaborate. They are his world making itself known, down to the finest detail, while overhead and over all the Word gathers its breath to speak the abstraction we are waiting for.

They are the signs we need that our poet has seen
what we have seen, that he is interpreting the landscape of our life.

> And as he, who with panting breath has escaped
> from the deep sea to the shore, turns to the
> dangerous water and gazes:
> So my mind, which still was fleeing, turned
> back to see the pass that no one ever left
> alive.

> As sails, swelled by the wind, fall entangled
> when the mast breaks: so fell that cruel
> monster to the ground.

> As a green brand, that is burning at one end,
> at the other drops, and hisses with the wind
> which is escaping:
> So from that broken splint, words and blood
> came forth together.

> We met a troop of spirits who were coming
> alongside the bank; and each looked at us,
> as in the evening men are wont
> to look at one another under a new moon; and
> toward us sharpened their vision, as an
> aged tailor does at the eye of his needle.

> Not otherwise the dogs in summer do, now with
> snout, now with paw, when they are bitten
> by fleas, or flies, or breeses.

> Then he writhed his mouth and thrust
> his tongue out, like an ox that licks
> his nose.

As the falcon, that has been long upon his
    wings — that, without seeing bird or lure —
    makes the falconer cry, 'Ah, ah! thou stoopest' —
descends weary; then swiftly moves himself
    with many a circle, and far from his master
    sets himself disdainful and sullen:
so at the bottom Geryon set us, close to the
    foot of the ragged rock; and, from our weight
    relieved, he bounded off like an arrow from
    the string.

And through the circular valley I saw a people
    coming silent and weeping, at the pace which
    the Litanies make in this world.

As dolphins, when with the arch of the back
    they make sign to mariners that they may pre-
    pare to save their ship:
So now and then, to ease the punishment, some
    sinner showed his back and hid in less time
    than it lightens.

In that part of the youthful year, when the Sun
    tempers his locks beneath Aquarius, and the
    nights already wane towards half the day,
when the hoar-frost copies his white sister's
    image on the ground, but short while lasts
    the temper of his pen,
the peasant, whose fodder fails, rises, and looks,
    and sees the fields all white; whereat he
    smites his thigh,
goes back into the house, and to and fro laments
    like a poor wight who knows not what to do;

then comes out again, and recovers hope,
  observing how the world has changed its face in
  little time; and takes his staff, and chases
  forth his lambs to feed:
thus the Master made me despond, when I saw
  his brow so troubled; and thus quickly to
  the sore the plaster came.

As up before the flame on paper, goes a brown
  color which is not yet black, and the
  white dies away.

There I see on either side each shade make
  haste, and one kiss the other without staying, satisfied with short greeting:
even so within their dark battalions one ant
  rubs muzzle with another, perchance to spy
  out their way and their fortune.

As a lady who is dancing turns her round with
  feet close to the ground and to each other,
  and hardly putteth foot before foot,
she turned toward me upon the red and upon the
  yellow flowerets, not otherwise than a virgin that droppeth her modest eyes.

As a cross-bow breaks, when shot at too great
  tension, both its string and bow, and with
  less force the bolt hits its mark,
so burst I under this heavy charge, pouring
  forth a torrent of tears and sighs, and my
  voice died away in its passage.

Gazing on her such I became within, as was
  Glaucus, tasting of the grass that made
  him the sea-fellow of the other gods.

For I have seen first, all the winter through,
   the thorn display itself hard and forbidding,
   and then upon its summer bear the rose.

And at the name of the lofty Maccabee I saw
   another move, wheeling, and gladness was as
   the lash unto the whipping-top.

As the bird amidst the loved foliage who hath
   brooded on the nest of her sweet offspring
   through the night which hideth things from us,
who, to look upon their longed-for aspect and
   to find the food wherewith to feed them,
   wherein her heavy toils are pleasant to her,
foreruns the time, upon the open spray, and
   with glowing love awaiteth the sun, fixedly
   gazing for the dawn to rise;
so was my Lady standing, erect and eager,
   turned toward the region beneath which
   the sun showeth least speed.

As under the sun's ray, which issueth pure through
   a broken cloud, ere now mine eyes have seen a
   meadow full of flowers, when themselves covered
   by the shade;
so beheld I many a throng of splendors, glowed on
   from above by ardent rays, beholding not the
   source whence came the glowings.

In form, then, of a white rose displayed itself
   to me that sacred soldiery which in his blood
   Christ made his spouse;
but the other, which as it flieth seeth and doth
   sing his glory who enamoreth it, and the excel-

lence which hath made it what it is,
like to a swarm of bees which doth one while plunge
 into the flowers and another while wend
 back to where its toil is turned to sweetness,
ever descended into the great flower adorned with
 so many leaves, and reascended thence to where
 its love doth ever make sojourn.

So did I turn again unto his teaching who
 drew beauty from Mary, as from the sun
 the morning star.

They are also the sign we need that the visionary to
whom we have entrusted ourselves can see more in
the landscape than is commonplace — can see, in fact,
the celestial landscape that lies within it as the fourth
dimension sleeps among the other three, visible only
to the deepest eyes. Midway through Paradise Dante
begins to fear that the brightness he gazes upon will
become such that "all similes fall short of it." But it
never does. His similes are ever more ethereal to match
the increasing subtlety of what he sees, yet they never
abandon the language of earth. Early in Paradise he
learns that the spirits with whom he is henceforth to
speak will to any gross sense be invisible. This is the
way he learns it:

In such guise as, from glasses transparent and
 polished, or from waters clear and tranquil,
 not so deep that the bottom is darkened,
come back the outlines of our faces, so faint
 that a pearl on a white brow cometh not
 slowlier upon our eyes;

so did I behold many a countenance, eager to
    speak; wherefore I fell into the counter-
    error of that which kindled love between the
    man and the fountain.
No sooner was I aware of them than, thinking
    them reflected images, I turned round my
    eyes to see of whom they were;
and I saw naught, and turned them forward
    again straight on the light of my sweet
    guide, whose sacred eyes glowed as she
    smiled.

Unlike Narcissus, who mistook a reflection for a face,
Dante mistakes for reflections the faces of the last
spirits he will see — and how faint these are three
figures measure with an accuracy found only in such
poetry as he writes.

The briefest metaphors flash in like manner, though
more rarely, as we make our way from line to sober
line.

    Among evil cats the mouse had come.

    And thus quickly to the sore the plaster
      came.

    To course o'er better waters now hoists
      sail the little bark of my wit.

    With the swift wings and with the plumes
      of great desire.

    Thus, by asking, did he thread the very
      needle's eye of my desire.

The ice which had closed about my heart
became breath and water.

Verily, I see how thou dost nestle in thine
own light.

The mind which shineth here, on earth doth
smoke.

Within its depths I saw ingathered, bound by
love in one volume, the scattered leaves of
all the universe.

Work of this sort is done by Dante quickly — as
nearly as possible in no time at all. These are the jewels
on which the wheels of his allegory turn; they must
be here, but he would rather that we watched the
wheels. It is a secret that Milton discovered from him
only to forget. Adam's few and powerful words concerning Raphael, whose coming is like another morn
at noon, suggest the words of Dante in Paradise as he
follows the eyes of Beatrice and looks straight into the
sun: "Meseemed that day was added unto day, as
though he that hath the power had adorned heaven
with a second sun." But too little of *Paradise Lost* is
like that, whereas the *Divine Comedy* is like that most
of the time.

Dante's figured speech might seem to reach its climax
when in Paradise he telescopes the senses whose experience he reports. We hear about "the song of these
lights," lights that ring out the name of Mary, and an
eternal yellow rose which breathes praise. Yet there
is in reality no climax; from the beginning of the work

its author has been master of the hidden illumination, the buried phrase which will not stay buried. He even knows how to be brilliant with no light at all, as when in the dark plain before Hell proper he meets the un-numbered trimmers who deserve neither Hell nor Paradise, and cuts them with cold whips of phrases which no imagery makes merciful:

> The dreary souls who lived without blame, and
> without praise...
> who were not rebellious, nor were faithful to
> God, but were for themselves.
>
> These unfortunate who never were alive.
>
> These have no hope of death.
>
> Report of them the world permits not to exist;
> Mercy and Justice disdains them: let us not
> speak of them; but look, and pass.
>
> I should never have believed death had undone
> so many.

Those who were neither good nor bad — the immense majority of mankind — Dante refuses to render visible. He regards them, lashes them with the driest thong of his wit, and goes on. The decision to do so is in itself a figure, but of a kind which only the intricate structure of this poem makes possible.

It is early in Hell that Dante meets Paolo and Francesca, perhaps the most famous of his persons. And they deserve their fame, for the passage in which they live is peculiarly powerful. But the reason for this power is not easily discovered. It lies deep in the images of wind and bird that alter so imperceptibly as we read. The alterations — italicized below — carry the meaning of the canto; they are the way in which Dante says what he has to say not only about these lovers but about all carnal sinners, in his view the least of sinners, and consequently so much to be pitied.

> I came into a place void of all light,
>     which bellows like the sea in tempest,
>     when it is combated by *warring winds*.
> The hellish storm, *which never rests*, leads
>     the spirits with its sweep; whirling and
>     smiting, it vexes them. . . .
> I learned that to such torment are doomed
>     the carnal sinners, who subject reason
>     to lust.
> And as their wings bear along the *starlings*,
>     at the cold season, in large and crowded
>     troop: so that blast, the evil spirits;
> hither, thither, down, up, it leads them. No
>     hope ever comforts them, not of rest but
>     even of less pain.
> And as the *cranes* go chanting their lays, mak-
>     ing a long streak of themselves in the air:
>     so I saw the shadows come, uttering wails,
> borne by that strife of winds; whereat I said:
>     'Master, who are those people, whom the
>     black air thus lashes?' . . .
> After I had heard my teacher name the olden
>     dames and cavaliers, pity came over me, and

I was as if bewildered.
I began: 'Poet, willingly would I speak
    with those two that go together, and seem
    *so light upon the wind.*'
And he to me: 'Thou shalt see when they are
    nearer to us; and do thou entreat them by
    that love which leads them; and they will come.'
Soon as *the wind bends* them to us, I raised
    my voice: 'O wearied souls! come to speak
    with us, if none denies it.'
As *doves* called by desire, with raised and
    steady wings come through the air *to their
    loved nest,* borne by their will:
so those spirits issued from the band where
    Dido is, coming to us through the malignant
    air; such was the force of my affectuous cry.
'O living creature, gracious and benign! that
    goest through the black air, visiting us who
    stained the earth with blood:
if the King of the Universe were our friend, we
    would pray him for thy peace; seeing that thou
    hast pity of our perverse misfortune.
Of that which it pleases thee to hear and to
    speak, we will hear and speak with you,
    *whilst the wind, as now, is silent for us.*
The town, where I was born, sits on the shore,
    where Po *descends to rest* with his attend-
    ant streams. . . .

Starlings, cranes, doves — the descent of the series
is from restlessness to rest, as the movement of the wind
is from war to peace, and as at the close the fall of the Po

is from the mountains to the sea, attended by obedient tributaries. No passage in any poem does better work.

The difficulty of reading Dante is the difficulty of seeing all that is there. No poet has a greater horror of being obscure, but no poet has put so much into an equivalent space; to put in less than everything would have been for Dante to commit the obscurity that matters most, the obscurity of incompletion. To put everything in, however, does not mean with him to be diffuse; it means the opposite, for every corner of this space is precious, every tick of this time suggests eternity. So Dante, who does not distinguish between poetry and truth, devotes himself entirely to his vision, strengthening its supports with any buttresses that will stand, and feeling no scruple when his concentration becomes crabbèd, when his earnestness becomes prosaic. He is never, perhaps, prosaic, but he does not mind sounding so to those who have missed the poetry of his plan. His plan is as rigid as he can make it, to suit the rigor of his theme: the verse-scheme is handcuffs, and the system of the cantos — a hundred in all, as equally divided as possible among the three parts, and substantially of uniform length — is a set of leg-irons in which he walks from room to room. There is no other way in which he can feel his freedom. He does feel it, constantly, against the limits of so much form. It takes this much form to press out of his subject the "strong-bitter flavor" it rightly has. His ancestor who in Paradise counsels him to write the *Divine Comedy* predicts that his voice will be "grievous at first taste, yet vital nutriment shall it leave thereafter when digested." The nutriment is the thing: "contracted words which shall note much in little space." "The long theme so chases me," Dante once explains, "that many times the word comes short of the reality." This could be an apology, but it may be a boast; for nobody could know better than he does that he leaves nothing unsaid after all. He describes little — less, it would often seem, than enough — yet we see everything that we should see. "Who, even with words set free, could ever fully tell, by oft relating, the blood and the wounds that I now saw?" The answer must be another question. Who thinks that Dante's Hell is empty of blood and wounds?

He regularly exclaims that the things he must tell cannot be told. The truth of his vision is ineffable — the more so as he approaches its beatific end. "I write it not, because all speech would fail to tell." So he excuses himself for one of his silences in Hell. But the silences are much more numerous thereafter. In Purgatory he calls upon Helicon to stream forth, and Urania to aid him with her choir, so that he may speak of things which are hard even to conceive. The freest citizen of Parnassus, attempting to sing of Beatrice's eyes, would seem to have "a mind encumbered." It is not merely that such things are by their nature unspeakable, but the confines of his form are tyrannous; the part of his poem reserved for Purgatory leaves him too little room. "Forasmuch as all the pages ordained for this second canticle are filled, the curb of art no

further lets me go." And in Paradise the complaint, if
complaint it truly is, becomes chronic.

> In that heaven which most receiveth of his light
> have I been; and have seen things which whoso
> descendeth from up there hath nor knowledge
> nor power to re-tell.

> To pass beyond humanity may not be told in words.

> If now there were to sound all of those tongues
> which Polyhymnia with her sisters made richest
> with their sweetest milk,
> it would not mount, in aiding me, unto the thou-
> sandth of the truth . . .
> And therefore, figuring Paradise, needs must the
> sacred poem make a leap . . .

> It is no voyage for a little bark, that which my
> daring keel cleaveth as it goeth, nor for a
> helmsman who doth spare himself.

> Thenceforward was my vision mightier than our
> discourse, which faileth at such sight, and
> faileth memory at so great outrage.

> Oh but how scant the utterance, and how faint,
> to my conception! and it, to what I saw, is
> such that it sufficeth not to call it little.

> To the high fantasy here power failed.

It is not truly a complaint. This is Dante's rhetoric for
that which is less to be written than to be seen. The
writing is there, but we do not see it for the brighter,
taller thing that shows behind it.

No poet takes a more natural delight in abridgement which proves that all truth is possessed. For Dante condensation is a duty, but he loves the command that he be brief. The doomed souls "are prompt to pass the river, for Divine Justice spurs them so, that fear is changed into desire." And the Hell they go to is simply a part of the universe "where there is naught that shines." What other poet has put Demeter's daughter in three lines? Says Dante to Matilda in Purgatory: "Thou makest me to remember where and what Proserpine was, in the time her mother lost her, and she lost the spring flowers." But again it is in Paradise, where the heart of meaning beats, that compression reaches its limit.

> And his will is our peace.

> No more free than water that should not
> flow to the sea.

> This glory which suffereth not itself to
> be surpassed by longing.

> Bound by love in one volume.

If the limit is sometimes overreached, the reason is that Dante has fallen in love with brevity rather than with the cause it serves. He rests in silence, not the God of silence.

> I did not die, and did not remain alive: now
> think for thyself, if thou hast any grain
> of ingenuity, what I became, deprived of
> both death and life.

Ingenuity — Dante can seldom resist it. He is frequently more intricate than his subject is, more elaborate than the truth allows.

> And that he might in very construing be what
> he was, a spirit from up here moved them to
> call him by the possessive adjective of
> him whose he all was.
> Dominic was he named.

"Dominicus," in simpler terms, is the possessive form
of "Dominus." But that is too much to say — or not
enough — concerning the subject at hand. The ingenuity of another tercet is more attractive:

> Devoutly as I may do I implore thee that thou
> speak to me; thou seest my will, and to hear
> thee the sooner I utter it not.

This still, however, is ingenuity, and noticeable as
such.

Dante is not above a predilection for puzzles, for
incidental intricacies such as sometimes seem to justify
the man who called the *Divine Comedy* a Swiss clock.
The suggestion might have come from a simile for the
singing of saints in Paradise:

> And even as wheels in harmony of clock-work
> so turn that the first, to whoso noteth it,
> seemeth still, and the last to fly,
> So did these carols with their differing
> whirl, or swift or slow, make me deem of
> their riches.

But it could have come equally well from any of a hundred other inlays of wit with which the poem is adorned. When the angels sparkle with joy at one of Beatrice's speeches about them, the spectacle is of a brilliance measured, Dante says, by the number of the angels, which runs to thousands "beyond the duplication of the chessboard." Chessboard would be as faithful an image as Swiss clock. It poses problems, and Dante is often pleased to give us little problems over which we must pause before we read any more in the book that day. The poem has scarcely opened before he tells us in which direction he bore as he started to ascend the holy hill whose top would be denied him. But see how he tells us:

I took the way again along the desert strand,
so that the right foot always was the lower.

The astronomy by which he denotes the hour, the day, and the season when things happen is a noble science which Dante sometimes plays with, fascinated by the figures on its celestial face. The signs that Dante is alive in Hell and Purgatory are never the same; he breathes, he casts a shadow, he moves what he touches — the poet never wearies of inventing ways for the shades to learn that he is not like them. Indirection is a sacred game; logic is the law of this poetry's being. Count Guido da Montefeltro tells Dante that he is in Hell because one of the Black Cherubim remembered something Saint Francis had forgotten. Saint Francis came for Guido when he was dead, but these few dark words kept him forever out of heaven:

'For he who repents not, cannot be absolved;
nor is it possible to repent and will a
thing at the same time, the contradiction
not permitting it.'
O wretched me! how I started when he seized
me, saying to me: 'May be thou didst not
think that I was a logician!'

Logic is Dante's law, but it can become in his poem a
whip which he cracks. So with the understatement of
which he is master. Understatement is proper to his
style, as logic is, for both can underscore connections,
forcing us to see them for ourselves; but it can tor-
ment the commentators with uncertainty as to what
he intended they should understand. Ugolino, relating
in Hell the starvation of his imprisoned sons and himself, comes at last to the famous moment when he
knew himself to be their survivor:

Even as thou seest me, saw I the three fall
one by one, between the fifth day and the
sixth; whence I betook me,
Already blind, to groping over each, and for
three days called them, after they were dead;
then fasting had more power than grief.

Do the last words mean that Ugolino ate his sons, or
that hunger left him no strength for further grief? Certainly the second, but we ache to have it plainer.

Dante is nowhere more ingenious than in the circumlocutions he scatters like live sparks across the
floor of his verse. They again are proper to his purpose,

for in a world conceived as his is every object has a right to several names. The importance of anything is measured by the number of names it can have. The circumlocutions of Dante are not too numerous, nor could they be better than they are. God, who must not be named at all, is of course their most frequent occasion. God is called:

> That Emperor who reigns above.
>
> That Will whose object never can be frustrated.
>
> Him who willingly doth pardon.
>
> He who ne'er beheld a new thing.
>
> He who hath the power.
>
> Another.
>
> Such.

Heaven is "where what is willed can be done." It is "that part where the world quickeneth most." Purgatory is "the mount where justice probes us," and "the mount which makes you straight whom the world made crooked." Virgil is "My Guide," "the Master," "the Poet," "the Sea of all intelligence," and "he who ever in front of me alert was going." Beatrice is "the sun which first warmed my bosom with love," and always "my sweet guide." Once the three archangels are named, yet the third one is not named either, except by indirection. Beatrice it is who talks with Dante of "Gabriel, Michael, and him too who made Tobit sound again"; for Raphael cured Tobias's father of his blindness. The poet could not permit his Lady to speak in series as many as three plain names.

The ironies of Dante are sunk deep into his texture. They are among his richest beauties, but they prefer not to call attention to themselves. We must dig them out. The poetry in the *Divine Comedy* is something we must work for; this least poetical of poets has a design upon us — it is to make us poets ourselves. We often have the pleasure of thinking that we see more than Dante did. We suppose it is our imagination that dresses the naked objects he leaves in our path; and forget the imagination that left them just there, in the position best calculated to suggest the costume they require. So in particular with his ironies, which he leaves for us to discover; as when Farinata, who burns in Hell because like Lucretius he insisted on earth — "yonder where men breathe" — that the soul dies with the body, rises out of his flaming tomb "upright with breast and countenance, as if he entertained great scorn of Hell." Farinata's heresy has been disproved, his soul has survived his body, and still he refuses to believe it.

Such things bring it about that the *Divine Comedy* must be read slowly or not at all. It cannot be hurried, any more than the earth can be induced to rotate faster than its hours decide. Dante's progress is too difficult for his pace to be other than circumspect. "Ye Christians," says Beatrice in Paradise, "be more sedate in moving, not like a feather unto every wind." This

might be a motto for the poem in which she is so fixed
a star, smiling gravely as she precedes her worshipper
among the spheres of understanding.

The poem is stiff with manners. Courtesy holds it
down to the respectful gait which for its author it must
have. Courtesy, indeed, is almost cumbrous here;
dignity can never be sacrificed, nor the scruple ignored
which urges against harsh and perhaps blasphemous
directness. If the courtesy of the *Divine Comedy* is an
exquisite thing, it is also exigent to the point of iron
decorum. It suggests a code, the code that obtains
between teacher and pupil when respect is mutual. For
the story we are being told is the story of how Dante
was taught, in turn by Virgil, by Beatrice, and by
Bernard. And the complexion this story has is given
to it by the hesitancy its persons never cease to feel
as they ask and answer; the asker, Dante, is loath to
interrupt the thoughts of his greater companion, and
the companion is loath to lecture before lecturing is
necessary. The teacher would rather that the pupil
learned by himself, and imputes to him the power of
doing so; while the pupil wonders whether he should
hold back his question until the truth is manifest without words. It is as if they all wished words did not
exist, so that things might speak for themselves. Not
that the poem does not largely consist of the words
they exchange, of the lectures they listen to and deliver. But Dante's fear lest he offend is never laid, and
his teachers never commit the fault of condescension;
though as often as need be they rebuke him, and some-

times they do this roundly. Virgil is plain enough when
he charges Dante with being too curious to overhear
a certain quarrel between two false spirits in Hell:

> I was standing all intent to hear them, when
>   the Master said to me: 'Now keep looking a
>   little longer and I quarrel with thee!'
> When I heard him speak to me in anger, I turned
>   towards him with such shame, that it comes
>   over me again as I but think of it.
> And as one who dreams of something hurtful to
>   him, and dreaming wishes it were a dream,
>   so that he longs for that which is, as if
>   it were not:
> such grew I, who, without power to speak, wished
>   to excuse myself and all the while excused,
>   and did not think that I was doing it.
> 'Less shame washes off a greater fault than
>   thine has been,' said the Master: 'there-
>   fore unload thee of all sorrow;
> and count that I am always at thy side, should
>   it again fall out that Fortune brings thee
>   where people are in similar contests: for
>   the wish to hear it is a vulgar wish.'
> One and the same tongue first wounded me so
>   that it tinged with blushes both my cheeks,
>   and then held forth the medicine to me.

But, as the passage makes clear, he at the same time
hurts and soothes his disciple. No such wound is ever
left unhealed. Virgil and Beatrice both, and upon
many occasions, grow impatient with Dante, calling
him a child in reason, an infant in discourse. But kind-

ness follows, and a grave smile smooths all away. Dante, nevertheless, does not forget to be modest with inquiry. Shall he put another question or walk on in silence? It is hard to decide, "and I remain in doubt; for yes and no contend within my head." His division of mind is not like that of Homer's or of Virgil's men. The problem is one of courtesy, and of courtesy alone.

The relation between Dante and Virgil is one of the most beautiful things in poetry. It is Virgil, of course, who for the author of the *Divine Comedy* is "the sovereign poet," though it is upon Homer that he fastens the phrase. The remark of Statius in Purgatory, "to have lived yonder when Virgil was alive I would consent to one sun more than I owe to my coming forth from exile," would do for Dante too. The deportment of the pair is ever distinguished by its delicacy. "With eyes ashamed and downcast, fearing my words might have offended him, I kept myself from speaking till we reached the stream." But what were the words that might have offended Virgil? Merely: "Master, now grant that I may know who these are." And Virgil had declined to answer, saying that Dante would soon know by himself that they were Charon's passengers, waiting to be ferried into Hell. Not that Virgil's silence can be cruel. It cannot, because he is the prince of courtesy; nothing could exceed the subtlety with which he apprehends his pupil's shames and fears. "That color," says Dante before the gates of Dis, "which cowardice painted on my face when I saw my

Guide turn back, repressed in him more quickly his new color," which was the color of wrath. "Be not dismayed if I get angry," Virgil remembers to say. His help in time of trouble is a constant thing, and boundless in its power to comfort the shy learner in his charge.

The relation between Dante and Beatrice, once Virgil disappears from the poem, is still more beautiful, but it is not a relation of courtesy. Courtesy is the code of earth. It is mortality's best imitation of the divine life it will never share. Virgil is a great gentleman, but Beatrice is more than a great lady: she is a saint, and so can dispense with the elaboration of codes. Yet even she is the kind of teacher, the perfect kind, who can take pleasure in being forgotten when the time comes for that.

> Never was heart of mortal so disposed unto
> devotion, and so keen to give itself to
> God with all its will,
> as at those words was I; and so wholly was
> my love committed unto him, it eclipsed
> Beatrice in oblivion.
> Her it displeased not; but she so smiled
> thereat, the splendor of her laughing eyes
> parted my erst united mind amongst things
> multiform.

The fancy of this poet is unlimited but it is never unregulated. What regulates it is his unremitting seriousness as he searches for the truth. Philosophy for him, as for Aquinas, is not the study of what various men have believed, but of how "the truth of things standeth." Virgil assures Chiron, who resents Dante's presence in Hell, that "necessity brings him to it, and not sport." Dante is better than curious; he is studious. He would know more rather than see more. His admiration of the angels is because they know — even because their eyes are dazed, "like a faculty which by excess is confounded." So will he be dazed by what he sees in the last canto, but he does not hesitate to travel that far, by any conveyance that will take him there, metaphysical or mathematical. He is master of the dry term which in the end is not dry, for it measures the warmth of the world, and takes us along tangents to where we can delight our eyes with such sights as that of Matilda in the Earthly Paradise:

> a lady solitary, who went along singing,
>     and culling flower after flower, where-
> with all her path was painted.

If the picture is delicious, we have paid for it with the intellectual effort that brought us to where Matilda walks. Nor shall we measure the beatitude of Dante in his final state unless we can share with him his joy in the spectacle of a circle squared; for that was how God's face, with man's face painted upon it, seemed to him when he looked and lost consciousness at last.

Philosophy may be the serious concern of one who is not a poet. Dante's intellect does not make him a poet, it simply makes him a better one. The systematic nature of the *Divine Comedy* is a nature that he knows how to elevate till it is art. All is system, yet little is mechanics; the serious poet in Dante is not dull. And for that matter we may easily overemphasize the symmetries we find. There also are incidental surprises — stories told at length, figures that go beyond our expectation in the splendor of their light, and wonderful meetings like those with Casella and Statius, not to speak of those with Virgil and Beatrice. The poem is as rich as the *Odyssey* in its recognition scenes, though each of them is briefer than Homer chose to be, and less occupied with extending a single line of narrative suspense.

But the system is not without its own beauty, nor does Dante permit us to forget it. The three stages of the journey are constantly recapitulated. "Down in the world endlessly bitter, and along the mount from whose fair summit my Lady's eyes uplifted me, and after, through the heaven from light to light" — so runs one sentence out of many whose ends are tied together, making a strong thread through the fabric. If Dante is not speaking such a sentence then Virgil is, explaining the traveler's presence to Cato or some doubtful spirit; or Beatrice is, pleased as she steadily is to remind Dante of the stages in his own life which correspond to these. These stages, of Hell and Purgatory and Heaven, receive an ever richer weight of allegory. They organize the poem, but the poem is organized about love, and so the three regions partake of love's geography, shining or lost in shadow in proportion to the distance they lie from that "good wherein the mind may find rest." In Hell there is no love and hence no rest; in Purgatory there is love that voluntary punishment will purify, and those who undergo the punishment are content with their pain; in Heaven, where there is no pain, activity itself is rest, the music of pure being.

The grammar of Dante's system is the grammar of sin. He is so skilled in it that no composition employing its terms is beyond his powers. And here as usual he is enamored of a scheme. The punishment suits the crime. In Hell the avaricious and the prodigal, because they were so undiscerning of the true good to be desired, are now "too obscure for any recognition." The sullen carry "lazy smoke" in their hearts. The carnal are driven in total darkness by unceasing winds. The evil counsellors are invisible to one another, each wrapped in the flame of his own consciousness. In Purgatory the proud go willingly under immense burdens of stone, and the envious, who once had looked without joy on the happiness of others, are pleased to suffer sutures through the lids of their eyes so that they may not see. But there comes a turn in the *Divine Comedy*, a pivotal point after which punishment is not only endured but sought for, not only suffered but enjoyed. This point, characteristically, is midway through Purgatory, the central point of all. Henceforth we encounter spirits who because they were gluttonous on earth are eager for famine in the midst of plenty, and spirits who because they once were lustful cannot be kept now from the flames that burn them.

The turn is at the right time, and so it is always with the changes that steal over the poem as colors, obedient to season, succeed one another in the foliage of a forest. The *Divine Comedy* is never the same in two adjacent cantos. Its three grand parts are of course different, for they visit the extremes of the moral universe; but less perceptible changes are incessantly taking place. The movement of the poem is through many progressions — simultaneous, since each is a function of every other, but clearly distinguishable by the memory which recalls them, once the end is reached that draws them together.

The movement of the *Divine Comedy* is from low to high, and this is the same thing as from dark to light. It is from slow to swift, which is the same thing again, though there is also a fourth form: from difficult to easy. As Dante ascends into light the rate of his progress is multiplied so many fold that he scarcely knows he is changing place, or that activity is involved as he does so. Harmonious with these movements is the movement from remote to near, which in one of its aspects is a movement from past to present, from the biographies of men to the states of the soul in bliss. Persons give way to figures of light — circles and wheels — and there is a parallel progression from sullenness or silence to unlimited bursts of generous song. Correlative with this progression is one from the expressible to the inexpressible, from the sensible to the abstract; which means that the poem grows less narrative and more lyric. For lovelessness and pain are being replaced by charity and joy. When charity and joy are absolute, all else is absolute: light is blinding, swiftness comes home to rest, the soul on high is perfect in its ease, *there* has become *here*, eternity has expanded all experience until it is contained in one present moment, and joy that cannot be expressed soars into a silence antipodal to the sick one with which we started.

If these advances are in a straight line, as manifestly they are, that line has the mysterious properties of one that is infinite, for it is also a circle. Movement at first is contrariwise: Hell is always darker and more terrible, and love less evident. But that is because we are visiting the nethermost extreme. The uppermost extreme is straight ahead; when we emerge at the foot of Purgatory's mountain we are still going in the original direction, though now the gravity of the sins decreases rather than increases. The carnal sinners are encountered last, not first, and Paradise is not too far beyond them.

Thus the movement of the *Divine Comedy* has many epicycles of meaning; and by the same token there is a host of minor progressions tucked into folds of the great one. The beauty of Beatrice, if indeed that is a minor thing, grows by degrees which are proportionate to the light reflected in her face. The song of Matilda is more articulate as Dante approaches the stream beyond which she stands among the flowers. The clairvoyance of the teachers — for their courtesy is best expressed by their power to anticipate the questions

Dante will ask — moves to its natural climax in Beatrice, whose radiant smile, signifying her willingness to instruct him, accompanies at last these words:

> I tell, not ask, that which thou fain wouldst
> hear; for I have seen it where every *where*
> and every *when* is focussed.

As for the light which Dante by some miracle always can increase, for in many a canto it seems that he has reached the very death of words in his struggle with the brilliance about him, and yet he has not — light grows as hope grows, and charity, and faith; and as, in the intellect and the will, activity replaces effort. Nor is it neutral with respect to these things. Itself is a great person, warm and joyful, sparkling in the eyes of saints who nevertheless are hidden in it as in their own gladness. Light conceals light, sphere within sphere, as the petals of the divine rose have other petals over which they curl, protecting some innermost scent, some most ineffable song.

The *Divine Comedy* is crowded with persons, even in Paradise where they are not corporeal. Dante cannot do without individuals. His thought is subtle, but it is not content with figments. In the only life that men can understand, the characters and deeds of other men are what they understand; these are the language in which truth is written. The poem, therefore, is among other things a roll call of emperors and popes, merchants and soldiers, friars, priests, thieves, murderers, liars, lovers, and ladies good or bad. In every canto Dante has his interlocutors who by their curses, by their confessions, or by the beatitude they breathe distil the meaning from whatever place they occupy. Cacciaguida, the ancestor of Dante who in Paradise directed him to write what we are reading, told him why persons would be necessary in his poem:

> Therefore have been displayed to thee, in
> these wheels, upon the mount, and in the
> dolorous vale, only souls known to fame;
> for the soul of him who heareth resteth not,
> nor fixeth faith by an example which hath
> its root unknown and hidden, nor other
> inconspicuous argument.

Cacciaguida meant real persons, with real names. So Dante's people are not invented; he takes them where he finds them, in his own experience or in the history of Florence, Italy, and the world. Without such verifiable individuals the argument will be "inconspicuous," and the truth without example. The result is sometimes deplored by those who call the *Divine Comedy* not only a clock and a chessboard but a gazetteer, a pedantical dictionary of biographies best forgotten. But Dante's people could be dispensed with only at the peril of losing his poetry, which if it is in any one thing is in the procession of persons he meets. Nor is it necessary to know of them all that he knew. Francesca lives chiefly here, and so does many another celebrated shade. Vanni Fucci, making his indecent and blasphemous gesture at God, is self-confessed.

Brunetto Latini, who as he turns away from Dante seems "like one of those who run for the green cloth at Verona through the open field," and of those seems "he who gains, not loses," is immortalized by that tender irony. The noble judge Nino, eager in Purgatory to send messages to earth, could not be better known than by the words he speaks:

> By that especial grace which thou owest to
>   him who so hideth his first purpose
>   that there is no ford to it,
> when thou art beyond the wide waters, tell
>   my Giovanna that she pray for me there
>   where the innocent are heard.
> I do not think her mother loves me more,
>   since she hath changed her white wimples,
>   which hapless she must long for once again.
> By her right easily may be known how long
>   the fire of love doth last in woman, if
>   eye and touch do not oft rekindle it.

Nor is anything added to the beauty of this passage by our learning that the widow who married again was Beatrice of Este.

Nino's concern is partly with himself but it is more with those he has left living behind him. The concern of the infernal spirits was with their own reputations. Dante could always use the promise of more fame — even a worse fame — than they already had as he sought to extract their stories from them; some grabbed at the bait, some growled that they did not care, some merely asked that their enemies on earth be got even with through tales carried back. In Paradise the thoughts of those with whom Dante speaks are entirely generous: they ask of others, not of themselves, and if they desire fame, it is the fame of them they love. Here is another progression which the reader's memory adds to a list already long.

The most interesting person in the poem, if it is permissible to except the one who is its Person, is Dante himself. He is no Narcissus; the poem is not a mirror he constructs so that he may contemplate himself. But he is a passionate man whose every utterance expresses him, and his qualities are of the deepest interest. His sin is pride, he tells Sapia in Purgatory. Not envy, though for one instance of that sin in his life he expects to have his sight taken from him.

> Greater far is the fear wherewith my soul is
> suspended, of the torment below, for even
> now the burden down there weighs upon me.

He still remembers the proud spirits bent double beneath their slabs of stone. And this seems proper, for he is indeed a person proud even to harshness and arrogance. Far from underestimating himself as a poet, he ranks himself at once with the greatest who have lived. The "lords of highest song" in Limbo, Homer and the rest, salute him when they see him, and make him one of their number, "so that I was a sixth amid such intelligences." Nor will he condescend to tell us what they spoke of among themselves:

> Thus we went onwards to the light, speaking
> things which it is well to pass in silence,
> as it was well to speak there where I was.

So in Purgatory it is a song of his own that Dante asks
Casella to sing. And if Dante is humble in the presence
of Virgil and Statius, walking behind them as they discourse of poesy, he permits Guido Guinicelli, whom
he has praised, to praise him in return by speaking of
those poems "so deep and clear that Lethe cannot take
them away, nor make them dim."

The wrath of which Dante is certainly capable is
nowhere represented as sinful wrath, nor within the
limits of the poem is he angry in his own person. But
he is a perfect scholar in the passion. The angers of
Virgil and the angel before Dis are accurately done, and
so are the ignoble furies manifested by the fiends.
Dante's own loathing of these fiends is expressed in
the iciest terms:

> Master, I should be glad to see him dipped
> in this swill ere we quit the lake.

> A little after this, I saw the muddy people
> make such rending of him that even now I
> praise and thank God for it.

> To be rude to him was courtesy.

The ice betrays what waters lie beneath, but itself is
never broken.

His pity — for Francesca, for Brunetto, for Pier
delle Vigne — is of such a sort that Virgil must rebuke

it, as he does when Dante weeps for the diviners: "Art thou, too, like the other fools? Here pity lives when it is altogether dead. Who more impious than he that sorrows at God's judgment?" So his desire for knowledge, so intense that it is painful to him, is something of which he represents himself as the victim, not the beneficiary. Only one pain is greater, "an anguished dearth of knowing more."

Dante like Milton carries with him a sense of being fallen on evil days. Florence too is fallen from its sober and chaste height. All cities are — Lucca, Pistoia, Siena, Pisa, Genoa, and Florence again — all are corrupt in manners and confused in government. There is no government, and hence no peace, in Italy.

> Ah Italy, thou slave, hostel of woe, vessel
> without pilot in a mighty storm, no mis-
> tress of provinces, but a brothel! . . .
> And now in thee thy living abide not without
> war, and one doth rend the other of those
> that one wall and one foss shuts in.
> Search, wretched one, around thy sea-coasts
> by the shores, and then gaze in thy bosom,
> if any part of thee enjoy peace. . . .
> For the cities of Italy are all full of tyrants,
> and every clown that comes to play the par-
> tisan becomes a Marcellus.

In such a world Dante is an exile, doomed to "make trial of how salt doth taste another's bread, and how hard the path to descend and mount upon another's stair."

Peace is as precious to Dante as it was to Virgil, whom here the pilgrim through eternity reminds of his fourth *Eclogue*. But Dante can mean by the "new world" of that eclogue more than its author meant. He can mean the Christian peace for which Virgil was perhaps only groping. His golden age lies ahead, but it will be nothing like the age of Augustus upon which Virgil pinned his pathetic faith. Dante well understands that the golden age of old was like the Garden of Eden in that both were nurtured by gods who walked there in the cool of the evening. He does not make Virgil's mistake of supposing that the better time to come will be of such a sort. No better time will come at all until men on earth have government. These evil days are blamed by some on heaven, but the fault is here.

> Clearly canst thou see that evil leadership
> is the cause which hath made the world sin-
> ful, and not nature that may be corrupted
> within you.

> There is none to govern the earth, wherefore
> the human household so strayeth from the
> past.

Not original sin is the cause of present chaos, but sin so recent that Dante can name the sinners; and he does, and certain popes are among the lowest. Boniface VIII has degenerated upon the seat which itself does not degenerate; when Saint Peter denounces him, all heaven blushes the color of clouds at sunset. The mo-

nastic orders have deserted their vows, and priests are
fat with the filth of gain.

> Now the modern pastors must need be but-
> tressed on this side and on that, and
> have one to lead them on, so heavy are
> they, and one to hoist behind.
> With their mantles they o'erspread their
> palfreys, so that two beasts travel be-
> neath one hide; O patience, that so much
> endureth!

So it is to themselves that men must look for the good
world that government makes possible. Virgil looked
to the gods, but they were lying gods, and Augustus
was among them. That is why Virgil must remain in
Limbo, the insubstantial underworld where all pagans,
no matter what their human greatness, live sadly in
eternal gloom. They have been put there, not for
punishment but in logic, by the God whose light they
never saw. He is a God whose peace burns like a rose
in each heart that knows and loves him. The peace of
earth he leaves to the laws of men.

Dante thinks and feels this with the intensity that
makes him everywhere unique. "Even now the recollection" — it is a frequent phrase with him, for things
that happen to him are too real not to last. They all
survive into some vast moment, some present moment, which is ideally the time of the poem. Scholars
work out time-schemes for the *Divine Comedy*, but
their effort is largely wasted; the poem happens all at

once, and if it seems long, that is because not even the best mortal imagination knows how eternity is spent. When Dante does know, for the ultimate canto takes him to this knowledge, his imagination is eclipsed, his tongue is tied.

Meanwhile he feels to the human limit every phenomenon he encounters. The beams of love are not for him the sunshine of an idle day; he must learn to bear them, for they are too much at first, as Blake's little black boy was told by his mother. The journey always threatens to become impossible, Dante is never sure he can go on. Each turn of his experience shakes him to the root. No wonder he thinks at the beginning, as he follows Virgil through the brown air, that he must prepare himself "to bear the war both of the journey and the pity." Even then he knows that to possess all understanding, to travel everywhere through truth, must be in a sense to die. The Word, unless we are stronger than we think we are, is a crushing weight. The strength of Dante is sufficient only because it is given him by his guides. They do not minimize the difficulty, but they protect him against despair. When in Purgatory he is smitten by the brilliance of an angel so that against his will he must turn his eyes away, Virgil comforts him by saying:

> Soon will it be that to behold these things
> shall not be grievous to thee, but shall
> be a joy to thee, as great as nature has
> fitted thee to feel.

But nothing becomes easy except the path his feet fly over. Physical progress is at last a thing of which he ceases to be aware, but the beams of truth and love are by degrees more difficult to sustain. The hymn he hears in the Earthly Paradise he cannot report, because he did not "endure its melody outright." He is filled by joy in Paradise because for once — when he is talking with Cacciaguida — his mind can fill with gladness "and yet not be rent." But the divine music that sounds as he beholds the golden ladder of Jacob does not sound for him; it would shatter his ears, as at this stage Beatrice would shatter his eyes if she turned her full smile upon him. Later, when he has withstood the blinding vision of Christ's triumph, she can say to him:

> Open thine eyes and look on what I am;
> thou hast seen things by which thou
> art made mighty to sustain my smile.

The effort to do this, however, is nothing to the effort he must put forth when the Infinite Worth is to be seen. At that moment, in fact, it would have been death to look away.

> I hold that by the keenness of the living
> ray which I endured I had been lost,
> had mine eyes turned aside from it.

Therefore he could be bold, and was; and the poem ends.

But there has been no moment, in Hell, in Purga-

tory, or in Paradise, when Dante's gaze at things has
not been of that intense sort which Giotto painted on
the faces, and indeed in the postures, of his men and
saints. "I drew near my Guide with my whole body,"
says Dante once in Hell. And in Purgatory, as he
walks beside the proud spirits, he is "all bent" — as
they are — from the sympathy he feels. All that he
is — and wears, for the folds of his robe are eloquent
— expresses the fullness of his response to what he
sees. It is not surprising, then, that we too see things
we shall never forget, things delivered to us by the
testimony of two unresting eyes.

> As the lizard, beneath the mighty scourge
>    of the canicular days, going from hedge
>    to hedge, appears a flash of lightning,
>       if it cross the way:
> so, coming towards the bowels of the other
>    two, appeared a little reptile burning
>    with rage, livid and black as pepper-
>    corn.

Nothing in any part of the poem, or in any other poem,
is so startling as that midget monster in the seventeenth
division of Hell.

The drama of Dante's recognition scenes derives its
intensity from a similar source — the poet's peculiar
power to drape human figures with the telltale garments of desire. Most of the recognitions are of course
by Dante himself, but there is one of which he is
spectator, and because he is thus the third party he can

make a picture of it such as Giotto would have made.
Statius, asked by Virgil in Purgatory who he is, identifies himself as a Roman poet to whom the *Aeneid* had
been nurse and mother, for without it he would have
been nothing. His praise of it is so wonderful that
Virgil turns to Dante "with a look that silently said:
'Be silent.'" But with the best will in the world Dante
cannot restrain a smile; which Statius sees, and this
leads to Virgil's permitting that Dante declare the
truth:

> He who guideth mine eyes on high is that
>   Virgil from whom thou drewest power to
>   sing of men and gods.

And he has more to say, but Statius needs no more.

> Already was he stooping to embrace my Teacher's
>   feet; but he said: 'Brother, do not do so, for
>   thou art a shade, and a shade thou seest.'
> And he, rising: 'Now canst thou comprehend the
>   measure of the love which warms me toward thee,
>   when I forget our nothingness.'

The three grand parts of the *Divine Comedy* are ordered in a relation which the careful reader never tires
of contemplating. The thought that ordered them is
an even greater poem than the one we read. The details
of the poem we read are supreme in power, but the
whole is greater than their sum. The ugliness of Hell,
for instance, does not prevent its relation to the rest of
Dante's world from being beautiful. The function of

Hell is to be the visible, the grotesquely visible, place which it is. No other kind of evidence than the kind here presented to the sinners who once would not believe that Hell exists — and so were already in it while they lived — could convince them now. In this Hell they are convinced, for there could be no clearer proof of Grace than that they know they do not have it; they cannot deny that they long for "the sweet light" and "the beautiful stars" — not of Heaven, for of Heaven they feel only the far authority, but of the earth on which they wasted their lives. Their incapacity to long for any more than "the sweet world" and "the memory of men" is something of which they know God makes them conscious. The fact is beautiful, nor is it anything that can be described. Dante does not even state it. It is for us to understand. And when later on we do, the immense distance that separates us from Hell's hideous objects clothes them for us in a livid light which we can love because it shows to us still, no matter at what height we ride, the under side of truth. Nor are all the objects in Hell hideous. Francesca is not, and Odysseus — Ulysses now — is not. Ulysses is there because

> neither fondness for my son, nor reverence
> for my aged father, nor the due love that
> should have cheered Penelope,
> could conquer in me the ardor that I had to
> gain experience of the world, and of hu-
> man vice and worth;
> I put forth on the deep open sea . . .

He put forth, driven by his insatiable curiosity, to visit even "the unpeopled world behind the Sun," urging on his comrades with words like those of Milton's Satan when he tempted Eve:

> Consider your origin: ye were not formed
> to live like brutes, but to follow vir-
> tue and knowledge.

But a mountain appeared, dim with distance, and a tempest rose, and the ship's prow went down, "as pleased Another, till the sea was closed above us."

All of Dante's dead except those who cannot leave Hell enjoy the stars. The subterranean gloom of Homer's and Virgil's Hades, where even the most glorious spirits walked in a dusk like that of Dante's Limbo, is transcended as soon as the poet and his teacher issue into the "sweet hue of orient sapphire which was gathering on the clear forehead of the sky" at the approach to Purgatory. Now are visible "four stars never yet seen save by the first people" — the four cardinal virtues, lost in their purity by Adam and Eve. And there is the look of life again in "the sweet grass" and "the trembling of the sea." All, indeed, henceforth is life as Dante knows life. It would be new to Homer and Virgil. It is the upper side of truth, the eternity that Christianity recovered.

The souls in Purgatory are relatively free, but only relatively. The infernal wailings of those who have in eternity what they wanted in time recede before the singing of these who want what can still be had if they hasten to get it. They are spirits "whose sufferings both justice and hope make less hard." They too are in a fire, but it is one that refines them. They are learning how to lose remorse, to look upward and not downward. Virgil cannot take Dante all of the way through this mid-region of the world. He must return to "the woeful realm" whence an angel had brought him thus far for Dante's comfort.

> There dwell I with those who clad them not with
> the three holy virtues, and without offence
> knew the others and followed them all.

Virgil may not possess even the relative joy that Purgatory makes possible. He must disappear as the intellect disappears when truth comes in sight. Beatrice, who replaces him as Dante's guide, is what Virgil could never be: "a light between truth and intellect." She of the shining eyes is a transformed and rapt Athene, a divine person whose wisdom is the love her gaze reflects. Virgil's speech of farewell is the speech of a great gentleman and scholar, but Beatrice is something greater yet. And the greatest thing is yet to come.

It comes in Paradise, where Dante's poetry demands of us the exercise of all the reason and imagination we possess. This heaven is not a work of fancy; for Dante it is what it must be, not what it may be. It is built out of the hardest mental stuff, although the bliss it pictures is impalpable. Its beatitude is graded, but there is harmony among the degrees, and no spirit but finds peace in God's will. In the politics of eternity, which Virgil never knew, peace is not made by man. It is made *for* him — if faith, hope, and love in him are perfect. The three holy virtues are tested in Dante by Saints Peter, James, and John; the stars disappear in pure light which puts them out:

> light intellectual full-charged with love, love
> of true good full-charged with gladness,
> gladness which transcendeth sweetness,

a light "in river form, tawny betwixt banks painted with marvellous spring"; Beatrice ascends to her circle among the saints; and now only Bernard and Mary remain as intercessors between the poet and the vision he has come so far to see. The vision is granted him in the ending canto, each tercet of which is itself a folded rose, a periodic sentence of the fullest and deepest rapture. All of them together move him with grave and steady ecstasy to the moment for which everything hitherto has been but preparation, the center toward which every line of the poem has been plunging. He is looking straight into the eternal light. He knows all things at once. The facts of life for him are found.

> Within its depths I saw ingathered, bound
> by love in one volume, the scattered
> leaves of all the universe;
> substance and accidents and their relations,
> as though together fused, after such fash-
> ion that what I tell of is one simple flame. . . .
> But already my desire and will were rolled — even
> as a wheel that moveth equally — by the love
> that moves the sun and the other stars.

# VII · THE
# FAERIE QUEENE

To CALL *The Faerie Queene* a philosophical poem is to compliment it, not to praise it. Whatever else it may be ordered by, it is not ordered by intensity. There is so little concentration in it upon a single visionary goal that many, indeed, have found it monotonous in its variety, and therefore, since it is endless, dull. The mistake of finding it so is most easily made by those who suppose that Spenser's queer masterpiece is to be compared with Dante or even with Lucretius; or by those who, refusing to credit its author with an intellectual design, look idly among its pages for the "mere" delight which legend says is there. Read slowly, and with a care which nothing at first glance seems to call for, it works its reward. The adventurer among its stanzas who listens to each word, each line, letting each unit of whatever length canter at its own pace through his understanding, will discover that a knight of poetry, on broad horseback, moves gracefully — if rather primly, with a certain old-fashioned and charming stiffness — through unbounded meadows of discourse.

Spenser insisted that they were moral meadows, and they are; and they are agreeable, even if unfenced. Spenser deserves the epithets that have so long been standard for him. He is sage and serious. He is nothing more. He is a virtuoso in verse, and the master of a certain style which nobody else can use; but at his center he is an intellectual amateur, a gentleman moralist, a high-Renaissance Englishman who writes better than he thinks and feels. He loves poetry more than he loves truth. And he is drunk with allegory. But he does not know how to make it his inspiration. The heroes whom he sends riding among the pitfalls set to test their virtue are priggish in their triumph, nor is the meaning of their triumph certain save in the book of manners which Spenser consults. Spenser is interested in virtue or he would not be a man; but he is not abstract enough — passionately abstract — to be either the philosopher or the story-teller he thought he was. When his Red Cross Knight is conducted by an aged holy man to the top of a mountain whence he can gaze at heaven, all that Spenser can say about this heaven is that it is built of pearl and precious stone. It is "too high" a subject for his "simple song." But his song is normally not simple, at least in the sense of lacking complication. It is all too bewilderingly subdivided, section within section; and there are times when Spenser boasts of the great things, unat-

tempted yet by other poets, with which he has to deal
— his poem, he says, must push itself through "strange
ways where never foot did use." He confesses to simplicity only when he is at a loss to say what he sees.
On such occasions his thought has not given him
enough to see.

His unconvincing heroes are virtues on horseback
— an impossible conception. Spenser has a beautiful
desire that their adventures should seem profound, and
he regularly has a right lyric feeling about the states
they represent. But that is it. They represent rather
than embody. The quaint pedantry which thus conceived them bears no resemblance to the passion we
find in Dante, or to the obsession we honor in Lucretius. Some stanzas in the fourth book are a translation
of the magnificent rushing lines with which the *De
Rerum Natura* opens. The difference is edifying.
Spenser is candid, transparent, clear; but his waters
show no depth. They are the waters of a poetry whose
source is not a single spring. Spenser, even more than
Milton, is an eclectic poet. Somebody else might have
made harmony out of philosophy and romance, out
of Aristotle's temperance and Prince Arthur's courtesy, but Spenser has not done so. He has made at
best a medley — of ancient reason and medieval
magic — and set it to the vaguely ideal music of his
"Antique Time." His faerie land is not the universe
anatomized. It is a gentle map of the moral life, a
colored chart of the human career, made from ma-
terials such as line the average man's imagination. The

imagination of Spenser was, and could be, no better than his thought. Too much of his poetry is borrowed without being paid for. He is called a scholar among poets, as Milton is, but neither of them is the success in scholarship that Dante is. For Dante, knowing what he needed, took only that. His vision did not fade as it was fed.

If Spenser dodges the responsibility of describing heaven, as Dante certainly does not, he accepts the dare of hell because he thinks it a less important place. But because he thinks so, the hell we find in the first book is no more than one out of a hundred picturesque places which ornament the poem. There is no detail in it that we shall necessarily remember. So with the little ship, the "feeble bark" which Spenser is always calling his poem. The metaphor is Dante's, but the rigging is too fancy in the present case; there are tackles, a main sheet, a card, a compass, a pilot, and stars to steer by; and the craft is loaded in one stanza with jolly mariners. Also, the metaphor gets abandoned for another; *The Faerie Queene* becomes a team of plowhorses that pull a coulter. The edges of Spenser's objects never shine with the special light which in Dante falls on things and defines them. Spenser commits himself as Dante does to light as a medium for truth and poetry. But when he apologizes to Queen Elizabeth for wrapping her identity in shadows,

> That feeble eyes your glory may behold,
> Which else could not endure those beamës bright,
> But would be dazzled with exceeding light;

or when he has the Red Cross Knight drop his eyes
before the man of God who has shown him heaven because they are dazed

> Through passing brightness, which did quite confound
> His feeble sense, and too exceeding shine.
> So dark are earthly things compared to things divine!

he merely reminds us that Dante, unlike himself, felt
light as a mystical force. With Spenser it is the common coin of a much less notable realm.

He knows Homer only in the accidents anyone may
know. He has his Circe, his Sirens, his Cyclops, and
his Penelope; and the mother of Marinell, Cymoent
under the sea, is to her son as Thetis was to Achilles.
But there is no suggestion of the simple power which
in Homer achieves the emphasis desired and leaves
every outline permanent. Spenser would scarcely have
perceived that Homer has his allegory too, though it
is not formal or confessed, as Dante's is. Achilles,
Athene, Odysseus, Penelope — they mean everything we can see them meaning, they rest on all the
ideas men possess. But Spenser's ideas are not the ideas
of men. They are the ideas of romance.

His allegory calls names. Abstractions become persons, mount horses, and ride off; and the farther they
go, the less distinct their definition. At the worst they
simply encounter other names — Strife, Fury, Occasion, Excess and Defect, Despetto and Decetto, Fidessa
and Duessa, Sansfoy, Sansjoy, Sansloy, Elissa and
Perissa, Priamond, Diamond, Triamond, Wrath, Lust,

and Despair. This is the worst, that is to say, unless the House of Alma is, that incredible dwelling whose rooms as we read are all too patently the parts of the human body, with personified agents directing each familiar process from judgment to digestion. Gardante, Parlante, Jocante, Basciante, Bacchante, Noctante — such people, nevertheless, prancing in verbal parades through halls that exist for no reason except to display them, are fair competitors with Alma's house for the honor of standing on the lowest sands ever surveyed by allegory.

From such antics of the imagination we can learn nothing. Didacticism in pictures is didacticism still. Nor can we be sure what thing it is we are supposed to be learning. Duessa stripped of her fine clothes is discovered to have rotten gums, a scurvy head, sour breath, dried dugs, and at her rump a fox's tail; furthermore, one of her feet is like an eagle's talon and the other is like a bear's paw. "Such," says Una who is Truth, "such is the face of Falsehood." But the face of Duessa who was so beautiful — how did it cover this one, and is it Falsehood that is so hideous, as of course should be the case, or is it merely Spenser's monster? If we learn anything, it is that we shall never know Falsehood when we meet her, for she will not look like this. So with Triamond in the fourth book. Friendship must be a relation of equals, but Triamond, who would be a friend to Cambalo, is only one third as good a man. He is not eligible, therefore, until his two brothers Priamond and Diamond have been slain and he has absorbed their souls. This is possible because the three brothers had natures as remarkable as their names:

> As if but one soul in them all did dwell,
> Which did her power into three parts divide.

Such truth as there is in the principle does not appear in the application. Indeed, Spenser's machinery mashes it as flat as conscious moralizing in him usually is. He is not without his morals, but they are never to be found in such fantasies as the foregoing.

Neither are they to be found in the preambles to his several books and cantos — where, as if he knows the ensuing allegory will not turn the trick, he gives us his doctrine straight.

> Whoever doth to Temperance apply
> His steadfast life, and all his actions frame,
> Trust me, shall find no greater enemy
> Than stubborn Perturbation to the same. . . .

> What war so cruel, or what siege so sore,
> As that which strong Affections do apply
> Against the fort of Reason evermore,
> To bring the soul into captivity! . . .

> What virtue is so fitting for a knight,
> Or for a lady whom a knight should love,
> As Courtesy: to bear themselves aright
> To all of each degree as should behove? . . .

Here is poetry at its weakest. It is written in the awareness that what comes after will be weak. For Spenser could not have been so happy among his personifications as scholars since have been. He would have done better if he could.

With all that he has, however, he goes manfully on with his business, which is to show how certain knights who are virtues in the flesh learn what is involved in the practice of those virtues. The Red Cross Knight of the first book is in love with Una as Faith is in love with Truth; but whereas she is a good lover, steadfast and wise, he is a poor one, for he is wandering and unaware. He is safe with obvious Error but he has no Judgment, he cannot penetrate disguises. Falling into the hands of Pride, he is rescued and disciplined by Humility and Reverence; then, made proof against Despair, he is ready to proceed and slay the dragon he had sworn to slay for Una's sake. His quest is not so much for the mean of his virtue, since Holiness can have no mean, as for the virtue itself, which Judgment merely perfects him in; but if we insist upon a defect and an excess, wishing to hold Spenser to his claim that he is Aristotelian, he supplies them in Sansfoy (No Faith) and Corceca (Superstition).

In the second book, whose hero is Sir Guyon (Temperance), the mean is very much in evidence. The House of Medina, where we find Elissa (Too Little) and Perissa (Too Much), is where it lives; as the House of Alma, besieged by the Seven Deadly Sins and the Five Temptations of the Senses, is Temperance's own dwelling. But it is not Sir Guyon's dwelling. It is merely one of the many places he visits, for he has far to go and much to learn. He must be tutored in the perils of Angry Passion, Worldly Power, Idle Mirth, Lasciviousness, and Foolhardiness. A Palmer goes with him, a lecturing Polonius, to explain what everything means, so that he issues from the book a thoroughly instructed knight — instructed, at any rate, in the book of his virtue. He knows, that is to say, as much as we do when the ordeal is done.

The third book has a heroine, not a hero. Britomart (Chastity) loves Artegall (Justice), whom she pursues through both this book and the next one, sharing the foreground she graces with three other ladies, Florimell, Belphoebe, and Amoret. The two books together explore the varieties and refinements of Friendship and Love, which by Spenser's analysis are made to appear in substance a single virtue, corruptible only when Suspicion, Jealousy, or Lust is present and operative.

The fifth book is all about the Justice which Artegall — the perfect lover for Britomart, since he is the prime public virtue as she is the prime one of the private life — studies in many places as he pushes his quest against Grantorto, who probably is political in his reference, standing for the King of Spain or for the Pope. We learn in this book about Distributive Justice and Corrective Justice, in the service of which terms we meet Deceit, Violence, Equality, Mercy, Cruelty, Pillage, and Slander.

The last book that Spenser was able to finish, the sixth book, containing the legend of Sir Calidore, or

Courtesy, deals with a virtue which has been Spenser's concern throughout, and which would have continued to be his concern in all of the eighteen further books he would have written had he been granted the good fortune to live forever. But the tale of Calidore provides an opportunity to handle at close range certain select articles of the creed. The hero is occupied with Decorum, Condescension, Simplicity, and Noblesse.

Such a summary of *The Faerie Queene* commits outrage upon it by ignoring a thousand nice details and by failing to distinguish between the two levels on which Spenser's allegory rides. It accentuates the lower level, which in one sense is fair. For only thus can the basic weakness of the poem, the weakness that has prevented it from becoming a poem of world importance, be thrown into clear relief. This basic or structural weakness is perhaps not balanced by the thousand nice details — the woodland scenes, the innumerable pursuits, the delicious bowers, the tantalizing mishaps, the delicate dames and vile ogres, the sweet vales and wild seashores — of a poem which sooner or later contains everything except life as men and women live it.

But it is almost balanced by the greater success which Spenser sometimes achieves in his delineation of the virtues — in, that is to say, the allegory by which he must have thought, and thought correctly, his poem would stand or fall. Any story stands or falls by its allegory: by what it is able to mean. But it had better mean more than words with capital letters. It means most, paradoxically, when we are not easily able to say what it means; when its truth is buried in its life as blood is buried in the functioning flesh. It means most of all when it is so much like what happens to us, or what could happen to us, that we remember and believe rather than interpret and annotate. Meaning of such a sort is found in Homer, Dante, and Shakespeare. And it appears, if imperfectly, in *The Faerie Queene*.

It appears there as soon as we feel, if we do, that Una and the Red Cross Knight love each other as persons instead of as qualities. To the extent that we can find their meaning in their acts, their moral in their love, we have something better than a narrative arrangement of ethical texts. Una and her learning lover do not wholly succeed in giving us this better thing, though Una touches us most tenderly. But Britomart does succeed — all alone, Britomart saves the poem from disaster.

She puts her poet's pedantry to rout. The first moment she appears, nature and human nature revive; and by contagion the other persons of the poem learn suddenly how to enjoy themselves. For she is not Love. She is in love. We never doubt her happiness when she is close to Artegall, her unhappiness when something separates them. We share her anxiety, we participate in her triumph. She is flawless in her constancy and strength, but that does not make us disbelieve her. On the contrary, we have in her the one thing we have a right to expect from romance — perfection miraculously alive. She is real as Shakespeare's

Imogen is real, in the completeness and frankness of her devotion, in the simplicity, both physical and unphysical, of her passion. With her there comes into *The Faerie Queene* a richer art, sumptuous and sentimental; the woods and seas are fresh again, and oxygen in the people tints their cheeks. Florimell and Marinell, Amoret and Scudamour, Timias and Belphoebe — they all pick up as soon as Britomart is there. All of Spenser's women surpass his men in naturalness and power, but the queen of them is Britomart. It is she who rescues the fifth book from the dulness which Spenser's ideas about justice threaten to kill it with. Her expedition in this book to save Artegall from Radigund is inspired as jealousy is inspired. For Britomart can be jealous, just as she can be overjoyed, and just as she can sweat. Invincible in combat, she yet can be disarmed; and the removal of her helmet reveals not only cascades of golden hair but flushed cheeks

> Dewèd with silver drops through sweating sore.

No single fact authenticates Britomart better than this one does, or more endears her to us. It has the force fact always has in poetry, a force with which Spenser too seldom is on intimate terms.

If Britomart does not altogether save *The Faerie Queene*, the reason must be that there was too much bulk to rescue. Sir Calidore throws in his weight, but it is not enough. Courtesy, as has been said, is Spenser's subject over all; and the sixth book is entirely dedicated to it. But it is a book in which Calepine, giving the childless Matilda an infant boy to bring up, can advise her that she has two alternatives with respect to his education: she can train him in chivalry or she can make him a philosopher. This is a strange thing to find in a poem which itself is trying to be philosophical. The distinction should be impossible. That it is not so with Spenser helps to explain why ethics for him is the same thing as etiquette. Virtue is what gentlemen do. It is a code both natural and contrived, as is proved by the marvelous manners of courteous Calidore,

> Whose every act and deed, that he did say,
> Was like enchantment, that through both the eyes
> And both the ears did steal the heart away.

The Savage Man who is so important in the sixth book tempts us at first to suppose that being one of nature's gentlemen is better than being one whom the court, that "great schoolmistress of all courtesy," has trained. But even the Savage Man turns out to have in him the noble blood which for Spenser is necessary to a virtuous life. Virtue is the property of a class, the gentleman class, as venery is. What else than hunting could "banish sloth that oft doth noble minds annoy"? Only one thing: horsemanship. Try as he may, the common man cannot deceive us once he is on a horse.

> In brave pursuit of honorable deed,
> There is I know not what great difference
> Between the vulgar and the noble seed,
> Which unto things of valorous pretence

> Seems to be borne by native influence,
> As feats of arms; and love to entertain;
> But chiefly skill to ride seems a sciénce
> Proper to gentle blood: some others feign
>    To manage steeds, as did this vaunter; but in vain.

Fighting, hunting, and riding — these are not for the "rascal many," the "rude rabblement."

Sir Calidore is handicapped as a hero not, of course, by having good manners but by having to be conscious of them. This makes him a prig, and, what is worse than that, a condescending prig. When he sojourns among the shepherds he assures them that their "mean food" will be good enough for him, and he takes part in their merrymaking — because he loves Pastorella — just as if he were one of them, though he knows they know that he is not. His endeavor is

> To shew the courtesy by him profest
> Even unto the lowest and the least.

And he does the best he can. But his best is only as good as Spenser's ideas of courtesy and virtue are. There is something the matter with Spenser's ideas, both here and in the book on justice, where his chief fear seems to be lest the poor get money and the gentry be disenthroned. Courtesy and justice are perhaps not very far apart, and Spenser is aware of this. But he misses the simple insight of Socrates and Hamlet, for whom justice is not so much what a man does as what he has or is. It is the harmonious result of other virtues. Spenser never penetrates so far into the mystery of good men.

Since he is not penetrating he cannot be brief. His lack of depth has to be made up for by a lot of breadth. Surface with Spenser is everything. But surface in poetry is no substitute; even this fragment of the poem Spenser planned is nearly thirty-five thousand lines long, and yet it is clear that *The Faerie Queene* could never have been long enough to count with its competitors. Its merits, which are real, are watered down.

The narrative art of Spenser keeps itself going with pursuits and surprises. These are innumerable, and most of them are nicely managed, but they are too uniform, too equal in their strength — which means, by art's arithmetic, in their mildness. Since there is frequent disguise there is frequent recognition, and Britomart's unveilings have indeed their special excitement; but even they are lost at last in the series, as are dozens of psychological details which in another context might have been powerful. Spenser, like any poet who has cut himself off from natural sources of power, must cultivate the artifice of sensation. In order to maintain our attention, for instance, he must keep his dames in peril. He likes nothing more than an opportunity to show delicate ladies undergoing dreadful damage. The damage in most cases will be repaired, but while it lasts we cannot help looking. The more snow-white the victims, the grimmer — or more grotesque — the violence. The lovely Florimell, so desperately pursued that she jumps from her palfrey into a fishing boat and rows away, discovers that the

old man asleep in it is himself a lecher, for when he
wakes up he at once assaults her, filling "her garments
gay with scales of fish." The still lovelier Amoret, kid-
napped by a wild man, awaits the double fate of
being deflowered and eaten. Both of Serena's tender
sides are ripped open by the Blatant Beast. And Pastorella, most delicious of all such girls, is buried to the
point of suffocation beneath the carcasses of brigands
who fight like boars to see who shall possess her. To
the point of suffocation, yet not past it. She too is
saved so that she may suffer again.

Sensation has its limits, however, and Spenser is
always reaching them; after which he has nowhere to
go save into more sensation. We have here an undistinguished series, as in the landscape of Spenser's
romance we have an undistinguished spread of standard wonders — a bleeding branch, a curative well, all
manner of magic herbs, all varieties of vanishing or of
metamorphosis. The poet's industry is amazing, but
he cannot amass enough such things to matter. So
with his pretty places — his Bower of Bliss, his Temple
of Venus, his Garden of Adonis, and his Idle Lake.
They have every familiar feature except the one feature, whatever it is, that would make us believe them.
They are concocted by recipe, like the pastoral world
which we often visit, and like the golden age which
by this time is but an inane memory:

> For during Saturn's ancient reign it's said
> That all the world with goodness did abound;
> All lovèd virtue, no man was afraid

> Of force, ne fraud in wight was to be found;
> No war was known, no dreadful trumpet's sound;
> Peace universal reign'd 'mongst men and beasts,
> And all things freely grew out of the ground:
> Justice sat high ador'd with solemn feasts,
> And to all people did divide her dread beheasts.

Neither Plato's thought nor Virgil's dream survives in such a stanza; nor, certainly, does Dante's indictment of a world that has forgotten how to govern itself.

The art of Spenser is in any of its aspects an extensive art. His world is spread thin — even by his words, which in spite of their great number seem all to have an equal force. In the long run this means a lack of force. Spenser depends at last upon his style, but it is a style that dodges difficulty and is most comfortable when most diffuse. The imagery never short-circuits itself, never generates heat by resisting convention. The epithets are the expected ones, the ones that have always come with these nouns; they do not add to our knowledge, they do not appropriate the function of substantives and verbs as Shakespeare's for example do. They supply at best the kind of color that comes in tapestry; no hue is independent of a general effect for which the name long since was lost. Una neglected is a "forsaken, woeful, solitary maid." Any dragon in the poem has a body "monstrous, horrible, and vast." Night is "grisly," with "visage deadly sad," and never dares to view the "cheerful face" of Phoebus. The enemies of Temperance are "wicked," "foul," and "ugly," and their numbers are "huge and infinite." Exceptions like the "bright dew-burning blade" of Una's champion or like the "sudden eye" of a certain Sarazin are pitiful in their fewness, and impotent to bestow upon Spenser's surface the genuine brightness it seems ever to be aiming at. For it is not true that Spenser is trying to be dull. He is trying to be brilliant. But the only trick he knows is exaggeration, just as the only narrative device he had at his command was more and more sensation.

> Therewith she spu'd out of her filthy maw
> A flood of poison horrible and black,
> Full of great lumps of flesh and gobbets raw,
> Which stunk so vilely, that it forc'd him slack
> His grasping hold, and from her turn him back:
> Her vomit full of books and papers was,
> With loathly frogs and toads, which eyes did lack,
> And creeping sought way in the weedy grass:
> Her filthy parbreake all the place defilèd has.

In the style of this famous stanza will be felt, perhaps, both sensation and exaggeration. The stanza which balances it in the first book — as Holiness balances Error — is famous too, and of course its contents are pleasanter to contemplate. But its subtlety is no greater.

> A little lowly hermitage it was,
> Down in a dale, hard by a forest's side,
> Far from resort of people, that did pass
> In travel to and fro: a little wide
> There was an holy chapel edifyde,

Wherein the Hermit duly wont to say
His holy things each morn and eventide:
Thereby a crystal stream did gently play,
Which from a sacred fountain wellèd forth alway.

Spenser must exaggerate because he has lost contact
with emphasis. This is the way he seeks it again, but it
cannot be found. We are not impressed by Clarinda's

private fire, which boil'd
Her inward breast, and in her entrails fried.

We cease to be horrified by inwards gushing forth
when churls are wounded, just as we tire of the endless
galleries where ideal paintings hang of sylvan bowers
and simpering beauties. The blood which in Spenser
flows so freely is there perhaps to intensify the tapestry,
but there is too much of it for the purpose. Sometimes
it is called "gore" for variety, and even "bloody gore."
Whatever it is called, it comes in streams, rivers, ponds,
lakes, and wells — Spenser's own terms, and they are
self-defeating. Who would have believed these faerie
people to have had so much blood in them? They never
had it. It is Spenser's brush at work, overtime and in
the wrong places.

Any poet who banks upon description as Spenser
does is bound at moments to go overboard. Worship-
pers of beauty have bad taste. Taste comes from a
deeper source than Spenser knows, or else he would
not have gone on with his account of Belphoebe's
charms until he reached her legs:

> Like two fair marble pillars they were seen,
> Which do the temple of the gods support,
> Whom all the people deck with garlands green,
> And honor in their festival resort.

If Belphoebe is Queen Elizabeth, that lady is substantially exposed. So is Frances Walsingham if Pastorella stands for her. For Pastorella rises on

> goodly thighs whose glory did appear
> Like a triumphal arch, and thereupon
> The spoils of princes hang'd which were in battle won.

A man who writes thus would seem to be without any sense at all of the value words can have. And it is true that Spenser scatters some of his words through lines which have never been matched for emptiness:

> My lord, my love, my dear lord, my dear love.

> We would and would again, if that we could.

> Come, daughter, come; come, spit upon my face;
> Spit thrice upon me, thrice upon me spit.

> He grinn'd, he bit, he scratch'd, he venom threw,
> And farèd like a fiend right horrible in hue.

> That is our Self, whom though we do not see,
> Yet each doth in himself it well perceive to be.

It is also true that he can put more than nothing in a little line:

> But he, my lion, and my noble lord.

> Whose life did lie in her least eye-lid's fall.

> Cover'd with cold, and wrapt in wretchedness.

Writing of such a sort, however, is rare in *The Faerie Queene*, and it never is dominant.

The dominant merit of Spenser is his music. This is a secondary merit, since it defies translation, but for any English reader it is real. Spenser is never at a loss to find melody in his matter, a sweet and unending melody which is none the less attractive because it is without accent. The triumph of *The Faerie Queene* is finally that it converts its weakness of sense into a charm of sound. Alliteration ripples through it as a light wind kisses the sea, not so much separating its tones as blending them into a oneness that whispers, a music that accompanies itself as with the rustle of brushes.

> And, more to lull him in his slumber soft,
> A trickling stream from high rock tumbling down,
> And ever-drizzling rain upon the loft,
> Mixt with a murm'ring wind, much like the sown
> Of swarming bees, did cast him in a swown.
> No other noise, nor people's troublous cries,
> As still are wont t' annoy the wallèd town,
> Might there be heard: but careless Quiet lies,
> Wrapt in eternal silence far from enemies.

It is a soprano music, attenuated in its vowels and rhymes; but it is music.

Its vehicle is the famous stanza which still is the most Spenserian thing about Spenser. If he did nothing else he fashioned a verse machine, a unit of metrical power, capable of carrying what he had to carry. It is in its stanzas that his poem lives. Unless they are heard, *The Faerie Queene* will not be felt. And they should be heard clearly, with no muting of their mechanics. They are meant to seem mechanical, to rock on their cesuras with the regularity of a horse's gait. Spenser has said that his poem is a ship he sails, a team he drives; he might better have called it a palfrey on which he canters. It picks its way forever through a landscape of light words, all equally important or unimportant, and in every ninth line performs a little skip, delivers to us a little jolt, which we must not miss. Once we do miss it we lose interest in what we read, and cannot go on. Its regularity ought by rights to be maddening, but the contrary is the case; only its absence would make us lose our way. Its presence is to be noted even when there is no punctuation to tell the eye where it is. It is for the ear, not the eye, and the ear will break every alexandrine sharply in two if it wants to keep awake. The cesura may come in the middle of a word, but that will not matter. At times, indeed, the delay thus caused has bearing upon the sense: it helps Spenser to get the effect that is latent in his words. All of the following lines, and all other ending lines in Spenser's countless stanzas, should be read as if a wide crack, a long pause, yawned between their halves:

Fierce wars and faithful loves    shall moralize my song.

O, help thou my weak wit,    and sharpen my dull tongue.

As one for knightly jousts    and fierce encounters fit.

Yet nothing did he dread,   but ever was ydrad.

Upon his foe, a Drag   on horrible and stern.

And by her in a line   a milk-white lamb she had.

The carver holm; the ma   ple seldom inward sound.

He brusheth oft, and oft   doth mar their murmurings.

Which from a sacred foun   tain wellèd forth alway.

Wrapt in eternal si   lence far from enemies.

Birds, voices, instruments,   winds, waters, all agree.

The gentle warbling wind   low answerèd to all.

So discord oft in mu   sic makes the sweeter lay.

Wise, warlike, persona   ble, courteous, and kind.

Through the green grass his long   bright burnish'd back declares.

And often to him call   ing to take surer hold.

As plain as at the first   when they were fresh and green.

But dread of shame my doubt   ful lips doth still restrain.

Was meant to her that nev   er evil meant in heart.

So on and on, through woods and over water, through
thick and thin, goes Spenser's steed — the only creature that will take us to the finish.

Nothing less, and nothing greater, explains the remarkable fact that *The Faerie Queene* is continuously readable, and indeed is more readable the longer it gets. Spenser's staying powers are powers of verse. Every stanza renews his spell, so that in spite of platitude, and in disregard of much that is dull, we live again to feel the peculiar freshness of his antique world. It is a trite world, but he has tuned it to some sort of truth. It is a world in which there is nothing but poetry, nothing but lines among which we can lie down, half-sleepy, half-alert, and take our pleasure month on month.

> Sweet Spenser, moving through his clouded heaven
> With the moon's beauty and the moon's soft pace —

it is Wordsworth's poet that we defend, even against his own claim that he is philosophical.

Had he been philosophical he would not have committed the tactical error of taking comic poets as his models; for that is what he did. Much of his failure follows upon the fact that he is out of his element. His genius is slender, and so is not at home in the loose ways of laughter, in the tough world which practical wisdom holds together. It needs form within which it can feel itself prisoner, and the more exquisite this form the better. Spenser simply does not know how to use his models toward the great end comedy has in view. He has his jests, his ironies, and his dutiful gallantries, but he is at bottom humorless; he is too sage and serious for either tragedy or comedy, each of which must have some kind of lightness in it, even if

in the case of tragedy this be lightning. Spenser is
softer than he is light, though he has chosen, of all
poets, Ariosto for his master.

Ariosto, who gives him his hero and heroine, who
teaches him how to seem the free and leisurely man
he is not, who shows him how to abuse form by break-
ing stories off in their middles and completing them in
distant cantos, who is always at his side with irrelevant discourse and innuendo — Ariosto is indeed the
master of lightness, but his essential secret is not
available to this English poet who set out to give him
a moral tone. Ariosto could break down all things in
poetry and life until they harmonized with the odd
Muse he worshipped. Everything becomes fluid with
him and pours into the medley he is making. He is
melancholy, gay, impertinent, and solemn; he simul-
taneously feels a thing and makes fun of it; he is, in a
word, the genius of comedy let safely loose among
knights and ladies whose sufferings he for some reason
has decided to sing. Being what it is, the *Orlando
Furioso* can do a justice to its knights and ladies which
*The Faerie Queene* cannot do to their counterparts.
Ruggiero, Bradamante, and the rest are taken by
Ariosto neither more nor less seriously than they deserve; he preserves them in their natural juice, as
Chaucer and Cervantes do their people.

Chaucer is Spenser's other hero. And while Spenser
lived, the perfect poem of chivalry was being prepared
in Spain. But Spenser would have benefited no better
by Cervantes, whom he did not know, than by Ariosto

and Chaucer, whom he did. Comedy, the most intellectual of delights, tempted him beyond his range. To
comedy, it may be, he sacrificed his one hope of complete success. The success of comedy can be complete,
and in Chaucer is. Just how successful poetry can be
when it is sage and serious, and nothing else, we have
still to learn.

# VIII · TROILUS AND CRISEYDE

CHAUCER takes his time with the simple story he has to tell of two Trojan lovers and their go-between. He is leisurely by nature as Spenser was leisurely by contrivance; he is long — for such a story; and he is light. *Troilus and Criseyde* has everything in it, yet it weighs nothing. Its wise author pretends to be the most ignorant of men. He is the finest instance in narrative poetry of the comic genius at work, and hence belongs in any list of Calliope's great sons — or nephews, if Calliope cannot bend. In that case he is the son of Thalia, her sister. But no matter, he cannot be missing from any account of poetry when it is important. It is never more important than when it laughs.

Comedy does not limit laughter, nor insist that it be loud. Chaucer's laughter is seldom audible at all. But it is steadily there, in the view he keeps of Troilus, Criseyde, and Pandar, and of the human life in which for a moment of old time they touchingly participate.

· 257 ·

Comedy as Chaucer makes us understand it is half of human life; or the whole of it, seen in a certain way, with a certain eye. How Chaucer sees it *Troilus and Criseyde* makes clear. And the man who looks is quite as interesting as the spectacle that engages him; though he never forgets the spectacle, nor will it be forgotten by us whose view of it is shaped by the arch of his brows.

Comedy has no beginning and no end. Its field is the middle distance where riddles are not resolved. Consequently its works are long, since anything that is endless must be long. Wit and tragedy may be short, and indeed they had better be, or we shall not accept them. But humor, the soul of comedy, will not be dictated to. The soul of tragedy, as Aristotle observed, is plot, is action, and there comes a time when we know what the action meant. Humor means itself. It distributes itself everywhere through the work it graces; it is in the style, the digressions, the asides, it is in fact the whole long body of that work. It tells its story as certain old men tell theirs, in such a way that the point, the end to be reached, interests us less than the voice, the intonation, and even the delays. Such a story could go on forever, and we hope it will. It is not an anecdote, and though serious events may be involved it is not a tragedy.

Tragedy depends on form, but form is the one thing that comedy escapes and refuses. Chaucer, Ariosto, Cervantes, Fielding, Byron, Melville, like animals at play, are more aware of the good way they feel than of the object they chase. The story they tell is not the thing. They interrupt it at will to talk of this or that, confidentially, with an audience at whom they are not too dignified to peer around the edges of the frame. Are you interested in all this? — they seem to say; but I am more real, and so are you; truth is not trapped by narrative. They prefer criticism to crisis; they rebuke romance, they disturb illusion, they wreck a mood, they reduce all things to the common dimension nature gave them first, and will give them last.

Comedy seeks and insists upon the ordinary. Tragedy cannot do without the extraordinary person, the extreme event, but such things embarrass comedy. It returns us to the commonplace, the limited world where people are only what people can be. And it makes us love that world, for now we recognize in it what we knew was there but had not had the courage to accept as glorious. Our minds had not been tough enough to take things as they are. This is done very rarely, and we might think it impossible if in a few classics of comedy it had not been done well; or if our acquaintance did not include a few of those natural persons who do it every day, and easily.

Such persons, like the poets to whom they correspond, are geniuses at talk. Tragedy is action, but comedy is talk. It is interested in what people say, and hence is addicted to proverbs — the intellect at work along the highways. If a proverb is the wisdom of many and the wit of one, comedy's concern is with the many who think they are so wise. It is amused by assurance, which it can always correct with another proverb. But it does not despise old saws. They are the sign that people have talked, and this is what comedy loves to know. It learns from proverbs that the truth has never been nailed down. For comedy no worse thing could happen, for then talk would cease.

Good conversation goes up and down, is important or trivial according as the wind blows, is by turns sententious and inconsequential. But the one thing that it must be is inconclusive. There must always be more to say; truth would be a tragic thing if it could intervene and command henceforward a dead silence. Comedy's best answer to one question is to ask another — not smugly, as if it knew there was no best answer, for it does not presume to know so much, but with a smile that doubts at the same moment that it hopes. The vision of the comic spirit is not self-defeating. We may think so, observing that it never rests on any point as final. But then we shall be confusing it with cynicism. Comedy is as remote from cynicism as tragedy is. Once it has found its vein it goes on talking because it sees more light ahead than behind. It accepts no substitute for the sense of being where all possible light is shining — all possible light, and of course no more. It prefers the sun to the moon, for it is really serious in its love of illumination. Seated in sunlight, it does not fret or grow fanatical. It has the courage to wait and see, for it will not act before it knows. It rarely acts — ideally, it never acts, but like any other precious thing it has not yet been seen among men in ideal form. Meanwhile it denies that there is any time which is not a time for comedy. This would be like saying that there was no time for itself, or for intelligence.

When Socrates said that comedy and tragedy were like each other he may have meant that both of them are techniques — twin techniques — for revealing the inner inconsistencies of theories, for exposing the fact that we still do not know all it is possible to know. If they are twins they are not identical, yet they are very close together. Great tragedy is not sad, and great comedy is not silly. We learn from both. But whereas the technique of tragedy is the technique of discovering, by action and in time, the flaw in a hero's knowledge, our comic poet seems aware of it from the start. His pity, if pity be in order, is leavened with a smile, the smile of an ancient understanding. Comedy is old, it has seen all this before. It is not weary, but it is wise. Its laughter expresses a mind not vacant but if anything too full. Not, however, too full for feeling. Life has been said to be a comedy for those who think and a tragedy for those who feel. Thought and feeling are not so separable. When comedy misses feeling it is farce, and when tragedy is thoughtless it is melodrama. Dante, choosing the "lower style" of comedy, the style that hugs the ground and makes possible the mention of all things, was not prevented by this style from taking the most passionate interest in human error. But he did not melt the error he saw, as tragedy

melts error, in the intense and blinding heat of catas-
trophe past which nothing else is visible. Dante, like
the author of the *Odyssey* and like Chaucer, wanted
always to see more. What all of them saw, however,
they certainly felt. Lucretius, seeing less than everything, felt as tragedy feels. He was his own hero, revealing in act, in dogma, the limitation of a faith to
which fanaticism committed him. Chaucer is committed to nothing except the pity of understanding, the
laughter of a perspective so long and wide that cruelty
dies out before a sound arrives.

The theory of life that Chaucer brings to ground in
*Troilus and Criseyde* is the theory of courtly love, according to which love is everything, and if it is not
secret, is nothing. To say that Chaucer brings this
theory to ground is not to say that he does so to bruise
or kill it. The ground is where he thinks theories belong. They need air, but it is not good for them to be
inflated. If they are true at all they can live where men
live; like Antaeus, they are too severely tested when
they are lifted off their feet. Chaucer searches for the
truth in courtly love, and finds it — on the ground.
More of the thing his comedy criticizes survives in
him than survives in a thousand solemn tales of sancti-
fied adultery. Such tales cannot see what is sensible
in their creed and what is not. Chaucer sees what is
there to see, with eyes made sharp by affection's wit;
what is not there he silently laughs away. As chivalry
lives in *Don Quixote*, and pastoral sentiment in *As You
Like It*, so courtly love now lives in *Troilus and*

*Criseyde.* Chaucer has reduced it to proportions that make it credible, and he has done so without touching it at the heart. At the heart it is true to men's experience.

Love too widely known
Yields bitter fruit, though sweetest seed be sown.

"Love should grow in secrecy" — Chaucer knows that as well as anybody. But he is not thereby prevented from concluding that his thoroughly conventional lovers make too much fuss over their reputations. "Some folk will talk," "my honor and my name," "my good repute and fame," and "every gossip's word" — such phrases are too often on the lips of *Troilus and Criseyde*, and too easily, to mean more than that this couple is sensitive to a code. It is natural for lovers to want to be alone. That is enough for Chaucer. The rest is rubbish.

How he does what he does is perhaps his secret, but it is well to begin by saying that he is different from any other poet. He pays his respects to Homer, whose great story includes his little one, by summarizing the action of the *Iliad* in a single stanza, the ninth of the poem, and lets it go at that. What he borrows from Dante and Boethius he subdues to the new soil he embeds it in. And the poem of Boccaccio which he rewrites, *Il Filostrato*, he transforms wherever he pleases. He makes it much longer; and the places where he lengthens it are precisely the places that invite his comic muse. If it seems a paradox that his additions to the lean tale of Boccaccio are additions that develop the power of an old legend to touch us — this at the same time that they include many passages of mockery — the reason is that the comic muse is more mysterious than any of her sisters: when she is most herself she is most moving. Chaucer extends his source as often as he sees the opportunity to render Troilus and Criseyde more real. And this is still truer of Pandar, the matchmaker whose importance increases with his age. For the man who in Boccaccio was Criseyde's cousin becomes in Chaucer's hands her uncle; he is older, he is more imaginative, and above everything else he is ironic. Comedy has lived long, seen much, and decided little; so Pandar provides a medium in which the helpless love of Troilus can be viewed as the unique yet typical thing it is. As for the lovers themselves, Chaucer has lavished upon them, and particularly upon the young widow Criseyde, his most searching wisdom. He has with the same stroke accentuated their weaknesses and made them more difficult to judge. The very dishonesty of Criseyde, if that is what it is, endears her to us; and the simplicity of Troilus becomes the simplicity of a child whom it would be senseless either to blame or to indulge. The scenes of their love-making, elaborated with a care which itself is love, have no equal in any comedy or in any romance.

The comedy in *Troilus and Criseyde* is never so overt as to make it possible for one to seize upon a passage and say: It is here. It is not alone in Chaucer's asides to the reader, though they make their contribution. It is not alone in the character of Pandar, that older Mercutio to a still more youthful Romeo. It is not alone in the devious, the seductive Criseyde. In nothing can it be alone, for comedy is social, and occupies all of the available air. The comedy of *Troilus and Criseyde* is in the tone of the whole, a tone so delicately maintained that if we hear it at all we understand the legend that comedy is divine: the gods know best how, when, and why to smile. Troilus is denied a tragic death; it is Achilles, not Diomede, who kills him in battle, though it was Diomede who stole his mistress from him. But even that is not it. No single item is. The genius of the poem enjoys itself constantly and everywhere. For this is a poet who knows perfectly how "to walk both light and soft" — as Shakespeare did not choose to do when he retold the tale in *Troilus and Cressida*, his most savage and least successful comedy.

> Tisiphone, now help me to endite
> These woful lines, that weep e'en as I write!

Chaucer's invocation is sincere, for the words he writes will caress their subject, will pierce that subject and let forth its tears. But they will also be sensible words, steady with health and sane with reminders that the world is a wide place where even love is not alone.

The infantile Troilus whose lovesickness runs so true to medieval form is Chaucer's hero only in the sense that it is he to whom love happens — love,

whose true terrors Chaucer knows better than any
love-calf could. "Almighty Jove!" cries Pandar at one
point,

> Who ever saw a grown man acting so?

The sign for Chaucer that Troilus is not grown is
that he has no humor. Once he smiles weakly at a jest
of Pandar's, as Romeo, stricken in like fashion though
he is, once rises to a jest of his own, and overjoys
Mercutio. Yet by and large he has lost his wits — a
calamity which Chaucer understands and pities, but
is careful not to praise. Chaucer is more interested in
the woman who has stolen them, and in the friend who
vainly tries to bring them back.

Criseyde's superior strength, though not her superior virtue, consists in the fact that she cannot be
lost in love as Troilus is. She responds to his madness, but she is never mad in kind. The wildness of
his delusion — the delusion that no other woman exists — cannot but astonish her, for in the sanity she
keeps she knows that this is not true. However sweetly
she gives him what seems to be herself, the gift is in-
complete; she saves something out, as if she knew that
another man than Troilus exists — and Diomede in
the sequel does. It is not that she anticipates her treachery, or that treachery is the word for what so naturally
she does. It is simply that she never belongs to Troilus
in the same way that Troilus belongs to her. Nor does
Chaucer appear to suggest that she should. He no sooner
indicts her for desertion than he softens the charge to

unkindness. He does not know her secret well enough
to be sure that he can decide her fate with us. He
counts on her to seduce us, as she must, but he does
not insist that we be angry when she turns away and
listens to a Greek.

He describes her only once: she is of even height,
her hair is bound with a gold thread, her brows meet,
and her eyes are bright. But the last line of the description is probably the one with which his thought
began:

> Sedate she was, simple and wise withal,
> Instructed in the arts most carefully,
> Goodly of speech, whatever might befall,
> With kindly grace, both dignified and free;
> Nor lacked her heart in sensibility
> In all the things which sympathy engage,
> But I regret I cannot tell her age.

The taint of mockery there, of her and of us, the sudden slip from fancy into fact, is his way of saying that
Criseyde is beyond our reach. We know that her coy-
ness has some calculation in it, but we never know
how much. We observe her indecision, but cannot
name its motive. Soft though her flesh and voice can
be, there is some hardness in her that makes us wonder
what on earth she means when she tells Troilus she
loves him for his "moral virtue."

> Believe me well that neither vain delight,
> Nor royal rank, nor yet the high respect
> Or you in war, or in the tourney fight,

> Nor pomp, nor wealth, nor dress, did aught affect
> My heart, and thy sole image there erect —
> No, moral virtue, firmly set and true,
> That was the reason why I first loved you.

We do not believe this, yet we do not know what else to believe. It was not "vain delight" either — the thing we should most enjoy believing. And of course it was not that the father of Troilus was Priam. Our uncertainty as to why she loves Pandar's friend is almost the same thing as our uncertainty whether she loves him. She calls him "sweetheart" and means it, just as she means the caresses that ravish him. But the center in which she means such things, though it may not be a deep center, is something she has the skill to hide even from Antigone, her sweet-tongued maid.

Chaucer permits us to doubt her ingenuousness without pushing us to impugn her integrity. She is artful, but what shall we conclude from that? When word comes that Criseyde must leave Troy, both lovers fall in a faint, and Troilus emerges from his with sword in hand, ready for suicide.

> But, thanks to God, she woke up from her swoon —

was it God's doing, or had she been watching all the time? As she departs for the Greek camp she swears by Juno, by every god and goddess, by every nymph and satyr, by Atropos and Simois, that she will never prove untrue to Troilus. Is this too many witnesses? The schemes she sketches whereby it may be that she

can return quickly, or not have to go at all — what is
there about them that makes her prostrate lover ex-
claim:

> Those little tricks of yours of which you've told,
> They fill me not with hope, but ghastly fear?

He seems to be saying that he fears their failure. Or it
could be that their very number has brought home to
him the heaviness of the fate now overhanging them
both. But it might be — is this it? — that so much
evidence of an ingenuity in her he had never before
suspected fills him with a sudden sense that if she can
play with others she can play with him. Or, what is
worse, has played with him. The triumph of Chaucer
is nowhere more final than it is here. We cannot answer
such questions. Nor, he insinuates, can he. Love is as
puzzling as that. Troilus has stuck his head in among
the bees of experience, not the butterflies of poetry.
The courtly lover is becoming the lover. But Chaucer
does not denounce Criseyde any more than he would
denounce the sting that comes with honey. Not even
in the Greek camp, where she is so careful never to
discourage Diomede too much — Diomede, who has
promised to be a brother to her but has meant much
more, and of course she knows it — does Chaucer
expose her utterly, not even, that is to say, in lines
like these:

> For love and I are very far asunder,
> And I am more inclined, as things now go,
> To spend my life in mourning and in woe;

Though how my heart may change, I cannot tell;
The future may, of course, my grief dispel.
. . . What I've said should be enough for you.
Come back tomorrow, if you so desire,
But do not push this matter now too far.
Come when you want, if that's all you require! . . .
I do not say I promise what you seek,
Nor yet deny. So do not fret or frown,
For thou hast need to fear no other Greek!

Such lines leave us little to go on with. This Criseyde is almost Shakespeare's trollop. But it is still possible that she does only what she must. If we ever loved her we can at least pity her for the promptness with which she kills in us the reputation she once cherished in others.

Pandar knows her through and through. His interviews with her are masterly for what they leave unsaid. He understands how important it is to pretend that she is as innocent as Troilus, how much it will please her if he plays on her sensibilities as though he feared them; but even while he does so he is quick to seize occasions when he can be bald, for he is sure she does not want him to fail in the office of which the name is now his name. At the same time he expects his baldness to be rebuked, and is prepared to accept the rebuke with a show of shame.

"To save his life, and with no other thought,
Except no harm to you, thus am I driven!
And for God's love, who all the world have wrought,
See thou that life to both of us be given.

And now to you in full my heart I've shriven,
And since you see that it is pure and clean,
You know full well that I no evil mean.

"I pray to God, successful may you be,
Who such a fish hath caught without a net!
If you are wise, as you are fair to see,
Well in the ring then is the ruby set.
You two will make the best pair ever yet!
And heaven bless the day which well assures
That you are his as much as he is yours."

"Oho! I did not say that," answered she,
"Such talk as that will help things never a deal."
"O niece," said Pandar, "pray you, pardon me!
For though I merely spoke out as I feel,
I meant it well, by Mars with helm of steel!
So be not angry with me, dearest niece!"
"O well," she said, "for this time I'll make peace."

Everything is there except the true tenderness he feels
for her. This tenderness is something we know
rather than hear. It is stated neither in his exaggerated
speeches of affection and respect nor in the cynical
figures — the fish, the ruby — by which he thinks she
will be amused. It is in fact not stated. But it is as little
to be disputed as his fondness for the lovesick prince.

Pandar's method with Troilus, however, has to be
of the opposite sort. He can soften his words to
Criseyde because he knows she is hard. To Troilus
he must be harder than he feels; if he is not, the shape-
less youth will melt away. His words to the lover are

like the slaps we administer as medicine for hysteria. Troilus, paralyzed by his infatuation, must be taught how to walk again like a natural man. Pandar's favorite criticism of him is that he cries before he knows how much he is hurt, and before it is clear that nothing can be done to cure him. The thing to be done is very simple. It is to say what ails him. And first of all it is to let Criseyde know that he lies sick for her sake; or rather, to let the anonymous lady know, for this bedridden lover is so set in despair that some surgery is required before he will say the name Criseyde.

> If you refuse to tell, just for faint heart,
> And for your sloth and wilful foolishness,
> And will no slightest hint to me impart,
> And why I should not help in your distress
> You will not give a reason more or less,
> But supine on your bed yourself you stretch —
> I ask, what woman could love such a wretch?
>
> And how can she account then for your death,
> If you thus die, and she knows nothing why,
> Except for fear you breathed your final breath
> Because the Greeks about our city lie?
> What figure will you cut in the world's eye?
> Then she and all will say in scornful tones,
> 'The wretch is dead, the devil have his bones.'
>
> You may here weep alone and pray and kneel,
> But if the one you love of this knows naught,
> How can she make return that you can feel —
> Unknown, unkissed and lost, who is unsought!

Troilus, in other words, must be enjoying his grief. But fools alone do that. Pandar does not spare his friend the name of fool, infant, or whatever else occurs to his rough tongue. He must run through a long list, for the trouble in Troilus is chronic. The lover never learns to be up and doing — or rather, up and learning what can and what cannot be done. When Criseyde is ordered to leave Troy he conceives the idea of abducting her and taking her off where they can live together; but he is cast down by the thought that she may refuse to go. Pandar, extracting this much from him, asks him sensibly enough whether he has found out what Criseyde would do. The answer is Nay.

> 'Well, then,' said Pandar, 'why are you afraid?
> You don't know if she'd be at all dismayed
> To be abducted! Why then all this fear,
> Unless some angel told it in your ear?'

"Why, Troilus," the word is a little later, "you are your own worst foe!"

> To meet the ax a man his neck may stretch,
> But why should that give pleasure to the wretch?

The similitude of the ax is typical — Pandar brings figures from the world of fact, and the more absurd they are the better for his purpose, which is to shock Troilus out of his conventional stupor. Troilus is proud to be love's fool, but Pandar has no use for any kind of fool.

Or so he says. He himself has been a lover, and still is; nor has the course been smooth for him. He knows all about the feelings his friend has, and he could not respect him if they were absent. It is simply that he must save his life — not from the cruelty of Criseyde, which is nonexistent, but from himself. To this end he speaks as he does, employing the therapy of tartness and suppressing, or seeming to suppress, the subtlety of which his mind is capable. Just as his figures are Philistine, so his imagination sounds like that of a literal brute. When the two of them are planning the episode at the house of Deiphebus, and deciding that Troilus will feign illness so that with luck he may have his first word with Criseyde alone, a bit of dialogue takes place which throws their whole relation into perspective:

> 'In truth,' said Troilus, 'there is no need
> To counsel me a sickness to pretend,
> For I am sick in very fact and deed,
> So sick it well may be my fatal end.'
> 'That's good,' said Pandar, 'no time need you spend
> On how to counterfeit the sick man's lot,
> For one who sweats is taken to be hot.'

If Troilus takes the last line as signifying that Pandar has no true understanding of his precious state, he is wrong.

So is he if he supposes that Pandar means what he says when he says that Criseyde is not unique, the only lady under heaven.

And here's another thing — I dare aver
This town is full of ladies round about,
Fairer indeed than any twelve like her;
And if you want me, I can pick one out,
Yes, more than one or two, without a doubt.
Be glad, therefore, my own dear chosen brother,
If she is lost, why, we can get another.

"There's plenty more who know the art to please."
But Pandar is aware that what may be art in Criseyde
is nature to Troilus, and that the mention of other
women in the world is always shocking, and properly
so, to him who has picked out one. Chaucer does not
leave us in doubt about the man who interests him so
much:

These wise and cheering words good Pandar spoke
To help his friend as helpless there he lay,
As one who any measures would invoke,
No matter how much nonsense he might say.

Of course it is nonsense. And of course it is horse
sense, not human sense, for Pandar to say on another
occasion:

Get up, pretend that nothing has occurred,
And wash your face.

It is not in the language of Pandar that Chaucer
criticizes courtly love. It is in his person, concerning
whose delicacy we are never left in the dark. Or rather,
it is in all of the relations that Chaucer sees among the
three members of his little cast. The trio is what counts
with him. The refinements of his research into their

several souls are so numerous that no list of them
would be long enough. Nothing human is missed, no
truth of life or love is violated, in the series of conver-
sations these people have with one another. And yet
the word over all is wisdom, and it is worldly wisdom
at that. "Go, little book, my little tragedy," writes
Chaucer at the close; but he has misnamed his poem.
And who can doubt that he knows it?

He has made something of the *hybris* which moved
Troilus at first to scorn the love that would destroy
him. He has broken the prince's heart — the final
letter, the final outcry can mean nothing less. He has
ravaged Criseyde's face with grief, and driven her to
wish she had never seen this lover.

> Woe worth the day, and specially the night,
> When first I saw him with my eyes so plain,
> Who causes me, as I cause him, such pain!

He has given her, while love lasted, words to speak
such as no man's mistress has matched for softness,
for the gentle power to pierce. "I am not angry." "Had
I not yielded before this night, I would not now be
here." He has permitted even Pandar to lose his head
on a certain occasion; he has given the babbler a sad,
a quiet end; and once he has put into his mouth a
beautiful, grave statement concerning the profession
that friendship has forced him unhappily to adopt, the
profession of him who makes women come unto men.
He has strewn the poem with sweet songs, hymns, invocations, and laments — Antigone's song in the gar-

den is famous, but it is no sweeter than those the heroine and hero sing as they anticipate or remember love.

Chaucer has done all this, and still he has produced the opposite of a tragedy. An envelope of sun surrounds even the darkest portions of his scene. It is a sun that dries the tears from metaphor, that substitutes the speech of men for poetry's vapors. "My old hat," "a hill of beans," "not worth a pin" — such motes of the vernacular are always dancing in its beam, as proverbs get up and stretch in the dry light of noon. Troilus says he grows tired of Pandar's saws.

> Now peace, and say no more,
> For I have heard your wisdom and your lore.

Sleeping dogs, the stable door locked too late, the fire that time will cool, the nine days' wonder, the grave too deep for medicine — he thinks them irrelevant to his epoch-making case. But they have their effect upon him as the poem ages, and so do they upon us. They remind us that love is long, though the life of one lover may be perilous.

Chaucer insists he is not writing a poem — not really. This is something more than that. Or less, if we believe poetry to be the greatest thing there is. He for one does not consider it so. "The stories old books tell" — he dismisses them as Pandar does. Pandar, asking Criseyde what she and her maidens have been doing on the day he pays his first visit to her, hears that they have been reading about Laius and Oedipus.

'O yes, I know all that,' Pandar replied,
'And all the siege of Thebes and that affair;
In twelve big books it has been versified.
But what's the news? What gossip's in the air?'

Chaucer is willing that we should think him less than
a poet if we please. In the opinion he has of himself, or
pretends to have, he is more. He is a historian.

He accepts no responsibility for the tale he tells. He
did not make it up. He consulted authorities, and un-
fortunately they are not always so explicit as poetry
might like them to be. He would not mind knowing,
for instance, whether Criseyde had any children by
her husband who is dead. "I have not heard, and therefore let it go." "For me, I merely state the facts." He
bothers a good deal about dates, and apologizes when
he has to guess concerning the contents of letters for
which no reliable text has come down. As for what
his people think and feel — well, that is a problem the
"ancient records" too often leave for him to solve. He
wishes he knew for sure; then he could be sure about
his heroine, whom he plainly confesses that in the
present state of the record he imperfectly understands.

I can but think, as I it written find,
That all of this was said with good intent,
And that her heart withal was true and kind,
And what she said, all that she truly meant,
And of her grief no part did she invent,
And ever thought to him she would be true,
But of her heart, not all of it she knew.

In this case he is glad to have authority for thinking well of her, but at other times he cannot discover the document he needs.

As things stand he doubtless will fail to satisfy our curiosity. One reason is his "feeble tongue" and his "weak art" — nor has he the facility at invention which regular poets have. But maybe it will not matter. After all, the reader has lived too, and probably loved. Then let him fill in the details. Chaucer's most elaborate pose is that he the historian is being assisted by us who are the stuff of history. He addresses us directly, dumping etceteras in our laps. And he is safe in doing so because we are citizens with him of the ordinary world. Troilus and his pretty widow seem to have thought their world was special, but it was not, for no world with people in it can be special. No matter how much time has passed since Troy, he counts on us to understand his lovers. "You know as well as I" — the phrase is inveterate with him. Consequently he will not bore us with matter we can just as well supply out of our own minds. Criseyde's inward debates were endless at one stage; he will merely suggest the way they went. So with the small talk at Deiphebus' house:

> But I don't mean to pass here in review
> The names of guests and all they say and do,
> For you can guess their greetings and their chatter,
> And we'll proceed to more important matter.

"And so on, all to much the same effect." "Not to stray too far among reflections manifold." "In short, to bring the matter to a close." "And now we're coming to the point right soon!" Chaucer never lets us forget our good fortune in having on our hands a poet who refuses to tell us what we already know.

> The manner of this meeting was again
> Somewhat as I have told and as you know,
> And so I shall not bother to explain. . . .

> O, I don't know, he said some thing or other,
> 'Twas all as well, one answer or another. . . .

> But if you think that I should now relate
> Each word of Troilus, each hope and fear,
> The little nothings, sweet and intimate,
> That he meant only for his lady's ear,
> I couldn't do it if it took a year;
> To tell you every passage of his wooing
> Would be a labor scarcely worth the doing.

> I do not find that ever anyone
> In telling such details has been minute —
> 'Twould be appalling if it were all done!
> In letters thousands of verses I compute
> They wrote, on which my author is quite mute;
> He was too sensible and wise to try
> To write all lovers say, and so am I.

He grows lengthy in his explanations of why he is not long. And he is willing to do so because he trusts us sooner or later to see his joke. In truth he is not for shortness — he likes to talk, and in his own person. He promises to pass by "all things collateral," but nothing pleases him more than to digress and discourse, as Fielding, Cervantes, and other "historians" since his time have done.

He is discursive because he is skeptical; to the comic genius everything is partly true and he is its priest, its garrulous vicar who in a minute can find his attention turned to something else of equal interest. Not that Chaucer is a holy fellow. "Well prayed," says Pandar after Troilus has finished one of his invocations to Love. It is an irreverent phrase, of the sort that Chaucer can almost be said to have invented. He tells us that Pandar swore to Criseyde "by sticks and stones and all the gods that high in heaven dwell." And he himself remarks, at the conclusion of another address by Troilus to the Venus who he hopes will always keep Criseyde soft at his side:

> His prayer he ended with a kiss or two,
> Which part of it at least was well received.

The reverence of Chaucer is for all that is, not for this or that person, god, or thing. The comic spirit is not committed, and cannot take seriously those who are, even though in this case they are a hero and a heroine. Chaucer's way of rebuking exaggeration is to exaggerate still more, till fate sounds funny. The rebuke to Troilus and Criseyde is affectionate, as to a pair of children, but it is clear. We learn that Troilus, in the first stages of his love seizure, changed color "sixty times a day." This was before he had told anybody what ailed him — anybody except himself, with whom he was most eloquent.

> These words, and more, within his room he spake,
> And begged his lady, in his grief profound,
> Some recognition of his love to make,
> And wept salt tears in which he nearly drowned —
> But all in vain, for not a single sound
> She heard, not being present to do so,
> Which made his griefs a thousandfold to grow.

If any stanza imprisons Chaucer's essence, that one does. But another comes near to doing so:

> And then in mind she canvassed up and down
> The count of all his gracious qualities,
> And all his rank and all his great renown,
> His wit, his figure, all his knightly ease,
> But that he loved her, most of all did please.

To Criseyde's good reasons for thinking well of Troilus, suddenly Chaucer adds the real one. The comic spirit can be as swift as it is slow. It descends wherever it will, on friend and foe alike. Chaucer is the best friend his lovers have — he is even a better friend than Pandar — but he will not spare them when they need a little taking down. The comic spirit grows giddy on great heights. Because it respects all things it respects no thing too much. The comic spirit is just, and loves the world entire.

# IX · DON JUAN

"I WANT a hero." Thus Byron begins, and we cannot
set it down as an accident that his first word is what it
is. He never finds a hero, and in a sense he never
finds a subject — Byron, that is to say, is a modern
poet. Subject matter has been hard of late to find, which
means among other things that comedy has been hard
to write. The enormous natural genius of Byron is
handicapped as even comedy must be by a want of
stuff to work on. Even comedy needs a mountain
that can be assaulted and reduced. Byron must be his
own mountain.

He is his own hero and subject, and so is free to talk
forever. But his freedom bores him. He would rather
have something distant, something dry, something
really high to talk about. He cannot be as perfect in
comedy as Chaucer was because he has no single story
to tell. Chaucer could assert himself against an object
— the legend of a certain love — but Byron has no
object. He inhabits a desert, the world after Waterloo,
and no amount of rage brings back sufficient echo.

This may or may not be Byron's fault, but in any case he pays with failure. All is conversation, and the intellectual force displayed in this is astonishing; but Byron has to stretch and strain himself too far, he has to become fantastic, he has to range between the titanic and the cute. Improvisation is his curse. He flounders brilliantly, now up, now down, and he is nowhere more amusing than in his many admissions that this is true. But he would rather have more to be amusing about.

He calls his comedy an "epic satire," suggesting by the phrase a world about him that is foolish — or vicious — without limit. The absence of limit takes some salt out of the satire; it is overseasoned, and still it cannot prove its point if it has one. Perhaps *Don Juan* is better than a satire. Its several stories — of Juan's education, of his shipwreck and short idyll with Haidée, of his stay with Gulbeyaz the Sultana, of his prowess in the Russian war, of his residence in Petersburgh as Catherine's favorite, of his falling ill and being sent to England for a rest, of England as he found it — are the rolling wheels of a vehicle which, considering its make, might be all the grander to ride in because it had no victims to run down. Its make is comic, and some of its lines are of the purest order. There is confusion in the whole design, but it is the design that counts, as always with comedy, and not the designation. Byron attacks plenty of individual things: tyrants, war, the Lake Poets of England, Castlereagh and Wellington, the life of the North as

seen by an exile among "countries near the sun,"
Plato, and England in every aspect. But that may be
the trouble. He attacks too many things. At bottom
he is trying to revive the comic spirit, and he is not
altogether clear that a poor way to do this is to shoot
every rascal in sight. The spirit in him suffers as he
wanders in search of game. If comedy survives at all
it survives in Byron. But it survives in him without
serenity.

Byron cannot be serene, cannot smile and be wise,
because he lacks confidence in the world. True comedy
trusts the world to be what it must: a foolish place,
but steady on its foundations, and ready to outlast
the loudest laugh at its expense. For something like the
same reason Virgil could not be tragic. He was terri-
fied. Byron too has lost perspective. War, the "brain-
spattering, windpipe-slitting art," is too much for
him. It doubtless should have been, but his poetry
does not withstand the shock. So with the England to
which Don Juan goes. Its society

> is now one polish'd horde,
> Form'd of two mighty tribes, the *Bores* and *Bored* —

a spectacle more than sufficient. It is suffocating. Byron
never knows what to make of the mad world he finds.
Or the dull world. They are the same one, and he has
no philosophy — or no theology — with which to
conquer it.

He promises at one point to write a canto which
will take us to Hades, but he never makes the promise

good. He forgets or abandons it as he does so many other things in the long fragment which *Don Juan* is — a fragment for other reasons, surely, than its author's death. The end which Chaucer was so slow in reaching was at least an end: not the end of comedy, which is boundless, but of the subject it had to deal with in one case. Byron has no subject because he has no world. Or he has one and cannot see its parts. He could not have built, as Dante did, a hell in which earth and heaven find themselves reflected. He is not sure, as Dante could be, that most things and people are undeserving of either wrath or ridicule. Dante's trimmers, whom Virgil advises him to regard and pass, are the majority of mankind; they are the uncreated mass wherein neither bad nor good resides. Dante can leave them and go on to the relatively few who by making choices have earned hell, earned heaven. Dante can do this because he can conceive hell and heaven; his universe has corners. His thought has top and bottom where it can be busy to some purpose. He wastes no anger on the many — rich or poor, famous or unsung — who are immaterial to his plan. For he has a plan, as his world has shape. He can take for granted the boredom and the meanness of most life. He can take them for granted and go on to imagine an eternity — on three levels — from which they are missing. That is why every nook of his poem contains important truth, and why we never say that he is wasting his strength.

Byron wastes at least some of his strength in satirizing things and people we cannot believe he will ever reform. He seems to think the whole world should be beautiful, intelligent, and good. He wakes up, as so many poets since his day have done, in a waste land which irks him because it is full of dishonesty and dulness. Above all, it is rotten with respectability. Respectability is morals from which the danger has departed. Byron is right in despising it, but he is mad in devoting to it the time he does. He tries to cure it with the medicine of insult, to outrage it till it learns to live again. But it was never alive. Nor will it learn anything from his diabolism, his game of saying that bad is good and good is bad. For the seven deadly sins he substitutes seven thousand — "that low vice, curiosity," and that poor thing, simplicity of wit. This is fun, but it will not make the world over into a fair place. Byron is bursting his heart with efforts to galvanize a dead body. It is the body of this life, concerning which both Chaucer and Dante are wiser than he because they have remembered how little at best was to be expected of it.

But *Don Juan* is not all satire, nor does its author think it is. He knows that comedy is talk, and he takes more than full advantage of the principle. More than full advantage, as must follow from what has been said. For Byron's talk is not about anything; or rather, it is about too many things, and searches too desperately for still further things to be about.

> I don't know that there may be much ability
> Shown in this sort of desultory rhyme;

> But there's a conversational facility,
>   Which may round off an hour upon a time.

The claim is too casual, as in another canto confession
is too frank. "I love wisdom more than she loves me."
This is as much a cover for carelessness as it is a piece
of humble pie.

Byron's talk of course is wonderful. No talk is like
it in the world of verse. His past, his present, his sins
and his better sides, his taste in wine and oysters, his
reading, his travel, his literary tricks, his opinions
about all trifles under the sun — nothing is excluded,
or should be if his subject is what he somewhere says
it is: *De rebus cunctis et quibusdam aliis.* "All things
and a few others." Whether or not it is Saint Thomas's
phrase, it will do for Byron, for

> *Me* — the present writer of
> The present poem.

That writer is always renewing himself. Long though
*Don Juan* is, it grows steadily fresher, even though
Byron says near the end:

> In youth I wrote because my mind was full,
> And now because I feel it growing dull.

This can scarcely be meant by one who after endless
cantos could improvise thus upon fashionable London:

> In the great world — which, being interpreted,
>   Meaneth the west or worst end of a city,
> And about twice two thousand people bred

By no means to be very wise or witty,
But to sit up while others lie in bed,
And look down on the universe with pity —

or thus upon lady-killers:

His manner was perhaps the more seductive,
Because he ne'er seem'd anxious to seduce;
Nothing affected, studied, or constructive
Of coxcombry or conquest: no abuse
Of his attractions marr'd the fair perspective,
To indicate a Cupidon broke loose,
And seem to say, "Resist us if you can" —
Which makes a dandy while it spoils a man.

No, it is never that Byron runs out of strength or wit. It is rather that he has so little to employ these treasures on. He is too ready to call his poem a bubble — "to play with, as an infant plays." We never quite decide that he is wasting our time, even when he parenthesizes about nothing, as he certainly does in two dozen lines of the thirteenth canto.

At Blank-Blank Square — for we will break no squares
By naming streets: since men are so censorious,
And apt to sow an author's wheat with tares,
Reaping allusions private and inglorious,
Where none were dreamt of, unto love's affairs,
Which were, or are, or are to be notorious,
That therefore do I previously declare,
Lord Henry's mansion was in Blank-Blank Square.

Also there bin another pious reason
For making squares and streets anonymous;

Which is, that there is scarce a single season
   Which doth not shake some very splendid house
With some slight heart-quake of domestic treason —
   A topic scandal doth delight to rouse:
Such I might stumble over unawares,
Unless I knew the very chastest squares.

'Tis true, I might have chosen Piccadilly,
   A place where peccadillos are unknown;
But I have motives, whether wise or silly,
   For letting that pure sanctuary alone.
Therefore I name not square, street, place, until I
   Find one where nothing naughty can be shown,
A vestal shrine of innocence of heart:
Such are — but I have lost the London Chart.

At Henry's mansion then, in Blank-Blank Square. . . .

But we would just as soon that he had something to say while he passed his mornings and filled his foolscap. "This narrative is not meant for narration" — we know that, and consequently have no reason to be surprised when in the middle of the twelfth canto we come upon the words: "But now I will begin my poem." In comedy the tale is not the thing, as Chaucer for one has told us. We can suspect, however, that some sort of action, delivered in some sort of order, is what even the comic spirit needs in order to feel free. Byron has more freedom than he can feel. Only a poet of stupendous powers could endure as he does, lacking proper food.

It is as if Byron, knowing that what he wanted was

serenity, said to himself he would have it at any price, even the price of thrashing his wits to exhaustion. The serenity beyond satire — he is always in search of that, for he keeps on assuring us that he means little or nothing of what he says. He protests too much. He exaggerates every comic gesture. Chaucer's pose of being a historian is repeated here, but without sly-ness, and toward no better understanding of the events at hand: the events of his story, which, as Chaucer never did with his, he despises and wants to spoil. The comic spirit looks at us around the edges of its work, but the work is there. Byron lounges in front of both the picture and the frame, obscuring as much of everything as possible.

> 'Twas on a summer's day — the sixth of June: —
>   I like to be particular in dates,
> Not only of the age, and year, but moon;
>   They are a sort of post-house, where the Fates
> Change horses, making history change its tune,
>   Then spur away o'er empires and o'er states,
> Leaving at last not much besides chronology,
> Excepting the post-obits of theology.

> 'Twas on the sixth of June, about the hour
>   Of half-past six — perhaps still nearer seven —

here is all the business of believing that "facts are facts," or of pretending to believe it — all the business, and little of the result.

> But all this time how slept, or dream'd, Dudù?
>   With strict inquiry I could ne'er discover,

And scorn to add a syllable untrue. . . .
All that I know is, that the facts I state
Are true as truth has ever been of late.

The last two lines go out of their way in this case to
confuse the result; the historian cannot conceal the
moralist, who is too insistent an intruder upon the
scene.

Without, or with, offence to friends or foes,
I sketch your world exactly as it goes.

There he is again, suggesting that the historian in him
is in fact one of those fellows for whom the truth is
nothing but the truth about his times — something
which nobody else knows. Yet the original gesture is
never altogether forgotten. It will do to fill a moment
or supply a rhyme.

Upon his table or his toilet — *which*
Of these is not exactly ascertain'd —
(I state this, for I am cautious to a pitch
Of nicety, where a fact is to be gain'd).

In such a case the gesture is but the jerk of an automaton — an automaton, furthermore, without memory.
For Byron can never recall whether it is history or
fiction that he would have us believe he is writing.
"Recollect, the work is only fiction." But how can
that be? "I detest all fiction even in song." Which
statement are we to understand?

'Tis the part
Of a true poet to escape from fiction

Whene'er he can; for there is little art
  In leaving verse more free from the restriction
Of truth than prose, unless to suit the mart
  For what is sometimes call'd poetic diction,
And that outrageous appetite for lies
Which Satan angles with for souls, like flies.

The answer seems again to be that Byron has contemporary game to kill.

  I hate all mystery, and that air
Of clap-trap which your recent poets prize.

"My poem's epic." But it is not, even on the comic level. Even on the level of its attempt to sweeten poetry with the prose of experience and sense — a worthy attempt, as Chaucer has proved — it weakens itself with worries about the failure of other poets to be doing the same thing. The comic spirit does not worry. It survives all the Wordsworths there are — for it is Wordsworth that Byron has paused to belabor.

The gesture that goes with the historical one, the gesture of leaving details to a reader who knows as much about life as the author does, is likewise made beyond all limit. It is made in macaronics, a sure sign that Byron is in extremity and knows it.

But just suppose that moment should betide,
  I only say suppose it — *inter nos*.
(This should be *entre nous*, for Julia thought
In French, but then the rhyme would go for nought.)

"Hail, Muse! *et cetera*" — insouciance could no further go, unless the limit is where Byron slaps and cuffs his story as if it were a little dog, a nuisance, on his lap.

> Meantime Apollo plucks me by the ear,
> And tells me to resume my story here. . . .

> But let me to my story: I must own,
>     If I have any fault, it is digression —
> Leaving my people to proceed alone,
>     While I soliloquize beyond expression;
> But these are my addresses from the throne,
>     Which put off business to the ensuing session.
> Forgetting each omission is a loss to
> The world, not quite so great as Ariosto.

Byron certainly knows, as Spenser certainly did not, what use to make of Ariosto. And he has learned from Chaucer.

> We live and die,
> But which is best, you know no more than I.

That could be Chaucer — with a little change, for Chaucer knew it is better to live, and he never doubted the wisdom of his reader. His knowledge was deficient, but not mankind's. Still, the accent is right. And so is Byron in his master's vein when he assures us that we shall be saved from lists of things we are as familiar with — and as tired of — as he is. "I spare you then the furniture and plate."

> I won't describe — that is, if I can help
>     Description; and I won't reflect — that is,
> If I can stave off thought, which — as a whelp
>     Clings to its teat — sticks to me through the abyss

> Of this odd labyrinth; or as the kelp
>   Holds by the rock; or as a lover's kiss
> Drains its first draught of lips: — but, as I said,
> I *won't* philosophize, and *will* be read.

The only difference is that Chaucer would not have said so much. He would have promised less, and quietly done more.

The ordinary world to which Byron returns us is no more to his relish than the poetical one he plays with and rejects.

> I've got new mythological machinery,
>   And very handsome supernatural scenery.

The scorn in these lines is proper to the "pedestrian Muses" with which in his dedication he says he wanders. And the motto he quotes from Horace,

> Difficile est proprie communia dicere,

is perfect for comedy. Of course it is hard to write well of familiar things. Comedy is rarely successful. It takes courage to "play upon the surface of humanity," and it takes genius to demonstrate while doing so that the depths there are deep indeed. But Byron doubts the depths. The waters he explores are brackish, and what sleeps under them he dismisses — not slyly, as Chaucer does, but with something slapdash in his contempt. "I hate all mystery." That again is right, but Byron races to the puerile extreme of know-nothingism. "Oh Plato! Plato! . . . You're a bore, a charlatan, a coxcomb." We can be amused by that without being matured by such discourses as the following:

Few mortals know what end they would be at,
　　But whether glory, power, or love, or treasure,
The path is through perplexing ways, and when
The goal is gain'd, we die, you know — and then —

What then? — I do not know, no more do you —
And so good night. . . .

My tendency is to philosophize
　　On most things, from a tyrant to a tree;
But still the spouseless virgin *Knowledge* flies.
　　What are we? and whence came we? what shall be
Our *ultimate* existence? what's our present?
Are questions answerless, and yet incessant. . . .

"Que sçais-je?" was the motto of Montaigne,
　　As also of the first academicians;
That all is dubious which man may attain,
　　Was one of their most favorite positions.
There's no such thing as certainty, that's plain
　　As any of Mortality's conditions;
So little do we know what we're about in
This world, I doubt if doubt itself be doubting. . . .

For me, I know nought; nothing I deny,
　　Admit, reject, contemn; and what know *you*,
Except perhaps that you were born to die?
　　And both may after all turn out untrue.

It is the language of sophomores, so daring in their
sadness, so sure that they have been everywhere and
come back with nothing — and that the bulletin will
impress us. Byron has a better language which he has

learned from Tacitus and Pope. The art of this language is the art of coupling terms which nobody else has coupled, toward the end of ironic, wry surprise. Don Juan has been trained to scale fortresses and nunneries. "No one likes to be disturb'd at meals or love." The seasick passengers who now realize that their ship is in danger "find it much amiss to lose their lives as well as spoil their diet." Haidée's "piratical papa" is slow in returning home because

> The good old gentleman had been detain'd
> By winds and waves, and some important captures.

Don Juan, musing in the last canto "on mutability or on his mistress," hears suddenly "a supernatural agent — or a mouse." If the trick is worked too often, as it may be, we forgive the fault because we cannot forget the alliteration which couples "passions and potatoes" in a certain essay Byron has seen fit to insert on the subject of population as Malthus taught his generation to conceive it.

If "trick" is the word for Byron, then we know that he has missed the heart of comedy at which he aimed. The margin may be slight, but when it exists it is a real measure of the distance there is between formula and form. The form of comedy is to be formless — really formless, as the large world is which the comic spirit ranges. But the form of Byron is the little form that "turns what was once romantic to burlesque" — his words, and he speaks them as one who never knew the difference between burlesque and comedy. It is the difference between reducing things and denying them. The highest comic spirit desires to level things as life levels them, so that all of them may last forever. The lowest desires that they should die of laughter — its laughter, which it cannot control. The genius of comedy is above formula because it is not convinced that tricks will do its work. It will be the slave of nothing, and certainly not of a technique. It is really skeptical, and therefore in the long run gentle. It saves everything it can out of the wreck when romance collides with candor.

But Byron has a formula. His muse is a trained mermaid who dives. From the sublime to the ridiculous — the phrase is musty, but Byron does not find it so. He never wearies of the practical joke which consists of coming up behind us and pushing us in. He has put there the water we admire, but only that we may flounder in its salt. The experience can be hilarious; it is even exhilarating at times. And one who cannot enjoy it at all will never enjoy *Don Juan*. But it has its monotony — its long, soaring flight and then its all too expected jolt as Byron's mermaid hits bottom.

> Sweet is the vintage, when the showering grapes
>     In Bacchanal profusion reel to earth,
> Purple and gushing: sweet are our escapes
>     From civic revelry to rural mirth;
> Sweet to the miser are his glittering heaps,
>     Sweet to the father is his first-born's birth,
> Sweet is revenge — especially to women,
> Pillage to soldiers, prize-money to seamen. . . .

No more — no more — Oh! never more, my heart,
    Canst thou be my sole world, my universe!
Once all in all, but now a thing apart,
    Thou canst not be my blessing or my curse:
The illusion's gone forever, and thou art
    Insensible, I trust, but none the worse,
And in thy stead I've got a deal of judgment,
Though heaven knows how it ever found a lodgment. . . .

"Farewell, my Spain! a long farewell!" he cried,
    "Perhaps I may revisit thee no more,
But die, as many an exiled heart hath died,
    Of its own thirst to see again thy shore:
Farewell, where Guadalquivir's waters glide!
    Farewell, my mother! and, since all is o'er,
Farewell, too, dearest Julia! — (here he drew
Her letter out again, and read it through.) . . .

And thus like to an angel o'er the dying
    Who die in righteousness, she lean'd; and there
All tranquilly the shipwreck'd boy was lying,
    As o'er him lay the calm and stirless air:
But Zoe the meantime some eggs was frying. . . .

And she bent o'er him, and he lay beneath,
    Hush'd as the babe upon its mother's breast,
Droop'd as the willow when no winds can breathe,
    Lull'd like the depth of ocean when at rest,
Fair as the crowning rose of the whole wreath,
    Soft as the callow cygnet in its nest;
In short, he was a very pretty fellow,
Although his woes had turn'd him rather yellow. . . .

The climax is probably reached when Byron's famous lyric apostrophe to the isles of Greece breaks abruptly off and is succeeded by a no less famous passage of literary criticism:

> Thus sung, or would, or could, or should have sung,
>     The modern Greek, in tolerable verse;
> If not like Orpheus quite, when Greece was young,
>     Yet in these times he might have done much worse.

The passage of criticism is among the cleverest things to be found in verse, but even at this climax we remember the monotony of the road by which we reached it.

It is a road that runs all the way from sentiment to cynicism — in neither of which regions comedy is at home. Byron has to be brutal because he has been mawkish. Just as his songs are softer at the center than those with which Chaucer dignifies his work and makes it beautiful, so his savagery goes beyond anything that the medieval poet would have thought proper to truth's muse — pedestrian, but it walked lightly, avoiding pits.

> Some odd mistakes, too, happen'd in the dark,
>     Which show'd a want of lanterns, or of taste —
> Indeed the smoke was such they scarce could mark
>     Their friends from foes — besides, such things from haste
> Occur, though rarely, when there is a spark
>     Of light to save the venerably chaste:
> But six old damsels, each of seventy years,
> Were all deflower'd by different grenadiers.

In such a stanza Byron not only falls but is confounded; comedy, tough thing though it be, soon dies from violence. It rarely survives an attack of the snickers.

The violence Byron does to all of his colleagues in the enterprise Calliope once set them is a sign that poetry with him has arrived at a stage of desperation past which there can be nothing but doubt concerning the direction henceforth to be taken. His delight in vulgarizing his peers is not the delight Chaucer had taken in reducing them to the proportions of human sense. "Troy owes to Homer what whist owes to Hoyle" — so much for the *Iliad*, and for the *Odyssey* this must do:

> An honest gentleman at his return
>   May not have the good fortune of Ulysses;
> Not all lone matrons for their husbands mourn,
>   Or show the same dislike to suitors' kisses;
> The odds are that he finds a handsome urn
>   To his memory — and two or three young misses
> Born to some friend, who holds his wife and riches, —
> And that *his* Argus bites him by — the breeches.

If it does very well for Byron's purpose, then the cheapness of the purpose is exposed. The purpose of such a poet is not to remind us of the world but to inform us, with a leer, that it is worse than simple folk suppose it is; and we are included among the simple folk. In like mood we learn that the "half-way house" where Dante found himself "at the age when all grow good" was the home of "abstruse ecstatics" whose meaning, being mathematical, is not to be searched with profit. And the little bark which Dante called his comedy does for Byron only when he has turned it into a steamboat. The end of the world that Lucretius saw with such seriousness becomes in *Don Juan* the story of a world

> Thrown topsy-turvy, twisted, crisp'd, and curl'd,
> Baked, fried, or burnt, turn'd inside-out, or drown'd.

Spenser is misquoted in passing:

> "Fierce loves and faithless wars" — I am not sure
> If this be the right reading — 'tis no matter.

And Wordsworth is regularly declared — nor always wrongly — to have mouthed noble nothings.

It is not that Byron should have tried to be the same poet as any of his peers. It is rather that he might have remained indeed their peer. He preferred to be a rogue. His roguery is indefatigable, and the amusement he affords us is immense. But the comic spirit which saves poetry is less evident in him than the devil's grin which damns it with all other things. And a few others.

# X · THE PRELUDE

"I WANT a subject." Thus Wordsworth would, or could, or should have begun his poem in fourteen books about himself. He did not so begin because he thought he had a subject — the only one in sight. Wordsworth created modern poetry when he decided that the man who writes is more important than the men and the things he writes about. Wordsworth had special reasons for deciding this: he did not know men, and the fountain of things had dried up. The world was a barren place, producing no further mythologies. The poet stood alone, and without a lyre. If poetry was to live again, he must make it live from nothing. He must make the dry bones sound.

Milton, searching for a subject, had found one that needed loads of ornament before it could seem substantial. Wordsworth, searching in the same fashion, found none at all; and ornament for him was not in order. He was honest, and furthermore there was no art of poetry extant, no set of pleasures with which he could play. The least sportive of poets — this cer-

· 303 ·

tainly he was — could not be expected to go forth
with a fowling-piece like Lord Byron's and litter the
waste land with carcasses of crows. If he was anything
he was a philosophical poet. Indeed he would have to
be one, for only such a man could build poetry again.
Intuition had departed; the rules for it must be redis-
covered. If the world was to bloom once more with
living truth, poetry must work the ground. Truth in
the fortunate ages had been something for poetry to
express. Now it was something for poetry to find.

But what is poetry? Wordsworth had first to answer
that simple question. At least it is simple before it is
asked. The greatest poets never asked it; they simply
went to work. Wordsworth, having no work to do
until he had produced a definition, devoted his life
to the discovery that poetry is the art of finding truth —
general truth, as distinguished from the particular
truths of science. It is an unsatisfactory answer, being
circular, but so have all subsequent answers proved
unsatisfactory. For Wordsworth started an inter-
minable series of attempts on the part of poets to say
what they thought they were doing. It is as if a secret
had been lost. It had been, apparently, and still is. If
we do not know what poetry is we shall never get
anywhere by arguing its definition; and, worst of all,
we shall not get poetry. It was a happier thing when it
could be taken for granted — even laughed at, as
Shakespeare laughed at it. For then it had natural
work to do. It could contemplate the actions of men.
Modern poetry contemplates itself, and makes grand

claims for what it is. But poetry that is sure of itself makes no such claims. It wastes no strength on schools, manifestoes, and experiments; or upon lamentations about the times, the ugly, unpropitious times which threaten to make poetry impossible.

Wordsworth wondered whether poetry had become impossible, and if not, by what superhuman efforts it might be restored. This is what he discussed with Coleridge during the long walks and talks they had at the turn of their century. Wordsworth emerged from those talks, and from meditations of his own, with notions which have become classic. Genuine poetry is ahead of its time; it is destined to a bitter struggle against misunderstanding — a struggle which it will win with the help of an original audience which is small but faithful. For only a few living persons can know at first the purity of its author's feeling. That is what matters. "The feeling gives importance to the action and the situation, and not the action and situation to the feeling."

Which is true, but Wordsworth takes it to the point where it means that the subject need be nothing at all compared with the nature of the man who treats it. Homer could have treated Troy without the distinction it deserved, but it deserved distinction, and he seems never to have doubted this, any more than Dante doubted the deep import of the universe his poem dared to enter. It was there before his poem was. But for Wordsworth there is no universe until he makes one with his poetry. All the power there can be is in his feelings. No meaning exists until his own "organic sensibility" has created it. The test of a poem is the character of its author. He must be like other men — "poets do not write for poets alone" — and yet he must be different too. Wordsworth would like to see this difference as a difference merely of degree, but every thought he has forces him to describe a difference in kind. The knowledge of which poetry is the "breath and finer spirit" is a special knowledge, and only special persons possess it. Poets are exalted men; they organize, ennoble, and educate the emotions of other men.

Which again is true. We learn from Shakespeare. But it was not the intention of Shakespeare to teach us — not the intention, nor the promise. With Wordsworth it is all promise. We never get beyond his proof that he will teach us if we listen — never, at least, in his masterpiece *The Prelude*. The business of *The Prelude* is to prove that Wordsworth is a poet; for he is ambitious to do great work, and he must first be sure he has the calling. The great work is to be a long poem to which this one is but preliminary. Hence its subtitle: *Growth of a Poet's Mind*. In 1814, when he published a fragment of the great work to be — a fragment, called *The Excursion*, which few have read or ever will — he explained how it was:

Several years ago, when the author retired to his native mountains with the hope of being enabled to construct a literary work that might live, it was a reasonable thing that he should take a review of his own mind, and examine how far nature and education had qualified him for such employment. As subsidiary to this preparation, he undertook to record, in verse, the origin and progress of his own powers, as far as he was acquainted with them. That work, addressed to a dear friend, most distinguished for his knowledge and genius, and to whom the author's intellect is deeply indebted, has been long finished; and the result of the investigation which gave rise to it was a determination to compose a philosophical poem, containing views of Man, Nature, and Society; and to be entitled *The Recluse;* as having for its principal subject the sensations and opinions of a poet living in retirement. The preparatory poem is biographical, and conducts the history of the author's mind to the point when he was emboldened to hope that his faculties were sufficiently matured for entering upon the arduous labor which he had proposed to himself.

Perhaps no more amazing statement was ever made by a poet about himself. If it is not amazing, then we have forgotten how Shakespeare, for one, came to his maturity — not by retiring to take an inventory of his powers, as yet unsuspected, but by staying in London and writing *Henry VI* and a dozen other plays in the course of which he developed those powers. That is the way of the apprentice, of the poet for whom there is an art that he will master if he can. For Wordsworth there was no art unless he dug it out of himself. He never climbed out of the excavation.

For the paramount fact in Wordsworth's biography is the fact that he did not finish his great work. He had almost half a century to do it in, but *The Recluse* as he planned it does not exist. He was too much interested in the preparation. *The Prelude* he kept always by him, revising it toward some perfection that he felt yet never found. It saw the light only when he was dead, and when the hope had died in him that he might serve Calliope as Homer, Shakespeare, Spenser, and Milton had. The preliminaries absorbed him: the preliminaries of defining what a poet is, and of deciding whether he was one. His only subject could be himself, for the only world he had was within his mind.

The world of poetry had gone, and with it every other world. Wordsworth then must live his poetry; he must be unique or nothing; he must make a mythology out of his faculties, a god out of his mind; he must cultivate a temperament from which wisdom once again might flow like waters from a long-forgotten spring. And all this in the absence of aid from the poor society around him. *The Prelude* is Wordsworth's announcement that he was successful — at discovering the power. The poem did not follow.

*The Prelude* has a special setting in its author's life. Like most modern poets, Wordsworth draws us into his biography; he lives not so much in his works as for them, or rather they live for him. They keep him going, and we must learn what they meant to him before we shall know what they can possibly mean to us. *The Prelude* is Wordsworth's answer to the French Revolution, which in its first stages he accepted but which as time went on he wanted to reject — and did not know how except by substituting for its public program of reconstruction by reason a private program of resurrection by feeling. The French Revolution had made him by 1792 the most miserable of men: sick of its excesses, but also guilty because he could not completely comprehend his desire to escape it. With all the discussion it brought in its wake it was not for him. He tried in London to maintain his original ardor, he tried to keep up with each new turn of thought, he tried to hold up his end of the human conversation which events inspired, but he grew weary and bewildered; and because he was bewildered he blamed himself — until, set free by the legacy of a friend to wander into the West Country and meet Coleridge, he realized with a rush that within his very self, his obscure and personal self, he had the makings of a religion — a "natural" religion — which might displace the revolution whose science he had not mastered. *The Prelude* begins at this point of rapture, this point of a scarcely articulate joy over being suddenly set free "from the vast city where I long had pined, a discontented sojourner."

> The earth is all before me. With a heart
> Joyous, nor scared at its own liberty,
> I look about; and should the chosen guide
> Be nothing better than a wandering cloud,
> I cannot miss my way. I breathe again!
> Trances of thought and mountings of the mind
> Come fast upon me: it is shaken off,
> That burthen of my own unnatural self,
> The heavy weight of many a weary day
> Not mine, and such as were not made for me.

The "dear friend" to whom he addresses the poem — Coleridge, of course — is asked to believe what we as readers must believe through fourteen books if the poem is to be successful with us: that in a single blessed moment, a mystical moment which quieted the earth and all men's voices on it, Wordsworth slipped into the heart of truth. It was

> a day
> With silver clouds, and sunshine on the grass,
> And in the sheltered and the sheltering grove
> A perfect stillness.

It was such a day as only Wordsworth could create, and anyone may envy him because he had it. But it does not follow that we shall find comprehensible the demonstration he goes on to provide of a past which had produced this present — a past which we are to understand as having been ordained to make him now the priest of a simpler and better life than revolutions and new laws will ever manage.

Wordsworth goes on to show how his life to date has prepared him to feel as poets feel, and therefore to teach all men how they should feel. It is important to him that he should show this beyond the shadow of a doubt. For there must be no mistake, he is indeed ordained. Without his knowing it, but no less certainly for that, Nature had been educating him all the while. The universe had conspired to make him its one philosopher of feeling. His favorite word is "thus." We are not to assume that he merely hopes or fancies.

He knows. And we must know — that the man he now is was always there, in the boy who played, a dedicated spirit, among those native mountains. The demonstration must be perfect.

But there is no demonstration. There is a series of pictures recovered from the past, and these are among the most beautiful objects poetry possesses; they are the reason *The Prelude* deserves talking about. And, alternating with them, there is a series of statements concerning what they meant and mean, there is a connecting tissue of proof, a web of words designed to convince us — and convince Wordsworth — that the man he now is has been "restored," after nightmares of reason and revolution, from the youth he once was. It is the statements that do not stand. *The Prelude* proves nothing except that Wordsworth remembered certain moments. They were worth remembering, and the poetry that preserves them is sure to live. But the intercalary verses do not live. They have been thought to do so, but such thought thins with the passage of time, which nothing fools forever. *The Prelude* is not autobiography. It is apologetics.

The first book establishes the pattern, which never again is quite so clear although it is discernible throughout. A vignette is given us — clouds lift from one of memory's peaks — and then, while another vignette is preparing, we hear Wordsworth's voice exhorting us to comprehend what he thinks he comprehends, namely, that the Spirit of the Universe sat brooding over all such scenes. As for the scenes — of

springes to catch woodcocks, of the little boat, of
skating, of games, of water off the sands of West-
moreland — nothing in poetry could be better than
the easy vigor, the effortless sublimity, with which
Wordsworth's verse renders their reality, their fact.

> Ere I had told
> Ten birthdays, when among the mountain slopes
> Frost, and the breath of frosty wind, had snapped
> The last autumnal crocus, 'twas my joy
> With store of springes o'er my shoulder hung
> To range the open heights where woodcocks run
> Along the smooth green turf.

Who could doubt that this is the way it was? The
movement of the words is the movement of the boy,
as again is the case when he finds a boat one summer
evening, tied to a willow tree, and steps into it to steal
a ride.

> It was an act of stealth
> And troubled pleasure, nor without the voice
> Of mountain echoes did my boat move on. . . .
> She was an elfin pinnace; lustily
> I dipped my oars into the silent lake,
> And, as I rose upon the stroke, my boat
> Went heaving through the water like a swan.

Or as when he and his companions hiss along the
polished ice:

> So through the darkness and the cold we flew,
> And not a voice was idle; with the din
> Smitten, the precipices rang aloud;

The leafless trees and every icy crag
Tinkled like iron; while far distant hills
Into the tumult sent an alien sound
Of melancholy not unnoticed, while the stars
Eastward were sparkling clear, and in the west
The orange sky of evening died away.
Not seldom from the uproar I retired
Into a silent bay, or sportively
Glanced sideway, leaving the tumultuous throng,
To cut across the reflex of a star
That fled, and, flying still before me, gleamed
Upon the glassy plain; and oftentimes,
When we had given our bodies to the wind,
And all the shadowy banks on either side
Came sweeping through the darkness, spinning still
The rapid line of motion, then at once
Have I, reclining back upon my heels,
Stopped short; yet still the solitary cliffs
Wheeled by me — even as if the earth had rolled
With visible motion her diurnal round!

But the voice of the prophet is a different matter.
The dissertations which intervene, the proofs which
press their way into the dead spaces between fact and
fact, come with a dull, cotton sound.

Dust as we are, the immortal spirit grows
Like harmony in music; there is a dark
Inscrutable workmanship that reconciles
Discordant elements, makes them cling together
In one society. How strange, that all
The terrors, pains, and early miseries,
Regrets, vexations, lassitudes interfused

Within my mind, should e'er have borne a part,
And that a needful part, in making up
The calm existence that is mine when I
Am worthy of myself! Praise to the end! . . .

Wisdom and Spirit of the universe!
Thou Soul that art the eternity of thought,
That givest to forms and images a breath
And everlasting motion, not in vain
By day or starlight thus from my first dawn
Of childhood didst thou intertwine for me
The passions that build up our human soul. . . .

Ye Presences of Nature in the sky
And on the earth! Ye Visions of the hills!
And Souls of lonely places! can I think
A vulgar hope was yours when ye employed
Such ministry, when ye, through many a year
Haunting me thus among my boyish sports,
In caves and trees, upon the woods and hills,
Impressed, upon all forms, the characters
Of danger or desire; and thus did make
The surface of the universal earth,
With triumph and delight, with hope and fear,
Work like a sea? . . .

                              Even then
I held unconscious intercourse with beauty
Old as creation, drinking in a pure
Organic pleasure. . . .

For they are not proofs. They are Wordsworth filling
in with metaphor, and a confused metaphor at that.
What he wants to believe is that Nature taught him

more than man, revolutionary man, will ever teach
anybody; and that the lesson was continuous. He does
not know that it was continuous, or even that it *was*.
All the more reason, then, to ransack his vocabulary
in search of terms which will seem to do the work of
demonstration. He finds too many terms, and he pours
them forth in too exigent a profusion. They do not
mix. A reader of *The Prelude* may be impressed by its
tendentious passages, and think them vaguely august
or grand. They are, but the emphasis is on "vaguely."
Another reader will not be satisfied so soon. He will
be embarrassed by the capital letters, the exclamation
marks; and he will be suspicious of the rhetorical
questions — suspicious that even Wordsworth does
not know their answers.

Above all, however, the careful reader of *The Prelude*, the reader who insists upon understanding the
words he sees, will be baffled in such passages by the
abstractions that fight for his attention. It will be clear
to him that Wordsworth is set on saying he was somehow taught by something; but sooner or later it will
be plain that the how and the what are misty matters
whereon this language throws no light. There is a
darkness, rather, of symbols that tangle with one another and choke their own art. Interfuse, intertwine,
intercourse — Wordsworth has a fatal weakness for
the prefix. Reconcile, build up, minister, inform, impress, create, and grow — he cannot decide which
verb it is that best will name the process of his teaching. There was a oneness, surely, between Nature and

himself in those good days, but how shall it be referred to — as union, as affinity, as connection, as association, as correspondence, as linkage, as impregnation, or as what? The terms pour together into a mixture too rich for reason and too dark for sense. The intercourse, furthermore, is "unconscious," and the workmanship is "inscrutable." The activity asserted is never seen.

There was no such activity. *The Prelude* is the work of an honest poet, and in its pictures it is the work of a very brilliant one, but at its core it is unintelligible. Wordsworth undoubtedly meant the preposterous prose of his concluding lines to Coleridge:

> And now, O Friend! this history is brought
> To its appointed close: the discipline
> And consummation of a Poet's mind,
> In everything that stood most prominent,
> Have faithfully been pictured; we have reached
> The time (our guiding object from the first)
> When we may, not presumptuously, I hope,
> Suppose my powers so far confirmed, and such
> My knowledge, as to make me capable
> Of building up a Work that shall endure.

But there has been no history, and the discipline has been too passive to be worthy of such a name. The most that Wordsworth now possesses is a faculty which he calls imagination. Imagination is what he will see the truth with — not such truth as shines in his vignettes and will shine forever there, but the truth that lies behind things, the "essences" and "forms" with which his mind is so infatuated. He says he has learned

> That Poets, even as Prophets, each with each
> Connected in a mighty scheme of truth,
> Have each his own peculiar faculty,
> Heaven's gift, a sense that fits him to perceive
> Objects unseen before.

With his own peculiar faculty he will go forth in the world and see into the souls of men —

> Souls that appear to have no depth at all
> To careless eyes.

And he will take most pleasure in scrutinizing rustic countenances:

> Nature for all conditions wants not power
> To consecrate, if we have eyes to see,
> The outside of her creatures, and to breathe
> Grandeur upon the very humblest face
> Of human life.

For man — or Man — is still his subject. Man is the creature he must save. And he can do this best by telling the world henceforth how noble are "the simplicities of cottage life," where shepherds sit in the shade with dogs and never once suspect how important they appear to the poet — or the Poet — who beholds them.

> How little they, they and their doings, seem,
> And yet how great!

The condescension seems not to bother Wordsworth, or the vanity. Having found his mind, he must give it work to do though the heavens fall. No poet ever knew less about people, but no poet has been so sure that he was wise concerning Man.

At its center, then, *The Prelude* yields little or nothing. It is barren of sense in the end, and so as poetry it was doomed from the start. The business of poetry is to tell men what they already know, not to convince them that what they have seen so far is vulgar illusion. The greatest poets have seen what was there to see. Wordsworth, insisting on more, finds less. His imagination, boasting of its power to deal with what is "really" there, suggests that nothing is there at all for men of sense to see. Such men withhold the final word of praise from such poetry as *The Prelude* is. And they are right. Its author promised to use the "language really used by men," but he did not keep that promise in what was for him the thinking heart of *The Prelude*.

It is a psychological, not a philosophical, poem, and as such it was bound to be obscure. It is not a poem that says things, it is a poem whose author is getting ready to say things. The world waited, and they were not said. *The Recluse* was never written. Nor could it have been written in the longest of eternities. If *The Prelude* proves anything it proves just that. For it has proved that a poet exists. The miracle having happened, nothing more is needed. The further miracle of poems about men and the actions of men, of poems with other subjects than their authors, of poems like Homer's and Shakespeare's, or even like Virgil's and Milton's, is not to be thought of yet. Poetry is possible. That, ye Ministers and Presences, is enough for now.

If *The Prelude* is a work of fancy after all — a work in which sensory magic has saved from oblivion a few moments out of one man's life — the blow to Wordsworth's shade must be very bitter. For he despised fancy as he despised fact. And he would not have liked to think that his little pictures were all he had to give us. He had a gospel to give, and used these pictures only to point its truth. But the truth is in them — so accidentally remembered, so immediately loved, and so sharply fixed in words. Between them there is only that semblance of truth, that rootless and useless wisdom, which in all times discredits poetry. In all times, including ours.

If poetry in our time is thought by most poeple not to be important, the reason is a good one. It is not about anything. Or about enough. Poetry has come a long way since Achilles and his mother, since Hector and Andromache, since Odysseus and Penelope, since Telemachus, since Nausicaa, since Eurycleia, since Dante at the gates of Dis, since Beatrice in Paradise, since Troilus and Pandar and Criseyde. Poetry no longer lives in people like ourselves: like ourselves, and greater. It lives in those who write it, and they are praised — when praised — for being different from us, for having souls when we have none. They are admired in proportion to their want of prudence, of tragedy, of mirth. They are envied because so little is expected of them: so little, or so much. For sometimes they are ordered to show us what we should believe — and not about the persons in some story, but about the secret of all life. The secret, not the facts. The facts of life are found in story, which poetry has ceased to tell. When it recovers the art, it will pay its way again.

# INDEX

(*The*) *Aeneid*—*see* Virgil

allegory, failure of, 184-186, 232, 235–236; perfection of, 176–182, 186

alliteration, 251

analogy, 170–171

Ariosto, made use of by Byron, 294

    *Orlando Furioso*, 134, 255

Aristotle, comparison of *The Iliad* and *The Odyssey*, 46; defining tragedy, 258

artificiality, 127

*As You Like It*—*see* Shakespeare

Boccaccio

    *Il Filostrato*, rewritten by Chaucer, 263–264

Boëthius, material used by Chaucer, 263

(*The*) *Book of Tobit*, 139

brevity, 200

Byron, Lord, 283–302; and Chaucer, 283, 286, 287, 290, 291, 293, 294, 295, 300, 301; and Dante, 286, 287, 301, 302; handicapped by lack of subject, 283, 289–290; and Lucretius, 302; as pretended historian, 291–292; and Spenser, 294

    *Don Juan*, 283–302; confusion in, 284; exaggeration in, 291; form in, 297–298; monotony, 300; perspective, lack of, 285; purpose, cheapness of, 301; reference to *The Iliad* and *The Odyssey*, 301; as satire, 284–287; savagery, 300; theme, 284

Castlereagh, attacked by Byron, 284

Cervantes, comedy of, 258; and Chaucer, 281; and Spenser, 255

characters, outstanding, 33–43, 74–85, 104–107, 125–126, 136–141, 144–145, 156–158, 194–196, 218–220, 223–225, 241–242, 266–275

Chaucer, Geoffrey, 257–282; and Byron, 283, 286, 290,

291, 293, 294, 295, 300, 301; and Cervantes, 281; and Dante, 261–262, 286, 287; and Fielding, 281; and Homer, 262; and Lucretius, 262; as pretended historian, 277–279; and Shakespeare, 265; as sovereign poet, 1; and Spenser, 255–256

*Troilus and Criseyde*, 257–282; characters, outstanding, 266–275; comedy, 258, 262, 264–265, 279–281; comic genius, 257; exaggeration, 281–282; theme, 262–266, 275–278; vernacular, 277

Coleridge, Samuel Taylor, 305, 309, 310, 316

color, 3–6, 31–33, 64–65, 169–170; use of animals for, 4

comedy, 258, 264–265, 279–281, 283; in Chaucer, 258, 262; compared to burlesque, 297–298; defined by Socrates, 261; discursive, 279–281; exaggeration of, 289, 291; failure of, 254–256; form of, 297–298, quality of, 254–255, 256, 285; survival of, 285

comic genius, 257

comic spirit, 291

courtesy, 70–71, 93, 206–209, 240, 242–244

Dante, 172–230; and Byron, 286, 287, 301, 302; and Chaucer, 261–262, 263, 286, 287; and Homer, 172–173, 186; and Milton, 127, 136, 183, 193, 220; as peer of Homer and Shakespeare, 172–173; as philosophical poet, 172–173; as sovereign poet, 1; and Spenser, 231, 233, 234, 235, 241, 247; treatment of subject, 305; and Virgil, 101, 121, 221

*The Divine Comedy*, 172–230; allegory, 176–182, 184–186; brevity, 200; characters, outstanding, 194–196, 218, 220, 223–225; comparison to Giotto's paintings, 225, 226; courtesy, 206–209; form, 182–183, 212–215, 226–230; imagery, 195–196; ingenuity, 201–202, 203–205; irony, 205; logic, 202–203; metaphor, 192–193; philosophy of, 177; recognition, 225–226; simile, 186–192; theme, 174–176, 178–179, 221–222

*De Rerum Natura*—*see* Lucretius

didacticism, 152–153, 166, 236–237
(*The*) *Divine Comedy*—*see* Dante
*Don Juan* — *see* Byron
*Don Quixote*, 262

eclecticism, 127, 233
*Eclogues* — *see* Virgil
Epicurus, 170; as master of Lucretius, 156, 158
epithet, 8–11, 64–65, 92–93, 129, 247–248
exaggeration, 281–282
(*The*) *Excursion*—*see* Wordsworth

(*The*) *Faerie Queene*—*see* Spenser
Fielding, Henry, comedy of, 258; compared to Chaucer, 281
(*Il*) *Filostrato*—*see* Boccaccio
form, 6–8, 14–15, 19, 31, 46–47, 63, 182–183, 212–215, 226–230, 297–298, 311–313, 316; of comedy, 297–298; confusion of, 284; repetition of, 211; rigidity of, 197–199

(*The*) *Georgics*—*see* Virgil
Gibbon, Edward, compared to Virgil, 99

Giotto, 225, 226
*Growth of a Poet's Mind*—*see* Wordsworth

harshness, 151
*Henry VI*— *see* Shakespeare
Herodotus, *History*, compared to *The Odyssey*, 47–48
Homer, 1–85; and Chaucer, 262; and Dante, 172–173, 186; ingenuity, 19; and Lucretius, 153–154, 169; as master poet, 1, 172, 319; mastery of perspective, 1–3; secret of his power, 2; servant of poetry, 308; and Spenser, 235, 241; treatment of subject, 305; and Virgil, 86–92, 98, 100, 101, 102–105, 108–109, 120, 121
  *The Iliad*, 1–44; and *The Aeneid*, 87, 90, 91, 109; characters, 11–14; color, 3–6, 31–33; epithet, 8–11; form, 6–8, 14–15, 19, 31, 46; irony, 20–24; movement, 3–4, 8; and *The Odyssey*, 14, 15, 46, 49, 50, 56, 63–64, 73, 79; and *Paradise Lost*, 132; pathos, 24–27; relief, 18, 19; repetition, 8–11; rhythm, 7–8; savagery, 16–18, 39–41; and Shakespeare, 42; simile, 8–

11; summary of, in *Troilus and Criseyde*, 263; suspense, 29–30; theme, 19–20; as a tragedy, 8, 14–18, 19

*The Odyssey*, 45–85; Achilles' funeral, 43–44; and *The Aeneid*, 88, 90, 91, 93, 100, 104; characters, 56, 74–85; color, 64–65; courtesy, 70–71; epithet, 64–65; form, 46–47, 63; gods, simplicity of, 73–76; and Herodotus, 47–48; home, importance of, 70–72; human body, importance of, 72–73; and *The Iliad*, 14, 15, 46, 49, 50, 56, 63–64, 73, 79; irony, 57; reality, 64, 66–67; recognition, 57–63; relief, 52–53; sadness, as opposed to tragedy, 49–52; savagery, 55; simile, 63–64; scope, 65–70; suspense, 56–57; theme, 45–48

Horace, quoted by Byron, 295
hyperbole, 91; Virgilian, 134–135

(*The Iliad*)—*see* Homer
imagery, 195–196
ingenuity, 19, 201, 202, 203–205
irony, 20–24, 57, 91, 105–106, 143, 205

Lake Poets of England, attacked by Byron, 284
Lawrence of Arabia, comparison of *The Iliad* and *The Odyssey*, 46
logic, 202–203
Lucretius, 148–171; beliefs of, 158–166; and Byron, 302; and Chaucer, 262; and Homer, 153–154, 169; and Milton, 149–150; as scientific poet, 152–156, 172; and Spenser, 231, 233; and Virgil, 95–96, 110, 148, 165

*De Rerum Natura*, 148–171; analogy, 170–171; characters, outstanding, 156–158; color, 169–170; comparison to *Paradise Lost*, 149; didacticism, 152–153, 166; harshness, 151; materialism, 155; paradox, 149, 168–169; theme, 148–149; tragedy, avoidance of, 154; translated by Spenser, 233
lyricism, 96–98, 108, 109, 136, 251

Malthus, 297
martial idiom, 133–134
materialism, 155
Melville, comedy of, 258
metaphor, 192–193; mixed, 127

Milton, John, 122–147; and Dante, 127, 136, 183, 193, 220; error of, 146, 172; and Homer, 122–123, 131, 140; and Lucretius, 149–150; and Ovid, 134; servant of poetry, 308; and Shakespeare, 140; and Virgil, 87, 101, 122–123, 131, 146; way of using the poets, 132; and Wordsworth, 303–304, 319

*On the Morning of Christ's Nativity*, 132

*Paradise Lost*, 122–147; artificiality, 127; characters, outstanding, 125–126, 136–141, 144–145; eclecticism, 127; epithet, 129; hyperbole, Virgilian, 134–135; and *The Iliad*, 132; irony, 143; lyricism, 136; martial idiom, 133–134; metaphor, mixed, 127; and *On the Morning of Christ's Nativity*, 132; and *Orlando Furioso*, 134; poetic diction, 143–144; poetic tact, 142–143; prolixity, 126, 128–131; style, 123–124, 126; symbolism, 135; theme, 124–127; viewed in perspective, 122

monotony, 300
morality, 92, 232

*(The) Odyssey*—*see* Homer
*On the Morning of Christ's Nativity*—*see* Milton
organization—*see* Form
*Orlando Furioso*—*see* Ariosto
Ovid, compared to Milton, 134

*Paradise Lost*—*see* Milton
paradox, 149, 168–169
pathos, 24–27
perspective, 86–87, 91; lack of, 285; poem viewed in, 122; of poet, 1–3
Plato, 96, 120, 247; attacked by Byron, 285; *The Statesman*, 111–117
poetic diction, 143–144
poetic tact, 142–143
poetic taste, 249
poetry, chief art of, 1; what it is, 304–305, 318; where it is, 319; Wordsworth's definition of, 305–306
Pope, Alexander, 297
*(The) Prelude*—*see* Wordsworth
prolixity, 126, 128–131, 245, 250

reality, 64, 66–67
*(The) Recluse*—*see* Wordsworth
recognition scenes, 57–63, 225–226, 245

relief, 18–19, 52–53
Rembrandt, comparison to character in *The Odyssey*, 77
repetition, 8–11
rhetoric, 90–91
rhythm, 7–8

sadness, as opposed to tragedy, 49–52
satire, 284–287
savagery, 16–18, 39–41, 55, 300
sensation, overuse of, 245–246, 248–249
Shakespeare, William, and Chaucer, 265; and Dante, 172–173; and *The Iliad*, 42; as master poet, 1, 319; matured, 307; and Milton, 140; as servant of poetry, 308; and Spenser, 241, 247; as teacher of poetry, 306; and Virgil, 87, 101, 109
  *As You Like It*, 262
  *Henry VI*, 307
  *Troilus and Cressida*, 265
simile, 8–11, 63–64, 92, 98–99, 105, 107, 186–192
Socrates, 171, 244; defining comedy and tragedy, 261
Spenser, Edmund, 231–256; and Ariosto, 255; and Byron, 294; and Cervantes, 255; and Chaucer, 255–256;

eclecticism, 233; and Homer 235, 241; and Lucretius, 231, 233; and Milton, 233, 234; misquoted by Byron, 302; qualities of, 232–235; servant of poetry, 308; and Shakespeare, 241, 247
  *The Faerie Queene*, 231–256; allegory, failure of, 232, 235–236; alliteration, 251; characters, outstanding, 241–242; comedy, failure of, 254–256; courtesy, 240, 242–244; didacticism, 236–237; epithet, 247–248; lyricism, 251; morality, 232; poetic taste, 249; prolixity, 245, 250; recognition, 245; sensation, overuse of, 245–246, 248–249; Spenserian stanza, 251–254; style, diffuse, 247; summary, 238–240
Spenserian stanza — *see* Spenser
(*The*) *Statesmen* — *see* Plato
style, 101–107, 123–124, 126, 247
suspense, 29–30, 56–57
symbolism, 135

Tacitus, 297
Tennyson, Alfred Lord, appraisal of Virgil, 102

theme, of poems, 19–20, 45–48, 91–92, 94–95, 110–121, 124–127, 148–149, 172, 174–176, 178–179, 221–222, 262–266, 275–278, 284

tragedy, avoidance of, 154; defined by Aristotle, 258; defined by Socrates, 261; inability to write, 285; quality of, 8, 14–18, 19, 254–255, 258, 259, 261–262

*Troilus and Cressida* — see Shakespeare

*Troilus and Criseyde* — see Chaucer

vagueness, 96–100

vernacular, 277

Virgil, 86–121; appraised by Tennyson, 102; and Dante, 101, 221, and Gibbon, 99; and Homer, 86–92, 98, 100, 101, 102–105, 108–109, 120, 121; and Lucretius, 95–96, 110, 148, 165; and Milton, 87, 101, 122–123, 131, 146; power exerted over Dante, 121; and Shakespeare, 87, 101, 109; tragedy, inability to write, 285; and Wordsworth, 87, 319

*The Aeneid*, 86–121; characters, indecision of, 104–105; characters, outstanding, 104–107; courtesy, 93; eloquence, lack of, 90–91; epic genius, absence of, 109–110; epithet, 92–93; hyperbole, 91; and *The Iliad*, 87, 90, 91, 109; irony, 91, 105–106; lyricism, 96–98, 108–109; morality, 92; and *The Odyssey*, 88, 90, 91, 93, 100, 104; perspective, 86–87, 91; reality, lack of, 89–91; rhetoric, 90–91; simile, 92, 98–99, 105, 107; style, 101–107; theme, 91–92, 94–95, 110–121, 172; vagueness, 96–100

*The Eclogues*, 108, 111, 118, 221

*The Georgics*, 88, 93, 111, 118

Wellington, attacked by Byron, 284

wit, quality of, 258

Wordsworth, William, 303–320; appraisal of Spenser, 254; and Byron, 304; creator of modern poetry, 303; criticized by Byron, 293, 302; his religion, 309, 311; meeting with Coleridge, 309; and Milton, 303–304, 319; as philosophical poet, 304; poetry, his definition of, 305–306; subject, search for, 303–304; and Virgil, 87, 319

*The Excursion*, 306

*Growth of a Poet's Mind*, 306

*The Prelude*, 303, 320; addressed to Coleridge, 310; as answer to French Revolution, 308–309; as apologetics rather than biography, 308–311; color, 312–313, 316; form, 311–313, 315–318; metaphor, 314–315; prolixity, 315; as psychological poem, 318; vagueness, 315–316

*The Recluse*, 307, 318

## PRODUCTION NOTES

DESIGNER: *Maurice Serle Kaplan*

TYPE: *English Monotype* Fournier, *based on a type cut in 1745 by Pierre Simon Fournier. The headings and title page are in* Deepdene, *designed by Frederic W. Goudy.*

TYPESETTING, ELECTROTYPING, PRINTING, AND BINDING: *The Plimpton Press, Norwood, Mass.*

DRAWING ON TITLE PAGE: *Paul McPharlin.*